What is Microhistory?

This unique and detailed analysis provides the first accessible and comprehensive introduction to the origins, development and methodology of microhistory – one of the most significant innovations in historical scholarship to have emerged in the last few decades.

The introduction guides the reader through the best-known example of *microstoria*, *The Cheese and the Worms* by Carlo Ginzburg, and explains the benefits of studying an event, place or person in microscopic detail. In Part I, István M. Szijártó examines the historiography of microhistory in the Italian, French, German and Anglo-Saxon traditions, shedding light on the roots of microhistory and asking where it is headed. In Part II, Sigurður Gylfi Magnússon uses a carefully selected case study to show the important difference between the disciplines of macro- and microhistory and to offer practical instructions for those historians wishing to undertake micro-level analysis. These parts are tied together by a Postscript in which the status of microhistory within contemporary historiography is examined and its possibilities for the future evaluated.

This book surveys the significant characteristics shared by large groups of microhistorians, and how these have now established an acknowledged place within any general discussion of the theory and methodology of history as an academic discipline.

Sigurður Gylfi Magnússon is the chair of the Center for Microhistorical Research at the Reykjavík Academy (www.microhistory.org) and Dr Kristján Eldjárn Research Fellow at the National Museum of Iceland. He is the author of seventeen books and numerous articles published in Iceland and abroad. His previous publications include *Wasteland with Words: A Social History of Iceland* (2010).

István M. Szijártó is Associate Professor in the Department of Economic and Social History at Loránd Eötvös University, Hungary. He is the author of three books and several articles published in Hungary and abroad. His previous publications include *Experience, Agency, Responsibility: The Lessons of Russia's Microhistory* (2011).

What is Microhistory?

Theory and practice

Sigurður Gylfi Magnússon
and István M. Szijártó

Routledge
Taylor & Francis Group

LONDON AND NEW YORK

First published 2013
by Routledge
2 Park Square, Milton Park, Abingdon, Oxon OX14 4RN

Simultaneously published in the USA and Canada
by Routledge
711 Third Avenue, New York, NY 10017

Routledge is an imprint of the Taylor & Francis Group, an informa business

British Library Cataloguing in Publication Data
A catalogue record for this book is available from the British Library

Library of Congress Cataloging in Publication Data
Sigurður G. Magnússon.
What is microhistory? : theory and practice / Sigurður Gylfi Magnússon,
István M. Szijártó.
pages cm
1. Microhistory. I. Szijártó, István M., author. II. Title.
D16.138.S55 2013
900–dc23
2012047337

ISBN: 978-0-415-69208-3 (hbk)
ISBN: 978-0-415-69209-0 (pbk)
ISBN: 978-0-203-50063-7 (ebk)

Typeset in Sabon
by Taylor and Francis Books

Printed and bound in Great Britain by MPG Printgroup

Contents

Acknowledgements

As author of Part I, István M. Szijártó would like to thank Mrs Maureen Lofmark for her kind assistance with the English text and Zoltán Boldizsár Simon for his advice and for making his yet unpublished text available for him.

The author of Part II, Sigurður Gylfi Magnússon, established some of his arguments early on as an independent scholar at the Reykjavík Academy and Chair of the Center for Microhistorical Research. Later, he enjoyed the good fortune to become a Dr Kristján Eldjárn Research Fellow at the National Museum of Iceland where he wrote his part of the book. He would like to thank his colleagues and friends at the Reykjavík Academy and the National Museum of Iceland, in particular: Margrét Hallgrímsdóttir, the Director of the National Museum of Iceland; Dr Davíð Ólafsson, a historian and Chair of the Reykjavík Academy; Dr Anna Lísa Rúnarsdóttir, the Head of Research and Collections at the National Museum; and other friends at both institutions. This book owes much to their generosity. It has been a stimulating and satisfying intellectual experience to work with such a talented and diverse set of people.

Part of Magnússon's argument has been published elsewhere, in two issues of the *Journal of Social History* – from 2003 and 2006 – and the book *Wasteland with Words* published by Reaktion books in London in 2010. He is grateful for their permission in allowing him to use some of that text in this book.

The extraordinary generosity of many colleagues around the world who have been in touch with Magnússon through the Center for Microhistorical Research at the Reykjavík Academy (www.microhistory.org) has been particularly influential in the development of Part II. Magnússon would also like to express his gratitude to Nicholas Jonse and Anna Yates, specialists in the English language, who helped with the text.

Magnússon had the opportunity to visit Budapest, Hungary, on a number of occasions. First he attended a graduate level workshop on teaching microhistory, financed by the Tempus Foundation and held at Collegium Budapest, Hungary, and later a conference held by the Central European University on the return of the 'social' in the humanities and the social sciences. István Szijártó came to Reykjavík, Iceland twice, first for a workshop on the concept of microhistory, financed by the Tempus Foundation in Hungary, and on another occasion as a visiting scholar, invited by the National Museum of Iceland, where he gave a talk on his part of the book. All this exchange has been important for the development of the book.

Both authors would like to thank the editors of Routledge for their cooperation in the creation of this book, especially Eve Setch (editor), Laura Mothersole (acting associate editor), Sarah Douglas (production editor) and also Ruth Jeavons (copy editor). Their support has proved extremely valuable, as have the comments of the four unknown critical readers. Both authors are grateful for their insights and constructive criticism.

Part I

Introduction

Against simple truths

Pighino and Menocchio

'My way is to begin with the beginning', wrote Byron in his *Don Juan*. If we follow his advice when searching for an answer for the question 'what is microhistory?' we should first turn to Italian microhistory. Within *microstoria*, it is the work of its best known representative, Carlo Ginzburg, that might serve as a starting point, and the obvious choice to demonstrate his scholarship is his world-famous book *The Cheese and the Worms*, published originally in Italy in 1976 (Ginzburg 1980). Two sixteenth-century Italian millers feature in this book. The leading role is played by Domenico Scandella, called Menocchio, and a minor character is another miller called 'the Pighino'.

He, Pellegrino Baroni, appeared before the inquisition of Ferrara. Since the mill had always been a social meeting place, millers were responsive to new ideas and capable of transmitting these. Peasants were traditionally hostile towards millers. A Flemish proverb named the miller as one of Satan's four evangelists, the other three being the usurer, the money-changer and the tax-collector (Greilsammer 2009: 17). Millers were therefore vulnerable to charges of heresy and this was the reason why Pighino from Savignano sul Panaro had to appear in Ferrara. A friar denounced him and reported that he had attributed his incriminated statements to a person lecturing in a noble's house in Bologna.

When Pighino was confronted by the friar, he denied the accusations, and listed all the noble households in which he had served – but when doing so he did not repeat exactly the list given the day before: instead of naming Vincenzo Bolognetti, he mentioned the name of Vincenzo Bononi. Paolo Ricci, also called Camillo Renato, a famous heretic who was later executed, served two years in Bologna in several noble households, including Bolognetti's, as a tutor from 1538. This was probably the reason why Pighino wanted to conceal his links to the Bolognetti family. Ricci writes about a peasant he met in Bolognetti's house. This peasant told Ricci that in bestowing grace, the Virgin Mary has a greater role than Jesus Christ. This person might have been our Pighino.

The historian of the case, Ginzburg, has noticed what, luckily for Pighino, the inquisitors had not, and he could render Baroni's connections to Ricci probable. But Ginzburg claims that Pighino was more radically materialistic than the known

Italian heretics of his age. Nor can his ideas about equality be traced back to humanists like Ricci: Baroni told the inquisitors that the great and the humble will be equals in paradise and emphasized Virgin Mary's low birth. Even Ricci's recollections suggest that ordinary people did not need humanists to teach them heretic ideas – whether it was Pighino or another peasant he was talking to in Bolognetti's house.

Pighino's many statements evoke those of Menocchio, another heretic miller, living in Friuli, several hundreds of miles away. Relying on inquisition records, Ginzburg reconstructed the world view of Domenico Scandella.

> I have said that, in my opinion, all was chaos, that is, earth, air, water and fire were mixed together; and out of that bulk a mass formed – just as cheese is made out of milk – and worms appeared in it, and these were the angels.
>
> (Ginzburg 1980: 5–6)

Hence the title of the book. Menocchio was born in 1532 in Montereale and died probably in 1599. He was first reported to the inquisition in 1583, questioned next year and sentenced as an 'heresiarch'. Let out of prison two years later, he stood once again before the inquisition in 1599, and this time he was executed as a recidivist.

Menocchio's theology, based on an insistence on the basic principles of the gospels, led him to extreme conclusions. It is enough to love our neighbours, he said, the Church is superfluous. The miller propagated a full tolerance, extending the equality of religions also to heretics. In conversations with his fellow villagers, later with the inquisitors, – he was glad to have a learned audience – Menocchio gave expression to 'a peasant religion, intolerant of dogma and ritual, tied to the cycles of nature, and fundamentally pre-Christian' (Ginzburg 1980: 112).

Ginzburg claims that the explosive mixture of Menocchio's thoughts was formed by elements of the popular and the elite cultures. The erudite historian reveals the probable or possible elite cultural background behind the miller's strange views, and he identifies among others the Bible, *Il fioretto della Bibbia*, a popular compilation from the Bible and other texts, the medieval story of John Mandeville's fictional journey, Boccaccio's *Decameron*, and perhaps even the Koran as pieces of Menocchio's reading – all in the vernacular, of course. Still, he maintains that Menocchio's particular world view, so shocking for the inquisitors, was not a result of his reading – just as Pighino did not need Ricci's teachings to be a heretic. Domenico Scancella used 'glasses' that severely distorted everything he read:

> Any attempt to consider these books as 'sources' in the mechanical sense of the term collapses before the aggressive originality of Menocchio's reading. More than the text, then, what is important is the key to his reading, a screen that he unconsciously placed between himself and the printed page: a filter that emphasized certain words while obscuring others, that stretched the meaning of a word, taking it out of its context, that acted on Menocchio's memory and distorted the very words of the text. And this screen, this key

to his reading, continually leads us back to a culture that is very different from the one expressed on the printed page – one based on an oral tradition.

(Ginzburg 1980: 33)

The roots of his views 'were sunk in an obscure, almost unfathomable, layer of remote peasant traditions' (Ginzburg 1980: xxiii). But the Reformation was needed with its discussions so that Menocchio felt free to form and express his own views about the world, as well as the invention of printing so that he had the words at his disposal to do so.

Ginzburg sees in Menocchio the representative of an ancient tradition, the oral materialistic popular culture. As a parallel to the picture of the cheese and the emerging worms, he evokes an Indian myth in the Vedas as well as a Kalmuck counterpart. He regards the miller's as a border case that points to 'the popular roots of a considerable part of high European culture, both medieval and post medieval' (Ginzburg 1980: 126). But with Rabelais and Breughel, the period of interaction came to a close, and 'the subsequent period was marked, instead, by an increasingly rigid distinction between the culture of the dominant classes and artisan and peasant cultures, as well as by the indoctrination of the masses from above' (Ginzburg 1980: 126). Menocchio 'is also a dispersed fragment, reaching us by chance, of an obscure shadowy world'; his 'case should be seen against this background of repression and effacement of popular culture' (Ginzburg 1980: xxvi, 126).

Ginzburg and the detective story

It is doubtful whether Menocchio could authentically represent popular culture if he did not really belong to it, but lived on its periphery as a miller, on the borderline of elite and popular, written and oral cultures. Dominick LaCapra writes: 'The idea that oral culture was Menocchio's primary grid seems particularly suspect in light of the way Menocchio was divided between the "world" of oral culture and that of the books that meant so much to him.' (LaCapra 1985: 66) According to Edward Muir, the guiding principle of Ginzburg's work is that inquisition records allow us to grasp the interactions of elite and popular cultures (Muir 1991a: x); but Ginzburg, although he stressed the importance of cultural interaction, did not really put this to effect in his book, but rather argued for the autonomy of popular culture, regarding Menocchio's 'glasses' as decisive in forming his reading experience, considering the books themselves secondary. Moreover, popular culture was not homogenous, argues LaCapra, and Ginzburg did not address the discursive process conditioned by power relations, the interplay of oppression and 'the interplay between domination and skewed "reciprocity"', which transformed Scandella's oral answers into the written source we know (LaCapra 1985: 62–63).

Ginzburg's colleagues, other Italian microhistorians, have also criticized his analysis of popular culture in *The Cheese and the Worms*. Edoardo Grendi reproached him for neglecting the miller's life and his social contacts: Menocchio mentioned a dozen of his friends and acquaintances in his confessions, but this social network has completely been left out of the book. According to Grendi, Ginzburg is only interested in culture: elite and popular culture as well as cultural forms (quoted by Cerutti 2004: 21–22, cf. Grendi 1996: 235). Simona Cerutti, another representative of the rival branch of the Italian microhistory, which is focusing on society, blamed Ginzburg for separating the analysis of cultural models from that of behaviour (Cerutti 2004: 19).

Reviewers sometimes compare *The Cheese and the Worms* with crime stories (for example Daniel 2004: 287). The culprit in this case is, however, not the inquisition, but the old Indo-European popular culture. LaCapra writes that 'the format of the detective story itself assures that the "whodunit" will reveal a single agent: oral, popular culture' (LaCapra 1985: 53). The young Hungarian historian, András Lugosi argues that while the hunter, the art expert and the detective can be certain that the traces they follow are the result of the activity of a deer, a painter or a murderer, the doctor, the psychotherapist, the sociologist and the historian lack this certainty. Ginzburg arrived at Menocchio's case from the study of popular culture, and his own implicit preferences prompted him to point to a pre-Christian, oral, popular culture as the inspirer of the miller's ideas, instead of understanding these from Menocchio's life (Lugosi 2001: 33–38).

Menocchio's story can be compared to Wolfgang Behringer's book, soon to be discussed. It is about the 'phantoms of the night' in the Alps, a widespread belief, which can be classified as white magic or shamanism. While on the basis of Menocchio's fantastic ideas Ginzburg supposes the existence of an ancient Indo-European materialistic oral popular culture, Behringer concludes that the surprising ideas of his protagonist, Chonrad Stoeckhlin, are merely the results of his 'bricolage'; in this particular combination these thoughts can only be found in his head (Behringer 1998). This is the key point: the representativity of Menocchio's or Stoeckhlin's case. At a conference in 2005, Ginzburg said that he was the first to stress the exceptionality of Menocchio. 'But it seemed to me that certain features of his behaviour are related to more general phenomena' (Ginzburg 2010a: 359). Although he could not convince all his readers that Menocchio's glasses are not unique pieces – as Behringer thinks that Stoeckhlin's are – but an ancient peasant heritage, one of a once widespread type, his book is no doubt a compelling read, the best known work of microhistory until this very day. According to Roger Chartier, it proves that 'it is on this reduced scale, and probably only on this scale, that we can understand, without deterministic reduction, the relationships between systems of beliefs, of values and representations on the one hand, and social affiliations on the other' (quoted by Ginzburg 1993: 22).

What is microhistory?

Microhistory is, in the first approach, the intensive historical investigation of a relatively well defined smaller object, most often a single event, or 'a village community, a group of families, even an individual person' (Ginzburg and Poni 1991: 3). Microhistorians hold a microscope and not a telescope in their hands.

Focusing on certain cases, persons and circumstances, microhistory allows an intensive historical study of the subject, giving a completely different picture of the past from the investigations about nations, states, or social groupings, stretching over decades, centuries, or whatever *longue durée*. Similarly to classical Greek plays, where we can find a threefold unity of place, time and action, the microhistorical approach creates a focal point, collecting the different rays coming from the past, and this lends it a real force. Microhistory, however – and this is the second and not any more evident element of its definition – has an objective that is much more far-reaching than that of a case study: microhistorians always look for the answers for 'great historical questions', soon to be defined, when studying small objects. As Charles Joyner said, they 'search for answers to large questions in small places' (quoted by Shifflett 1995). And finally, the third main feature of microhistory, and here first of all the original Italian *microstoria* is meant, is the stress put on agency. For microhistorians, people who lived in the past are not merely puppets on the hands of great underlying forces of history, but they are regarded as active individuals, conscious actors. These elements of a definition are evidently interconnected. It is the 'great historical question' that legitimates the micro-analysis, while, as Brad S. Gregory put it, it is on the micro-level that the agency of the ordinary people can be preserved (Gregory 1999: 101). The first element of the above definition seems straightforward – in fact, this is the single element defining microhistory in common-sense or hostile interpretations. But the two other elements and their corollaries are far from being evident. They will be treated in Chapters 3 and 4.[1]

Enumerating all the elements of a set is not the only way of defining it. In fact, the name 'definition' derives, too, from the other possibility: we may try to explore its boundaries. This method is to be followed in Chapters 1–4. Examining the border area of microhistory, several works of history will therefore also be mentioned that do not belong to microhistory in the sense of the above definition. It cannot be justified, for example, to narrow microhistory down to the Italian *microstoria*: a wider interpretation can also be used. If we do so, its intertwining with historical anthropology is evident. It is an open question whether we should classify as 'incident analysis' some works that display no effort to reach a general conclusion, or include these, too, as microhistory. These problems will be explored when treating Anglo-Saxon microhistory in Chapter 3, after having addressed Italian microhistory in Chapter 1 and its French and German reception in Chapter 2.

The place of microhistory in the discourse of history

Microhistory came into being in the 1970s, in the decade when the different historical approaches that can be most conveniently summed up under the heading of 'cultural history' also emerged.[2] Cultural history, to use a simple definition, puts the stress on lived experience and the representations that the actors themselves form to interpret their own experiences. Cultural history, as we shall see, first of all strives to find meaning: it has a distinctly hermeneutical character. Microhistory was probably most fashionable in the 1990s, when the star of postmodernism and cultural history stood at its apogee. There are therefore several factors that tie microhistory to cultural history. Capturing experience is claimed to be a distinct feature of microhistory (Christiansen 1995: 9; Brown, R. D. 2003: 13). Still, we cannot simply claim that microhistory is one of the branches of cultural history. This is clearly demonstrated by the hostility of most Italian microhistorians towards postmodernism, to be explored in Chapter 1. The fact that microhistory seeks answers for 'great historical questions' also links it to older schools of history – especially to traditional quantitative and structure-oriented social history.

The problems that orientate historical investigations always originate from the outside, from contemporary society, so 'great historical questions' are never defined within the discourse of history itself, they are determined by social and cultural factors. They may be different in Paris and in Budapest, and they are different today from what they were half a century ago. For Ginzburg, popular culture, interpreted as counter-culture, was a 'great historical question' in the 1970s, while later popular culture was rather regarded as a discourse, and the essentiality attributed to it by Ginzburg had disappeared (Szekeres 2003: 88–89). Colonization, globalization and Shakespeare's art are more generally ranked among 'great historical questions' as the problems linked to a particular community. Social history usually regards problems concerning structural factors as 'great historical questions.'

The fact that microhistory is trying to find an answer to such types of question attests to its being committed to the preferences of traditional social history. Although we could interpret this as a lop-sidedness or even backwardness – suggesting that microhistory was not able to move fully to the more up-to-date approach of cultural history, and is stuck with one of its legs in old-fashioned social history – it might also be seen as an advantage. The reason is as follows: neither social nor cultural history are thematically defined sub-sections of history; both represent the investigation of the past in its entirety from a special point of view, using a special approach. Cultural history regards society as a discursive phenomenon that is invested with meaning – so the historians' main task is to search for meaning. But the approach of the cultural historians, who seek *verstehen* and only want to find meaning, cannot take them closer to the past than where the authors of their sources were; cultural historians cannot learn more about the past than they knew about it. This fact makes it necessary for the historian to employ different approaches, and also to look for explanations – as social history, for example, has always been doing.[3]

Whether it is the restricted character of cultural history or just the accelerated change in fashionable historical trends, the search for meaning and analysis of representations that has kept historians busy for a few decades seems to have more or less come to an end at the beginning of the twenty-first century. Old topics such as the state and politics, as well as more traditional approaches, as among others that of social history, have come to the foreground again. One of the strongest arguments for microhistory in the early twenty-first century is, therefore, that it makes possible a harmonious blend of social historical and cultural historical approaches.[4]

For this reason, microhistory is not seen here as a fashion that was born in the 1970s, reached the peak of its popularity in the 1990s, and is already on the decline, i.e. a historical approach that belongs to the past, but as one that has a bright future, with the capacity to bring social and cultural history together, as an approach that can both supply the explanations of social history and grasp the meanings of cultural history within a single very circumscribed investigation. Microhistorians try to show the historical actors' experiences and how they saw themselves and their lives and which meanings they attributed to things that had happened to them, while they also try to point to deep historical structures, long-lived ways of thinking and global processes using a retrospective analysis – factors that were absent from the actors' own horizons of interpretation. All this can only be brought together, without running the risk of over-simplifying the past, when historians investigate a narrowly defined subject. It is exclusively on this level that we do not risk 'losing the complexity of the relationships that connect any individual to a particular society' (Ginzburg and Poni 1991: 5). The complexity of the past can only be represented for readers at the micro-level where both the actors and these readers live their lives. This kind of narrative is easiest to digest. If historians choose a higher level, a bigger object of investigation, they risk losing either the complexity of the past or their readers.

The historian's microscope

Chapters 1–4 of this book are fundamentally historiographical in character. They use both a geographical and a problem-centred approach. First, the different currents of microhistory are presented on a geographical basis, while certain problems will be highlighted and given a special treatment. These are the second and third elements of the definition of microhistory – the 'great historical question' and agency, the relationship of microhistory with historical anthropology and postmodernism, and finally the sore point of microhistory: the link between the micro and macro levels, or, in other words, the representativity problem. In Chapter 4, we shall come back to these questions, try to suggest some answers as well as address the new problems that are brought up in the discourse of history at the beginning of the twenty-first century.

Chapter 1 is about *microstoria*, the original Italian version of microhistory into which Giovanni Levi's classical *Inheriting Power* will serve as a point of entry (Levi 1988). Special attention will be paid to the ways in which Italian microhistorians have addressed the central theoretical problem of microhistory: the link between the micro-investigation and the macro-level conclusion. The concepts of the 'exceptional normal' and 'changing the scale' will be evoked. The relationship of postmodernism and microhistory will be also briefly dealt with, and we shall encounter a few works of Ginzburg, the best known Italian microhistorian and leading personality of the branch of *microstoria* focusing on culture. In passing, we shall also get to know a few representatives of the social history line of *microstoria*. Finally, the problem of microhistorical narration will also be addressed.

In Chapter 2, we shall proceed to the direct effect of *microstoria* on French and German historians, especially on the third and fourth generations of the *Annales*: why did French historians think that *microstoria* could bring a solution to their problems? Arlette Farge's and Jacques Revel's book about the riots in Paris in 1750 will serve as an introduction (Farge and Revel 1991). The micro–macro link will be once again in the foreground: if microhistorians limit their investigation to a single event, how can they make general statements, how can they answer 'great historical questions'? The French reception of the *microstoria* has developed the idea of 'changing the scale' into the theory of 'multiscopic' historical investigation. While the French reception seems to focus its attention on theory, the German reception of *microstoria* brings the German school of everyday life, *Alltagsgeschichte* into the discussion.

In Chapter 3, English and American microhistories will be investigated, the objectives of which may not be any more identical with those of the *microstoria*, and can therefore only be called microhistory using a looser definition of the term. The renowned American historian, Robert Darnton's famous essay about the 'great cat massacre' will serve as a starting point for our survey (Darnton 1985: 75–104). It calls our attention to the relationship of microhistory and historical anthropology. It was also he who coined the term 'incident analysis' for books that share the intensive micro-investigation with microhistory, but do not want to make statements on a general, macro-level. We have to think about the boundaries of microhistory, and in doing so, the second element of the definition of microhistory, the 'great historical question' will be focused on. Meanwhile, having met the forerunners of microhistory as well as microhistorical works with a social historical approach, we shall proceed to recent English and American microhistory.

Following three chapters that share a geographical outlook, Chapter 4 will be more problem-oriented, trying to furnish a few possible answers to open questions as well as exposing those new questions that the twenty-first century has introduced into the discourse on history. While doing so, the geographical scope of the investigation will also be enlarged: Hungarian, Scandinavian, or Russian microhistorical works will be addressed.[5] Hungarian microhistory suggests the hypothesis that microhistory is a fractal and gives priority to the historical context, while works on the microhistory of Russia expose the importance of agency. The place for microhistory in present-day historical discourse is explored, with a special respect to experimental history and global history, and the characteristics of microhistory are summed up. All this is, of course, just one possible interpretation of microhistory, and readers will meet another in Part II of this book, in which Sigurður Gylfi Magnússon takes over.

The test case discussed in Chapter 5 evokes nineteenth-century rural Iceland, specifically death and people's attitude to death. First, a general picture is presented using a classical macro-approach, then a micro-approach is contrasted with this, a view from below, based on a set of private letters, diaries and other material. The differences between these approaches will be evident, how they provide historians with different possibilities, how and to what extent these methods can assist our understanding of historical developments, and how different pictures may result from applying these approaches.

As a theoretical case study, an important and highly illuminating case, with important implications for the status of microhistory both in Europe and America, is considered in Chapter 6. The case in point is the well-known story of Martin Guerre, a series of events that occurred in sixteenth-century France. It leads us to the discussions of the criticism levelled at microhistory during the 1980s and how microhistorians responded to it, in part under the influence of postmodernism.

In Chapter 7, the focus moves to contemporary debates within microhistory, in particular on the impact of ideas stemming from postmodernism and post-structuralism on microhistory and its future development. The theoretical issues discussed have led Sigurður Gylfi to an advocacy of 'the singularization of history'. It incorporates a plea to historians to move away from letting their research findings be led and governed by the grand narratives (or the idea that has been addressed in Part I as 'the great historical question'). Behind this belief lies also the view that microhistory had had less influence on historiographical practice than it perhaps warranted.

The attempts made by microhistorical research to come to grips with the ego-documents are worthy of attention. Sigurður Gylfi presents in Chapter 8 what may be called an instructive case study from his private life: he uses his own love story to illustrate the problems of such sources: how to form a clear idea why these sources were created and how their authors selected the material included in them. The exercise highlights the importance of analysing any 'text' used by historians in as minute detail as possible. At the end of the book, in the Postcript section, Sigurður Gylfi presents his main arguments to outline the position of microhistory in contemporary historical studies and consider its possibilities for the future.

Both of us are advocates of microhistory. Sigurður Gylfi is chair of the Center of Microhistorical Research at the Reykjavík Academy, as well as editor of the *Journal of Microhistory*. István M. Szijártó is Associate Professor of History at Eötvös University, Budapest, founder of the Microhistory Network, an international group of historians interested in microhistory. Both of us have been teaching microhistory as well as publishing books and articles about it since the mid-nineties. We have been in contact since 2006, working together on various projects related to the use of microhistory in historical scholarship. In writing this volume, we do not intend to smooth over differences in our ideas about microhistory, for there is evidently an underlying debate going on between the two of us which it would be silly to hide or deny. Disagreement will emerge, for example, on the boundaries of microhistory, or when we evaluate Natalie Zemon Davis's *The Return of Martin Guerre*, when we place microhistory in the development of the discourse of history, when the relationship of microhistory and posmodernism is concerned, and especially when we consider the goal of microhistory: whether a 'great historical question' is an attribute of or a hindrance to microhistory.

Hence, this book should be read as a dialogue or a debate on microhistory. From time to time, we will have a disagreement which will usually prove manageable, but which may sometimes be rather significant. A Hungarian joke might give some indication of our position: At the tender of the new Budapest metro line, German builders claim that the two tunnels drilled from the opposing directions will meet at maximum 10 centimetres' difference. The Japanese firm's offer says that this difference will not be more than 15 millimetres. The Russian company's representative shrugs his shoulders: 'Well, you might end up with two tunnels.' So, readers should be prepared: they might end up with two distinct interpretations of microhistory. For Chapters 5–8 and the Postscript are not simply a set of examples of microhistory, or a discussion of current theoretical debates about microhistory, but a contrast to the Introduction and Chapters 1–4. They represent a different approach to microhistory. Sigurður Gylfi does not share the view that despite its micro-level subject matter, microhistory has a goal situated on the level of the general. He argues that the strength of microhistory lies in its capacity to break with metanarratives. He advocates a view of microhistory that should side with postmodernism, and that breaks with most traditions of social history. Instead of efforts to reach general conclusions, he suggests a 'singularization of history'; 'to analyse the interlinking of *events, narratives, analysis*, and *new events*' through the research model which he calls 'textual environment'.

Part I, including this Introduction, written by István M. Szijártó, tries to be descriptive as opposed to this approach of Part II, emerging from a highly personal narrative. Chapters 1–4 will rather concentrate on how microhistorians themselves see their position and offer a loose interpretive framework. Based on the original objectives and practices of the Italian *microstoria*, a definition of three elements is set up (micro-analysis, agency and the intention to answer a 'great historical question') and used as an analytical tool when touring the landscape of microhistory from the Italian core territories through the neighbouring French and German lands to the Anglo-Saxon landscape and beyond. Several works of history with a more or less pronounced microhistorical character will be investigated and such key theoretical issues are visited as the relationship of microhistory with postmodernism and historical anthropology, as well as the problem of the micro–macro link. As for the latter, in Chapter 4, a concept of microhistory is suggested based on its fractal-like character and the notion of 'abduction'. The sometimes didactic text of Part I, therefore, gives an overview of what microhistory looks like now, while Part II, written by Sigurður Gylfi, advocates another view of what microhistory should look like. This book intends to be an introduction to microhistory with a survey of books that are microhistorical, or at least could be called microhistorical, as well as with a presentation of the most significant theoretical problems of the genre. Beyond this – renouncing the illusion of an objective judgement – its authors would like to take a stand for microhistory, arguing that it is an especially promising approach. As we have seen, the two voices of the book, with two different views on microhistory – one based on and presented within a general historiographical overview, the other on a deeply personal research history and a confrontation with current theoretical debates – are sometimes contradictory. But both are arguments for microhistory and not against. Albeit trying to offer some reliable information about microhistory, the main goal of this book – just as of micro-history, as a matter of fact – is to work against oversimplification and superficial historical judgement. Although some works of microhistory try to give answers to 'great historical questions', they should always be regarded as contributions to a colourful discourse. Microhistory does not want to establish new orthodoxies. Life has never been straightforward and simple truths should be regarded with suspicion. They can be best unmasked if historians use a microscope.

Notes

1 There are certainly other ways of defining microhistory. An early example of the application of this term is the title of Luis González y González's book. He wrote about four hundred years of the Mexican village of San José de Gracia (González 1968). Such a long-term local history may be called microhistory nowadays, too: (Li 2009).

2 The term 'new cultural history' is also in use, first of all in the United States, highlighting its opposition to older currents of cultural history. Since, however, it is not generally used as a self-designation of all the new currents referred to, the looser term 'cultural history', applied for example by Ute Daniel, is preferred here (cf. Daniel 2004).

3 It seems advisable that historians give several parallel explanations so that their readers can see their arbitrary character right away.

4 Similarly, John Brewer argues that 'social and cultural history unite in the micro-processes of everyday life' (Brewer 2010: 8).

5 Unfortunately, due to a lack of language competence, this overview cannot aim to be fully comprehensive. Books of and about microhistory in Spanish will be, unfortunately, ignored (e.g. Serna and Pons (2000), Aguirre Rojas (2003), Espada Lima (2006) (cf. Ginzburg 2011: 10) or Barriera (ed.) (2002)).

1 Italian microhistory

An exorcist in Santena

Darnton gave the advice to his colleagues that they should try to enter the cultures of the past at points where they do not understand something.

> When we cannot get a proverb, or a joke, or a ritual, or a poem, we know we are on to something. By picking at the document where it is most opaque, we may be able to unravel an alien system of meaning. The thread might even lead into a strange and wonderful world view.
>
> (Darnton 1985: 5)

The picture of ripe cheese and worms emerging from it as a model for the birth of angels is surprising enough to be regarded as such a point of entry, from which Ginzburg has tried to map an ancient oral popular culture. And what was Giovanni Levi's point of entry when writing about Giovan Battista Chiesa and his village? Chiesa was the vicar of Santena, and he was summoned before the archepiscopal court of Turin for his exorcisms. Despite our initial expectations, it was not any element of the exorcism but the particular system of land prices in Santena.

Surprisingly, the closer the seller was to the buyer, the higher the price was. The highest was paid by a relative, the average price by a neighbour, while the other extreme was represented by 'outsider' buyers. In the latter cases, the price was low because sellers could not find a relative or neighbour to buy their land, and they could hardly find anyone at all: nobles or notables often bought these plots as an act of charity. The paradoxically high land prices found among relatives served for Levi as a point of entry into the world of seventeenth-century Santena. Prices were high in these transactions because buying someone's land was just 'the last in a series of gestures of aid' (Levi 1988: 92). When relatives took over the land from a kin in trouble, all the previous financial help was added up and they called this a 'price'. This is proved by the fact that in land transactions between relatives often no direct payment in coin took place. Although other sources suggest that peasants were living in nuclear families composed of parents and their children, they were, in fact, cooperating in a much larger circle.

We can see this in the case of the male members of the elite of the agricultural population: the *massari* lived in separate households, but they jointly possessed and rented large plots of land. These were more important than their own land, which played the role of a security reserve. The heads of the extended *massari* families directed the work of twenty to thirty adults. It was through family cooperation that they tried to reach security, a goal more important for them than prosperity. The notables of Santena also cooperated within the framework of their extended families. In the Tesio family, the jobs of grain merchant, physician, apothecary or priest passed from one generation to another, usually inherited by the nephew from the uncle. In each generation, family land was concentrated in the hands of one or two persons, for example in that of the priest who enjoyed tax immunity. Land circulated relatively fast in the family, and actual ownership stood in no connection with its cultivation. Cooperation was the rule:

> Divided formally, families were administered as a coordinated entity, and they shared in a common politics of prestige. This enabled them to operate within society like a wedge, with a pyramidal hierarchy of nuclear families and individuals. It also allowed them to put all their resources toward a unified strategy in order to advance one conjugal group or, more often, an individual, from whom, in return, resources, prestige and security flowed back to all the nuclear families that made up the lineage as a whole.
>
> (Levi 1988: 146)

The manner in which a village in late seventeenth-century Piedmont was ruled, is presented by Levi with the example of one of the notables, Giulio Cesare Chiesa. He was Giovan Battista's father, *podestà*, that is chief administrator and judge, and notary of Santena. Appointed by the consortium of local feudal lords, he was a successful broker between them, the peasants and central authorities. In the middle of the seventeenth century, Santena tried to evade the jurisdiction of Chieri. The case was far from being clear-cut: Santena had no charter but had the organs of an autonomous community. For the decades of the jurisdictional quarrel, Giulio Cesare Chiesa managed to erase Santena from the tax lists.

Interestingly enough, the *podestà* did not buy land to stabilize his social standing. He invested into his prestige and social network: he gave substantial dowries to his daughters and good education to his sons. It might be said that he bequeathed his social standing to his children. But the deterioration of the economy, the war at the end of the century, and the ensuing debates among Santena's landlords after Giulio Cesare's death ruined the Chiesas' standing. The village came to dislike Giovan Battista for his mismanagement of confraternal funds, his greed and his occasional failure to say mass, and finally he proved to be unable to uphold the prestige inherited from his father. The exorcism represented his desperate attempt to regain this, and the intervention of the Church meant his final defeat.

The *podestà* of Santena

The changes preparing for the coming of modern states are usually portrayed in a way different from that of Levi. He concentrates on the micro-level and gives an unusual picture in which ordinary people are active, not puppets but decision-makers. Behind this thinking is the anthropologist Fredrik Barth. Leaving behind the structuralist and functionalist explanations, in Barth's model we can find limited rationality, uncertainty, non-deterministic causality, the incoherence of normative systems, the plurality of social forms and a wide scope of action for the active and rational human beings, pursuing their own goals. 'Since social acts are thus not simply "caused" but "intended", we must consider these intentions', researchers should focus on the 'actors' strategies of instrumentality and the aggregate social consequences of such strategies' (Barth, F. 1981: 2–3; Rosental 1996: 142–47; quotations: Barth, F. 1981: 2–3). Microhistory is therefore, according to Levi or Davis, first and foremost a tool to discard deterministic history (quoted by Gyáni 1997: 152). *Inheriting power* suggests that a peasant in Santena was no *homo oeconomicus*; his main goal was not maximizing profits, but minimizing risks. Behind the success of Giovan Battista Chiesa's exorcism we can find the same strategy: peasants aspired to a control of their bodily and psychic problems.

Levi's thesis has, however, two weak points. He argues that Giovan Battista's 'immaterial heritage' was power, but he has only the negative evidence that Giulio Cesare did not, in fact, buy land. But does it follow that the *podestà* had a conscious strategy not to do so? He educated his sons, which might have been a successful strategy save in the case of Giovan Battista – without sources we have no way of knowing – and it was to him that he bequeathed his local power. The vicar, however, lost this 'immaterial heritage' within four years. Why does not Levi conclude that this strategy, if this was indeed one, led to failure and Giulio Cesare Chiesa should have bought land, for even this case suggests that it was the only solid basis for social status in this period?

Acquiring this power is attributed by Levi to Giulio Cesare's exceptional brokering skills. About his activities, however, we have yet again only indirect evidence. His success is therefore demonstrated by the absence of conflicts: there was no strife between Chieri and Santena; Giulio Cesare could *de facto* govern the whole village, the landlords' conflicts ceased and peasants' move-ments also. But what guarantees for us that all this was a direct result of his activities? Levi could also have argued that Giulio Cesare was *podestà* in a favourable, peaceful period, in one when no taxes were paid to Chieri, so he was able to preserve his position for a long time and make his son vicar of Santena. After his death, however, Piedmont became a theatre of war; famine came and natural disasters followed. Moreover, the Chiesas tied their fate to the Tana de Santena family, and when their star was on the wane, also that of the Chiesa family became eclipsed. So no wonder Giovan Battista was unable to keep the family business running: changing conditions and not personal qualities may have been decisive.

Levi's microhistory is clearly different from Ginzburg's. In Ginzburg's presentation, in accordance with the Foucauldian thinking of the 1960s and '70s contrasting institutional and social levels (Revel 1995a: 74–75), the state is still seen as an oppressor. From the 1980s on, however, writes Renata Ago, this simple model seemed untenable. The state and its institutions, like the law, were no longer regarded as mere tools of power in relation to which people have only two choices: to resist or to give in. Since the 1980s the relationship between norms and practices has been seen in a different light. For Levi, the social actors' goal is already manipulation: they try to exploit the contradictions of an inconsistent system of norms, they have the scope for action and initiative (Ago 2004: 45–47). Behind the micro-event, that serves as the focus of his book, Levi paints a socio-economic background on the basis of much deeper analyses than Ginzburg or, as we shall see, Davis. Anna Jacobson Schutte writes that this even goes to the point of tipping the balance between analysis and narrative, desirable in microhistory (Jacobson Schutte 1986: 962).

In Chapter 1, having introduced *microstoria*, its social historical and cultural historical branches, we shall address the relationship of postmodernism and microhistory, and also meet the concepts of the 'normal exceptions' and 'changing the scale'. We shall then concentrate on Ginzburg's work, particularly on its theoretical aspects, and a few other works of Italian microhistory will be briefly presented. Finally the role of narrative in microhistory will be discussed.

'A history with additives'

Microhistory was invented by Italian scholars with a Marxist background.[1] They grouped around the Bologna periodical *Quaderni Storici* (1966–) – which was exceptionally open to minority opinion in the extremely polarized Italian academic life of the time – and the book series *Microstorie* (1981–91, 22 vols) published by Einaudi in Turin.[2] In 1977, Edoardo Grendi suggested a programme of research based on 'micro-analysis'. This term was later replaced by 'microhistory' (Ginzburg 1993: 10–16; Levi 1991: 94; Muir 1991a: ix; Grendi 1996: 240; cf. Grendi 1977). Its programme was proclaimed by Ginzburg and Carlo Poni at an Italian–French conference in Rome in January 1979. Their paper was later published under the title 'The name and the game' (Ginzburg and Poni 1991).[3]

Ginzburg and Poni claimed that without adequate financing and organization, Italian historians were unable to follow the French way of writing history, something they should not do anyway, since doubts had arisen in connection with macro-historical methods: serial or quantitative history is losing life's reality. Instead of the social science history of the *Annales*, they suggested, as we have already seen, an 'analysis, at extremely close range, of highly circumscribed phenomena – a village community, a group of families, even an individual person', a history that stands closer to anthropology. In the labyrinth of the archives, historians should follow the name as Ariadne's thread, as usual in the reconstruction of families by nominative demography. This way they can find the individuals under investigation in 'different social contexts': in parish registers their births, deaths and children, in property registers they feature as owners and tenants, in criminal records as accused, plaintiffs or witnesses – and thus the network of their social relations will emerge (Ginzburg and Poni 1991: 1–5, quotations: 3, 5).

Following the decades of dominance by social science history, focusing on the great structures and Braudelian *longue durée*, a concentration on details was to a certain extent a predictable counter-effect. The characteristic feature of Italian microhistory is, however, that the goal, answering 'great historical questions', reaching general conclusions, remained unchanged. 'The purpose of microhistory is to elucidate historical causation at the level of small groups where most of life takes place and to open history up to peoples who would be left out by other methods' (Muir 1991a: xxi) True to their leftist thinking, Italian microhistorians have always put an emphasis on marginals, the losers of what Karl Polányi called the 'great transformation' (Polanyi 1944) As we have just seen, Menocchio also entered the stage as a representative of the popular culture, understood as a counter-culture, opposed to the ideology of the ruling classes.

From Ginzburg's and Poni's programme, it will be evident that microhistory – using Franco Venturi's ironic expression, 'a history with additives' (quoted by Ginzburg 1993: 32) – had no intention of completely departing from the traditions of social science history.

> We propose, therefore, to define microhistory, and history in general, as the *science of real life* [*scienza del vissuto*], a definition that seeks to comprehend the reasoning of both the supporters and the enemies of the integration of history with the social sciences, and for this, no doubt, it will not be pleasing to either side.
>
> (Ginzburg and Poni 1991: 8–9)

This way, *microstoria* is, on one hand, able to bridge the approaches of social history and cultural history, on the other, it can be characterized by a corresponding internal division. It is generally agreed, that one of the branches of Italian microhistory is social historical, the other cultural historical in its outlook, and there is some tension between them (Muir 1991a: xv; Rosental: 1996: 141; Szekeres 1999: 3). Cerutti, one of the series editors of *Microstorie*, remembers Alberto Banti dividing Italian microhistory into two in 1991, calling social historians parachutists and cultural historians truffle hunters (Cerutti 2004: 18). We have seen Grendi criticizing *The Cheese and the Worms* for neglecting the social and focusing only on the cultural. For Grendi, *microstoria* is a more detailed and better-founded social history (Grendi 1996: 239). According to Gianna Pomata – from the cultural side of the divide – the tension between the two currents of *microstoria* became sharper in the mid-1980s; then social historians got the upper hand and *microstoria* became hostile to cultural history, to those in search of meaning (Pomata 2000).

But microhistorians who emphasize social history, claims Cerutti, do not intend to separate analysis of the social and the cultural contexts, rather they try to grasp the cultural context at the level of the individual under investigation. She postulates a convergence between microhistorians with social and cultural preferences (Cerutti 2004: 19–20). Renata Ago also argues that since social structure is a result of human interactions, microhistorians wanted to reconstruct these, so they concentrated on human relations. Although they first focused on social networks, it is also possible to explore action and its meaning, and how these actions form the whole system. The most important thing is to understand what action means for the actors themselves: their culture should be revealed (Ago 2004: 41–44). So we might conclude that the undoubtedly existing difference in preferences between the two branches of Italian microhistory is not decisive. The arguments pitting *microstoria* against postmodernist epistemology seem much stronger.

Microstoria and postmodernism

The heat of the epistemological debates that comprised the so-called 'linguistic turn' is due to the fact that the impact of postmodernism – articulated from the 1960s and '70s – and the belated impact of modernist theories, already present from the early years of the twentieth century, arrived at the theory of history at the same time, amplifying each other's effect. Before this the impact of modernist philosophy on history remained rather superficial.

Conveniently, we can distinguish between modernist and postmodernist positions on the basis of their views about language. Historians could have learned long ago from Ferdinand de Saussure or Ludwig Wittgenstein that language cannot be ignored; it is not just a tool but the form of human existence (Bókay 1997: 133–34). Modernism argues that language is not mimetic but generative; it does not reflect the world but forms it. Postmodernism goes even further and claims that language cannot be dominated, the author is 'dead'; not even he/she is in control of meaning (Spiegel 1990). These contrasting views about language seem to stand behind the cardinal difference as to the theory of history: there are those who maintain that there is a correspondence between past reality and the historical text, and those who deny it.

It is not by chance that the 'linguistic turn' coincided with the challenge of cultural history. Joyce Appleby, Lynn Hunt and Margaret Jacob claim that cultural historians have given up finding causes in history, so cultural history became intertwined with relativism. According to them, those who endorse postmodernism deny the existence of truth; they claim that historians just produce reality effects, they deny the validity of macro-history, and they do not want to write anything but microhistory (Appleby, Hunt and Jacob 1995: 223–28). We see that this interpretation, hostile to postmodernism, links microhistory directly to it. Similarly, a Dutch philosopher of history, Frank R. Ankersmit, who, however, stands on the other side of the divide, regards microhistory as one of the recent currents, a fruit of postmodern times (Ankersmit 1995). According to him, postmodern history concentrates on small objects of investigation; it has a literary, narrative character, its narratives are incommensurable, and it has given up hope of getting to know the past. Among others, he even names Ginzburg as a postmodern historian (quoted by Ginzburg 1993). Some representatives of microhistory endorse this interpretation. For example *Casus*, the periodical of Russian microhistorians, claims in its slogan to address 'the individual and unique in history'.

Microstoria, however, emphatically denies this link with postmodernism, first of all because of its sceptical-agnostical epistemological outlook, albeit in the background of the birth of microhistory we can find the end of a belief in metanarratives. Levi writes that, in the crisis of the 1970s, Italian microhistorians went against the tide of the relativist 'linguistic turn', against 'the reduction of the historian's work to a purely rhetorical activity' (Levi 1991: 95). On the other hand, Levi acknowledges the similarity of the approach of microhistory to that of the anthropologist Clifford Geertz's 'thick description', arranging a set of signifying signs into an intelligible structure, and interpreting them with the help of a context. But here, for Levi, the power of the interpreter and the danger of relativism are too great. Opposed to Geertz's anthropology, microhistory does not attribute a homogenous meaning to signs and symbols, does not presuppose the existence of a homogenous cultural context, but takes its starting point in social differentiation, and, finally, does not sacrifice the individual to generalization (Levi 1991).

Notwithstanding inner debates, Italian microhistory seems to be unified in its refusal of postmodernism (Ago 2004: 43; Ginzburg 1993: 32–33; Ginzburg 2010b: 10; Grendi 1996: 242; Pomata 2000). The German historiographer and microhistorian, Otto Ulbricht also regards the classification of microhistory as postmodern as false. He says that its empiricism rules this out (Ulbricht 2009: 37). Richard D. Brown hints at the possibility that due to its well-based truth claims, microhistory might indeed be the adequate response to the 'post-modern challenge' (Brown, R. D. 2003: 20).

'Normal exceptions' and 'changing the scale'

Ginzburg and Poni have suggested that detailed qualitative research should be combined with a focus on the lower social strata. This, however, cannot ever be exhaustive. How to choose then, the relevant and significant cases? The answer of the *microstorian* to this theoretical challenge is the concept of the 'exceptional normal' (*eccezionalmente normale*) or 'normal exceptions'. According to this in preindustrial societies, breaking certain rules was in fact the norm. But it also means, and this is its more important meaning, that a really exceptional document, a marginal case can reveal a hidden reality, when the sources are silent about the lower social strata, or when they systematically distort their social reality (Ginzburg and Poni 1991: 7–8, cf. Ginzburg 1993: 21, Grendi 1996: 238). Hans Medick argues that the meaning of this opaque term,[4] opposed to statistical representativity, has broadened to denote the capacity of deep and contextualizing analyses of individual cases to go beneath the surface and reveal what was possible and what was not (Medick 1994: 46). *Microstoria* has worked out another theoretical category, too, to address the relationship of the micro and macro levels.

The leading personality of the Italian microhistorians with a social history outlook, Giovanni Levi, regards 'changing the scale' as being at the heart of microhistory, it is 'a practice based on the reduction of the scale of observation' (Levi 1991: 95) According to him, microhistory is not defined by the micro-dimension of its subject. Microhistorians analyse general phenomena on individual details. It is defined instead by the way microhistorians proceed: microhistory, in Levi's interpretation, is an intensive microscopic investigation; the scale of observation is changed in the hope of revealing previously unobserved factors. Microhistory is, therefore, capable of furnishing a more realistic account of human behaviour (Levi 1991: 94–97).

Ginzburg points to a forgotten forerunner of the idea of 'changing the scale' in the person of Siegfried Kracauer, a member of the Frankfurt school of critical social theory, who had no direct influence on *microstoria* in its formative years. Kracauer used the term 'microhistory' earlier then the Italians (Ginzburg 1993: 26; Medick 1996: 30, 32). In his posthumous *History: The Last Things Before the Last*, he devoted a chapter to the dilemma of micro- and macro-history. He maintains that micro- and macro-realities exist independently and both are equally authentic. A part of historical reality has a macro-dimension, insofar as it cannot be broken down to microscopic elements; certain developments happen above the micro-dimension. We should not, however, overrate the relative autonomy of the macro-level: the higher the level we observe, the poorer will be the historical reality: we are losing experience, macro-narratives are artificial, for they are too logical. Kracauer does not think that a mixture of both approaches is possible; he advocates an alternation of macro- and micro-histories,[5] giving priority to the latter and dedicating short overviews to the macro-aspects of history. An expert on film, Kracauer evokes the example of the 'blow-up':[6] microhistory is similar to the isolation of a small detail and its blowing up, to use Antonioni's term, in order to learn more about the whole (Kracauer 1969: 104–38).

Inquisitors and witches

Robert W. Scribner argues that for historians, 'it might be better to give up the pretence that we can recover the *status quo ante* and concentrate on the dialogue as the central hermeneutical context' (Scribner 1997: 31).[7] In Ginzburg's *The Cheese and the Worms*, we, in fact, witness the dialogue of the miller and the inquisitors, that is the dialogue between the popular and the elite cultures. Similarly, in his first book, Ginzburg unveiled a particular cult in Friuli. He was not presenting a microcosm of the local society, the way of life, the relationships or the world view of ordinary people, but the transformation of local beliefs under the pressure of the inquisition. He said himself that he was looking for class struggle but instead he had found a fertility cult (quoted by Daniel 2004: 286). For five decades, stupefied inquisitors listened to the so-called *benandanti* from

Friuli claiming that they were not witches, just the opposite: they were fighting the witches four nights a year to ensure a good crop for the community. This is an exceptional case, argues Ginzburg, in which the inquisition recorded exactly what the accused stated, because they did not understand any of it: these are the best sources of popular beliefs. Usually, the accused broke and confessed what the inquisitors wanted to hear (Ginzburg 1989b: 156–65). This was the end of the *benandanti*'s story as well: after decades of investigation the fertility cult was forcibly transformed by the inquisitors into witchcraft and the witches' sabbath (Daniel 2004: 286).

According to Cerutti, Ginzburg takes a document as his point of departure, then he identifies the relevant contexts; first the meaning given by the actor himself, then those contexts farther and farther from him – and for Ginzburg the most important of all these is the one that is the farthest from the actor. Evoking Luc Boltanski, Cerutti claims that historians should reveal why historical actors preferred one way to others, why they handed down one tradition to their children and not others. Relevance would be attributed in this 'emic' approach according to the actors' and not the historians' preferences (Cerutti 2004: 33–35). In the case of Menocchio, the most important thing for Ginzburg was to identify an old, oral, materialistic, Indo-European popular culture. We can, therefore, conclude that in certain cases one of the objectives of microhistory, the central importance attributed to agency, can only assert itself at the cost of the other, the wish to find the answer to a 'great historical question'. This contradiction might be solved by an 'emic' approach: looking for the 'great historical question' that was important for the actors of the past, too.

In the first volume of the *Microstorie* book series, Ginzburg chose Piero della Francesca's three major works as the subjects of his analysis. His reader can experience the thrill of a crime investigation as Ginzburg identifies those who commissioned and those who feature in the paintings, and solves the mystery of one of the paintings by revealing the context of its genesis and analysing the little details (Ginzburg 2000). When he draws conclusions from the shapes of the ears, noses or beards of those who figure on *The Flagellation of Christ*, or analyses the gestures made by their hands, he evokes the art historian Giovanni Morelli's method (Burke 2000: xvi–viii).

Ear-lobes and fingernails

In his well-known essay on the 'index paradigm', too, Ginzburg relies on the thoughts of Morelli, who attributed paintings of dubious authorship not on the basis of the great masters' typical features, copied by imitators, but analysing similarly characteristic little signs, for example the shapes of the ear-lobes and fingernails, neglected by imitators. Ginzburg draws a parallel between Morelli's method and those of Sigmund Freud and Arthur Conan Doyle's famous hero, Sherlock Holmes. Their similarity is based on their common model, medical semiotics. The essence of each of these is to approach a directly inaccessible reality through analysing small clues.

Calling this the 'index paradigm' or 'evidential paradigm', Ginzburg elevates it to the position of a rival of the dominant Galilean-Cartesian paradigm of science, based on quantification. He claims that sciences that use an individualizing approach and that are unable to employ quantification (for example medicine) are characterized by this paradigm. History also belongs to these, because of its individualizing strategy and indirect knowledge, based on conjecture. He claims that this knowledge is not inferior to quantifying science, just different from it: both medicine and history are characterized by a richer knowledge, in which instinct and intuition are at work (Ginzburg 1989a).[8]

A very similar phenomenon is described by the American pragmatist philosopher, Charles S. Peirce as 'abduction'. We look for a theory, he explains, taking our starting point in facts. We proceed by a 'trial and error' method; we do not make random guesses, however, but use our intuition instead. The sudden regrouping of hitherto unconscious information into a new form is called by Peirce 'abduction'. Abduction is the single way to forming new hypotheses, it is therefore indispensable for progress (Muir 1991a: viii, xvi–ix, cf. Sebeok and Umiker-Sebeok 1980).

In 2005, a conference was held in Lille to explore the aftermath of Ginzburg's concept of the 'index-paradigm', which he, as he explained, had since tried to deepen in three directions: towards the analysis of the proof, the rule and the case (Ginzburg 2010a: 353–59). The latter way, the method of 'thinking by case' was also explored in a volume edited by Jacques Revel and Jean-Claude Passeron. As they argue, this way of thinking seeks to deepen the particular qualities of observed singularities 'in order to establish an argument of more general interest' (Passeron and Revel 2005: 285). Ginzburg also argues that the theory deduced from a case is richer than explicit theory. According to him, the case may indicate the weak points of dominant epistemological paradigms (Ginzburg 2010a: 361–62). His argument reflects the fact that for Ginzburg the value of microhistory still rests mainly in its subversive capacity.

Turin, Florence and Genoa

The real heroes of the quantitative social history were not individuals but social groupings, constructed by the historians. For social historians, the first step towards change was using the categories of the period under investigation; then their attention was directed to how this system of categories had come into being and which conditions had formed it (Czoch 1999: 22). The best example is Cerutti's book about seventeenth- and eighteenth-century Turin, in which we can observe the multiple intertwinings of social reality and its representations (Nagy 2010: 243). Cerutti argues that to reconstruct the emergence of categories used by a society in the past to describe itself, historians should not accept that certain persons belonged to certain social groups as a proven fact; instead they should analyse the interpersonal connections and show how these result in solidarity, alliances and constitute finally social classes. She therefore advocates the use of social network analysis.

In the early eighteenth century, the former simplified picture of Turin that the inhabitants had had of their own city disintegrated: an elite composed of the army, the high office holders and the aristocracy versus the plebeians represented by the city council. The system of guilds was extended and differentiated and people started to think about themselves in professional terms, fragmenting the hitherto unified picture they had of themselves. When looking for the cause of this development, Cerutti compares the history of the guilds and that of the other possibilities of organizing people. Taking experiences, a multiplicity of life courses and individual rationality as her starting point, she analyses how social groupings were constituted, and how individual rationality was linked to collective identity (Cerutti 1990).

Network analysis and microhistory can be easily matched. Christiane Klapisch-Zuber's case study of Lapo Niccolini is an example. Sketching the social network of this Florentine merchant, the historian concludes that the tightly-knit group of his kin was most important for her hero, most of whom also shared a dwelling. Affinal kin gave him new opportunities, helping upward mobility. Finally godparenthood, a proxy for friendship, was more of a local character, directed downwards socially. These differences are demonstrated by the typical form of social contacts: relatives lived together, affinal kin were brought together to banquets held on important occasions, while friends were occasionally called in from the street for a cup of wine (Klapisch-Zuber 1985).

Cerutti's Italian colleague, Maurizio Gribaudi, also working in Paris, wrote about a working quarter of Turin between the two world wars. Instead of supposing the existence of a homogenous working class, characterized by a unified identity, he took the plurality of migration experiences as his starting point. What he saw then emerging, was not a social group, but a social situation (*condition ouvrière*), to which he could couple a particular local workers' identity. The passing from one generation to the other coincided with the incursion of fascism into the community that led to its disintegration (Nagy 2010: 250–57, cf. Gribaudi 1987). Gribaudi has shown that in the micro-analysis of the precise context, macro-structural causes lose their validity (Gregory 1999: 104).

Other important works of *microstoria* are Grendi's book on Cervo and Osvaldo Raggio's on Fontanabuona. Their research on the environs of Genoa paints a totally new picture of the emergence of the early modern state, because instead of the central organs of the state, they concentrated on local politics and the interrelation of central power and local society (Szekeres 1999: 3–5, cf. Raggio 1990, Grendi 1993). Grendi demonstrates the falsity of presentations of local community that are based on a description of the elite's political behaviour and macro-statistical data (Muir 1991a: xv). Works of the *microstoria* induce their readership to see the past differently, claims Ginzburg. Just as Raggio's book changes our ideas about the birth of the early modern state, Franco Ramella's microscopic investigation of the Val di Mossi changes our views about proto-industrialization (Ginzburg 1993: 33, cf. Raggio 1990, Ramella 1983).

Microhistory as narrative

> The experimental attitude that brought together, at the end of the 1970s, the group of Italian students of microhistory [...] was based on the definite awareness that all phases through which research unfolds are constructed and not given: the identification of the object and its importance; the elaboration of the categories through which it is analysed; the criteria of proof; the stylistic and narrative forms by which the results are transmitted to the reader.
>
> (Ginzburg 1993: 32)

One of the distinguishing features of microhistory is the central importance attributed to the text of the historian: his narration. Gianni Pomata preferred Ginzburg's microhistory to Grendi's because the former did not want to write social science but competed with authors. She claims that E. P. Thompson or Ginzburg can produce the same effect on readers as novelists (Pomata 2000). Many have pointed out that historians use narrative, and this tool exerts a significant influence on the results produced. Jerome Bruner asserts that there are two ways to construct reality, 'two modes of cognitive functioning': the 'narrative' and the 'paradigmatic' modes. Both a well-formed argument and a good story can convince the reader, '[y]et what they convince of is fundamentally different: arguments convince one of their truth, stories of their lifelikeness' (Bruner 1986: 11). Although narration is thus a key element in all kinds of history, in microhistory the stakes are especially high. Here the research process itself becomes a subject of the historians' reflexivity (Christiansen 1995: 7). Ginzburg wrote, that in his *The Cheese and the Worms* 'the hypotheses, the doubts, the uncertainties became part of the narration' (Ginzburg 1993: 24). Since the most interesting moments of the historians' work are when they actually find something in the documents, it is evident that it is worth trying to build the research process itself into historians' texts. If historians are able to convey the excitement of this pathfinder or detective work to their readers, history could be a much more arresting read.

Peter Burke has suggested to his colleagues that they should use modern narrative methods such as alternative endings or multiple viewpoints, that they should step into the foreground and make their preferences explicit instead of staying in the background and acting as all-knowing narrators. But most important, he maintains, is to write a narrative that is 'thick enough' to address not only events or intentions but also structures. To be able to do so, Burke suggests the use of micro-narratives, evoking first Carlo Cipolla's work on the plague in the Tuscan city of Prato in 1630, then Davis's book about Martin Guerre (shortly to be discussed and later in detail) which is about an event that uncovers social structures, and finally Jonathan Spence's many books (Burke, P. 1991: 241–43, cf. Cipolla 1973, Davis 1983). Spence's highly acclaimed *The Death of Woman Wang* uses narrative and literary sources to bring us close to the experience of ordinary people's lives in the turbulent conditions of the late seventeenth-century Shantung province of China through a set of stories (Spence 1978).

It is paradoxical that the special attention paid to narrative is generally regarded as one of the distinctive features of microhistory, while the micro-approach also lends it a stronger reality: so we can say that microhistory is both closer to and farther from literature than history is in general.

Levi's example or Burke's insistence that micro-narratives should address structural issues brings us back to the cardinal feature of the *microstoria*: the special attention paid to 'great historical questions' or, to put it in another way, to structures. This element of the definition of microhistory demonstrates that one of its feet stands firmly in the tradition of social history. This characteristic made it possible for microhistory to exert a significant direct influence on French and German historiography.

Notes

1 For an impression of this milieu, see: (Pomata 2000).
2 The first book to be published in the series *Microstorie* was Ginzburg's book about three major paintings of Piero della Francesca; then Raul Merzario's book on matrimonial strategies in the diocese of Como; then the dialogue of Pietro Mercenaro and Vittorio Foa about historical consciousness; Antonio Foscari's and Manfredo Tafuri's book about the Renaissance rebuilding of a church in Venice; Alessandro Portelli's 'oral history' about the town of Terni; Pietro Redondi's reconsideration of Galileo Galilei's trial; as well as books by Franco Ramella, Osvaldo Raggio and Giovanni Levi. The series was also open to translations: it published Paul Boyer's and Stephen Nissenbaum's book about Salem witchcraft, as well as the story of the return of Martin Guerre by Davis, Anton Blok's book about the mafia of a Sicilian village, and also a selection from E. P. Thompson's essays (Muir 1991a: xxii, cf. Levi 1988, Ginzburg 2000, Ramella 1983, Raggio 1990, Redondi 1987, Davis 1983, Blok 1974, Boyer and Nissenbaum 1974).
3 *Il nome et il come* – according to Simona Cerutti, they are referring to the historical actor's name and the form of social action (Cerutti 2004: 20).
4 Its various interpretations as well as somewhat diverging translations highlight this opaqueness. Jacques Revel therefore calls this oxymoron a 'dark diamond' (Revel 1996a: 31).
5 Maybe a good example of this is the way in which Tolstoy describes the battle of Borodino: alternating long shots – what is happening on the battlefield – with close-ups – what individual participants can see, e.g. Count Pierre Bezuhov or the soldiers in Prince Andrey Bolkonsky's regiment.
6 Michelangelo Antonioni's famous *Blow-Up* (1966), based on a short story written by Julio Cortázar, is repeatedly evoked in connection with microhistory. As we can see, Kracauer evoked this parallel earlier.
7 We have seen Muir's similar thought expounded in discussing *The Cheese and the Worms*.
8 The concept is given a different evaluation by Sigurður Gylfi Magnússon in Part II.

2   Under the impact of *microstoria*

The French and German perspective

The vanishing children

According to Michel Vovelle and Roger Chartier, in the 1750s and '60s, the loss of authority by the French monarchy reached a level when the popular reverence for it suffered serious damage (quoted by Baker 1987: xvii). Arlette Farge and Jacques Revel's book, *The Vanishing Children of Paris* (1991) gives a micro-analysis of this phenomenon. The strange case leads the authors to take an anthropological stance – that is, they also follow the path suggested by Darnton: that thorough analysis of unintelligible detail may serve as a point of entry into an alien culture.

In 1750, the rumour spread in Paris that the police were not only arresting tramps but also children found in the streets, who had to be ransomed by their parents, or they were transported to colonies overseas. On 1 May, when six youngsters between 13 and 15 years of age were arrested, a battle ensued between policemen on one hand and local inhabitants and soldiers who joined them on the other. It lasted for several hours. Somewhere else, the crowd attacked a cart transporting archers because they thought the archers intended to abduct children. Several wounded and one dead were left on the scene. 'Forty years later, the glazier Ménétra still remembers that his father came to fetch him from school "with seven strong cooper lads each carrying a crowbar over his shoulder"' (Farge and Revel 1991: 10–11). This atmosphere gave birth to an open revolt on 22–23 May, which in fact comprised a series of unconnected disturbances. On 22 May, six serious incidents happened. They all took their starting point from a street scene that was interpreted collectively.

> In one case, a disabled veteran from Les Invalides who had celebrated his leave by getting drunk, forced a street musician to play the hurdy-gurdy outside the collège des Quatre-Nations. That was enough for some to cry, 'He's no soldier, he's one of those constable rascals in disguise come to kidnap the children!' The crowd of onlookers, who had been amused by the soldier's antics up to that point, then hurled themselves at him intending to lynch him. The only safety lay in flight.
>
> (Farge and Revel 1991: 11–12)

The majority of incidents followed the same pattern. Those attacked by the crowd usually tried to find shelter in the local police commissioner's residence, but that was often stormed, too.

The authors stress that both parties claimed that they wanted public order, only the crowd regarded kidnapping children as an infringement, while for the police it was the unrest itself. The police saw sedition and conspiracy in the background of the revolt. They were most of all afraid of networks of organized crime. Those inhabitants of Paris who resorted to force regarded the police as the source of conflict. Parallel to the traditional type of police, under the control of the *parlement*, familiar to local inhabitants, in the eighteenth century a new, not territorially organized, police force was developed: inspectors with special tasks, also operating a network of spies. Because of their secret activity, they were unpopular with the public. The royal decree of 12 November 1749 entrusted them with rounding up vagrants. The new police chief, Berryer firmly instructed them to step up their activities and policemen were paid on the basis of the number of arrests made. His erroneous appraisal of the situation was triggering the unrest.

The revolt itself constituted a persistent search for meaning, argue Farge and Revel. Participants made sense of it in the current of events. Authorities later charged marginal elements rather than decent citizens, no women and only one artisan. Although decent citizens were clearly implicated in the unrest and there was often evidence against them, they did not fit the picture the police formed about the revolt retrospectively. After the events, these people did not identify themselves with the unrest, but earlier they were, in fact, ready to revolt for their children, for public order and for the meaning they gave to the events.

People were directed by rumours. The most serious of these concerned a leprous prince bathing in children's blood. Although not mentioned in the sources of the revolt, the authors claim that it was there in its background. This rumour likened King Louis XV to Herod, and charged him with all the sins, the corporeal manifestation of which is leprosy according to popular belief. As D'Argenson noted in the summer of 1750, the King is no longer loved by his people. According to Farge and Revel, the unrest following the kidnapping of children in Paris represents one of the milestones on the way to the estrangement of the King and the people of France (Farge and Revel 1991).

Discussing first the forerunners of microhistory in France, especially some of Le Roy Ladurie's books, we shall then consider the influence of the *microstoria* on the *Annales* school. Theoretical questions will come to the fore: the upgraded version of the concept of 'changing the scale', called multiscopic history, and the representativity problem of microhistory in general. We shall then proceed to German microhistory by presenting *Alltagsgeschichte*, the German school of the history of everyday life, as well as a few Göttingen historians and certain other works that we can classify as microhistory.

The battle at Bouvines and the carnival at Romans

There is no reason to think that the method of micro-analysis was taught to French historians by Italian microhistorians. In 1973, one of the outstanding figures of the third generation of the *Annales*, Georges Duby, wrote *The Legend of Bouvines*, one of the forerunners of microhistory which we might even call an early example. One single day stands at the centre of the book, 27 July 1214, the day of the battle of Bouvines. Duby not only evokes the battle itself and its background, but also demonstrates to the reader the – very different – meanings of war and battle in the thirteenth century. The final section of his book shows the development and later forms of 'the legend of Bouvines' (Duby 1990).

But Duby's micro-analysis is no fully-fledged microhistory. It is not the deep analysis of the battle, in which Philip Augustus, King of France won a great victory over the imperial troops and their allies, that shows the readers the world of the Middle Ages. Neither does it serve as a point of entry into an alien culture. The author does not build on it a general thesis, nor the refutation of another. The battle rather serves as a pretext for the famous medievalist to share his knowledge with us about the relevant contexts, synchronous or diachronic connections.

On the other hand, some of Alain Corbin's books are really centred on an event, and approach the general through this, so they can be described as microhistory. *The Village of Cannibals* has at its centre the brutal lynching of a young nobleman who had allegedly cheered the republic in Hautefaye in Western France in 1870. Analysing crowd violence, Corbin goes back to the French Revolution in order to interpret this last spectacular example of peasant rage in France (Corbin 1992). One of his other books is the result of a strange experiment: how to write a micro-analysis about a randomly selected person, Louis-François Pinagot (1798–1876) about whom no special sources have been conserved (Corbin 1998).

Similarly, there are good reasons to claim that Emmanuel Le Roy Ladurie's much earlier book, *Carnival*, is also microhistory. Unlike the case of *The Legend of Bouvines*, the individual event is not just a pretext here, it really stands at the heart of the analysis. In the province of Dauphiné, in south-west France, the nobility was divided along confessional lines during the civil war. In this uncertain situation, masses of peasants were armed and fought the marauders terrorizing the countryside. In February 1579, the agitation spread to the city of Romans. After the carnival procession, the artisans took over the militia as well as control of the city gates and walls. One year later, however, carnival celebrations as well as carnival 'kingdoms' (*reynage*) made it possible for the royal judge Antoine Guérin to organize the elite and their allies and stage a bloody take-over of power. Le Roy Ladurie places events at Romans at the centre of his narrative of events at Dauphiné in 1579–80. When Romans is re-taken by the earlier ruling elite, there is nothing left for him but to cut his story short. But the carnival at Romans was, in fact, nothing but an episode, and far from being the most significant event of the civil war in Dauphiné. The artisans' defeat at Romans was hardly felt by the peasants' league, which was only defeated by the king's army later. However, since Le Roy Ladurie had detailed documents about the events in Romans at his disposal, among them Guérin's narrative, he wrote his microhistory about the carnival at Romans. Narration, however, does not preclude analysis, and most of the chapters consist of traditional social historical analysis. The author tries to define partisanship by the average tax paid by the district's population as well as its professional composition, while he employs methods of cultural anthropology when interpreting the symbols of carnival (Le Roy Ladurie 1980).

Revel writes that the extraordinary event reveals historical layers of *mentalité* and society, left over from the early years of the *ancien régime*, just as geological layers are revealed in the Grand Canyon. Le Roy Ladurie resurrected the 'event' with this book, but only in order to analyse structures (Revel 2001).[1] The anthropologist Victor Turner defines 'social drama' in very similar terms, as 'an extended case study [providing] a limited area of transparency on the otherwise opaque surface of regular, uneventful social life. Through it we are enabled to observe the crucial principles of the social structure in their operation' (quoted by Macfarlane 1981: 24). Though using different metaphors, Turner and Revel refer to the same phenomenon. *Carnival* can be best interpreted as an example of 'social drama'.

Cathars in Montaillou

Le Roy Ladurie's best known work is *Montaillou*, based on the protocols of the inquisition of the diocese of Pamiers, in the south of France, from 1318 to 1326. It is the procedure of the bishop, Jacques Fournier, the future Pope Benedict XII, that gives these a special value: he was not only a clever and intelligent man, but he was also untiring in revealing truth and willing to work with meticulous care and go into minute details. He himself led the interrogation of all the suspects, most of them accused of the Cathar heresy, and torture was employed only exceptionally in his court. From a village in the Pyrenées, Montaillou, no fewer than 25 people appeared before his court. In his book, Le Roy Ladurie presents the everyday life of this tiny mountain village, reflected by the documents in unusual detail. *Montaillou* follows the example of the community studies of anthropology, and the author's questions are prompted first of all by the history of *mentalité*. His favoured themes are sexuality, beliefs, and ideas about time, space and the other world. He depicts the conflict of the, mostly ecclesiastical, oppressors and the, at least secretly, Cathar villagers. This picture is not as black and white as *The Cheese and the Worms*, partly because the 'main character' of the book, Pierre Clergue, Montaillou's womanizer parish priest, at first supports the Cathars and later becomes the local agent of the inquisition, denouncing his personal opponents in the village as heretics, only finally to die in the prison of the inquisition when Bishop Fournier's relatives, the clan Azéma, turn against him (Le Roy Ladurie 1978).

This book enjoyed a success rare among historical works, due to its subject and novelty. It is generally referred to as one of the classic works of micro-history. Undoubtedly, his unusually rich source material gives Le Roy Ladurie a chance to conduct a micro-investigation, and bring medieval life and thinking closer to the reader than at any other earlier time. Certain figures appear as active individuals – we can think of Pierre Maury's elaborately painted character. Le Roy Ladurie's interest in the medieval mentality might finally qualify as his 'great historical question'. His aspiration to reach more general conclusions is highlighted by contrasting *Montaillou* to René Weis's *The Yellow Cross*, which first of all wants to realize a topographic reconstruction of events. Reading his narrative, following a simple chronological advance, some details may be better understood then from *Montaillou*, but in Weis's book the stress is on the solidarity of the Cathars, suffering persecution for their faith, some even going to the stake for it (Weis 2000). In contrast to *The Legend of Bouvines* (Duby 1990), in Le Roy Ladurie's book it is from the particular under investigation that the general is unfolded. So we seem to have good reason to include *Montaillou* in the ranks of forerunners of microhistory.

Mark Salber Phillips, however, contrasts this book with *microstoria*. He claims that unlike *Montaillou*, *The Cheese and the Worms* speaks openly about problems posed by the sources – what establishes distance between the subject and the reader. Le Roy Ladurie takes inquisition minutes as direct manifestations of the peasants' ideas, whereas Ginzburg stresses the role of the inquisitor and that of the historian in historical reconstruction (quoted by Brewer 2010: 13, cf. Phillips 2003). Leonard Boyle's critical review points to the fact that one of the volumes containing documents of Fournier's inquisition sent to Rome has been lost and we know nothing of its contents. Le Roy Ladurie portrays Pierre Clergue as a resistance fighter in the last period of his life, but he might have behaved in a different way and his eventual confessions might have led to the arrests of many of his parishioners. Boyle claims that the author should not have taken everything stated during the inquisition procedure at face value, also that translation and written reports have modified original statements (quoted by Klaniczay 1998: 175–76, cf. Boyle 1981).

The most serious way to criticize *Montaillou* has been the writing of a quite different book on the basis of the same source material, just as Matthias Benad has done. He not only blames Le Roy Ladurie for continuously repeating spicy details, but also for neglecting the chronology of events and thus misreading the development of processes in Montaillou. Benad claims that the author oversimplified local processes by dividing Montaillou into two hostile clans. Instead he tried to show in his book the meaning of Catharism for a medieval family: how this religion, involving a special value system and world view, was exercised (quoted by Perényi 1999: 210, cf. Benad 1990).

Microhistory as a relief force

When *microstoria* appeared on the historiographical scene, it seemed to come to the relief of the *Annales* in crisis. '*La nouvelle histoire*' of the third and fourth generations resulted in a more culturally oriented history, for example the famous *histoire des mentalités*, but also such a diversification that was even called 'crumbling history' by François Dosse (*histoire en miettes*). Collective research and quantitative and social scientific approaches, which had given a distinct profile to the *Annales*, fell more and more into neglect. This situation was increasingly regarded as a crisis, and the *Annales* reacted with its '*tournant critique*', an effort for renewal at the end of the 1980s (Editors of the *Annales* 1988 and 1989). The fourth generation put together two important volumes (Lepetit (ed.) 1995; Revel (ed.) 1996), which concentrate on the social actors and their rationality while also demonstrating the readiness of the *Annales* to embrace epistemological debates. As the flag of *microstoria* was unfurled at a Franco-Italian conference of historians in Rome, a similar conference in Paris demonstrated that leading figures of the *Annales* embraced the propositions of microhistory. The latter volume was based on papers given there.

One of the key figures of the French reception of *microstoria*, Revel, writes that Italian microhistory was born as a reaction to macro-oriented social history. According to him, the following points sum up its lessons: picking a certain level of analysis influences knowledge; the micro-level is not preferred, because micro- and macro-versions are all true and complementary; and, finally, historical actors participate simultaneously in processes that take place at different levels, therefore the main thing is to change the focus of research (Revel 1996a: 15–26).

Ironically, the best actual works of microhistorical outlook were written in France prior to the direct influence of *microstoria*, and we have just seen these as 'forerunners', and the most important feature of recent French microhistory is theoretical reflection. The other key figure of the reception of microhistory in France next to Revel, Bernard Lepetit, developed Levi's idea about 'changing the scale' into a full-fledged theory. He writes that 'changing the scale' is not to be found in the stages of research, but reflects the fact that social actors appear in different contexts, micro- and macro-, at the same time. According to Lepetit, 'changing the scale' serves 'to identify those systems of context, that form the framework of social action. The goal of this dynamic cartography is to draw a variety, a set of maps, each of which corresponds to a social terrain' (Lepetit 1993: 126). In agreement with Kracauer and Revel, Lepetit also writes that no scale has precedence: 'macro-phenomena are not less real, micro-phenomena are not more real, (or vice versa): there is no hierarchy between them. [...] The controlled multiplication of the scales of observation is likely to produce additional knowledge'. If we change the scale, we get fresh insights, we look at reality being organized by different principles, interpreted on the basis of different causal interconnections (Lepetit 1993: 137).[2]

In Lepetit's model, different levels have a relative independence, and micro-level has no special place. This is not microhistory any more, objected Paul-André Rosental, but 'multiscopic' history.[3] According to Rosental, the thinking of *microstoria* is basically different from that of Lepetit, because micro-level has a special value. Microhistory regards past people as conscious historical actors who make individual decisions, and these decisions produce the social forms observed by the historian. According to Rosental, effective causal processes happen on the micro-level. He bases his opinion on the ideas of Barth, whom we have already met (see, p. 15).

This Norwegian anthropologist is interested in 'form in social life', that is constituted by the regularity of individual behaviour. His 'generative model' does not envisage itself as 'homologous with observed social regularities', but 'designed so that they, by specified operations can generate such regularities and forms'. It is to be discovered which 'particular constellation of the variables in the model' generates the forms corresponding to the 'empirical forms of social systems' (Barth, F. 1966: v). Gribaudi's monograph on Turin (see p. 23) can be seen as an attempt to create a generative model. He has found different mobility with the identical socio-economic background, that is, macro-level explanations do not work, they are incompatible with the principle of agency (Nagy 2010: 245). We shall come back to the question of multiscopic history versus microhistory in Chapter 4. Lessons of Hungarian microhistory might provide us with fresh insights into this debate.

How can we avoid trivial history?

There is an evident tension between the process of microhistory, characterized by micro-analysis of a circumscribed object of investigation, and its claim to find the answer for a 'great historical question'. As Muir asked: 'how can historians concerned with trifles avoid producing a trivial history?' (Muir 1991a: xiv). As we have seen, at the outset Ginzburg and Poni suggested Grendi's concept of the 'normal exceptions' as a reply of *microstoria* to this theoretical challenge, but Paul Ricoeur justly claimed in 2000 that the problem had not been solved, it is therefore worth making a new effort (Ricoeur 2000: 276–77).

Generalization is a key element in microhistory due to the fact that people, for example readers of historical works, are usually convinced that the rule is a better compass in life than the exception. They are fascinated by the exception, but they buy the rule. As E. H. Carr wrote, the historian is 'not really interested in the unique, but in what is general in the unique' (Carr 1961: 80). If Niklas Luhmann is right and the function of social systems is to reduce the complexity of life, then finding rules is the historians' downright duty. It is therefore an elementary interest of microhistory to find a way to link its micro-investigation to the level of the general, if it is to avoid being classified as 'trivial' history. In Part II, Sigurður Gylfi Magnússon will present his ideas, which are diametrically opposed to this view.

As quoted, Medick thinks that the 'exceptional normal' has come to denote the process of microhistory, and reveals what was possible in a given age for a human being (Medick 1994: 46). Similarly, Revel writes about Levi's book that 'testing the validity of the model does not consist of a statistical verification but its analysis among extreme conditions' (Revel 1996a: 32). Davis's book, *Women on the Margins* is an excellent example of definition of the area of human possibilities by perambulation. The three protagonists are not typical figures from the seventeenth century; they rather probe the limits of female existence. Telling their stories, Davis pegs out the field of possibilities open for early modern women (Davis 1995).[4]

A procedure close to that of microhistory is Erich Auerbach's famous experiment (1946) to write about certain periods of European literature on the basis of twenty little episodes, twenty short texts. He actually thinks that interpreting details of *Hamlet*, *Phaedra* or *Faust* can result in a deeper knowledge of Shakespeare, Racine and Goethe than systematic chronological accounts of their lives and work. Auerbach does not even try to achieve representativity, but nevertheless maintains that arbitrarily selected details might reveal the order and the explanation of life (Auerbach 1959: 509).

In Chapter 4, we shall revisit the theoretical problems exposed in this section, and we shall briefly come back to Auerbach, too. Here, we proceed to the other national historiography besides the French, directly and significantly influenced by Italian microhistory: that of Germany.

The history of everyday life

German historiography followed the French model with a significant delay. The belated institutionalization of the structure-oriented social history did not take place earlier than around 1970. Soon thereafter, however, new currents of cultural history also appeared on the scene: *Alltagsgeschichte* (the history of everyday life), historical anthropology and microhistory. Quantitative social history – first of all, Jürgen Kocka's and Hans-Ulrich Wehler's *Historische Sozialwissenschaft* (social science history) and their school organized around the University of Bielefeld – did not have the time to run its full course before being confronted by even more recent currents. It was therefore not their representatives who made a further step towards cultural history, having exhausted the capacities of macro-oriented social history, as happened in the case of the *Annales*. This fact resulted in violent attacks by representatives of *Historische Sozialwissenschaft* against the new currents in Germany on one the hand and the relative weakness of the latter on the other.

As for these more culturally oriented approaches, Thomas Nipperday advocated a social history based on American cultural history around 1970, and Martin Broszat proposed a new approach towards Germany's Nazi past: to reveal people's desires, expectations and fears, in order to understand Nazism (Daniel 2004: 299–301). *Alltagsgeschichte* was born, the German school of the history of everyday life that concentrates specifically on twentieth-century dictatorships, especially the dozen years of Nazism and later the history of the German Democratic Republic as well. What started as a history of experiences (*Erfahrungsgeschichte*) ended up as a research of individual lives and the everyday, how personal fates interacted in the behaviour of a crowd – centred on the investigation of the relationship of ordinary people and Nazi violence (Majtényi 2001: 243–44). Dorothee Wierling thinks *Alltagsgeschichte* is microhistory (quoted by Gregory 1999: 102). Although Otto Ulbricht disagrees (Ulbricht 2009: 49), it is worth having a closer look at this school of historiography.

The editor of its representative volume (Lüdtke (ed.) 1995), Alf Lüdtke stresses agency just as microhistory does. He claims that ordinary people have always had room for action, even in the Third Reich. *Alltagsgeschichte* tries to reconstruct people's actions and behaviour, statements and feelings step by step – with a stress on complicity (Lüdtke 1994: 78–79). But Lüdtke also points to the fact that everyday life is not just a struggle for survival, it brings about historical change as well: people are both objects and subjects of their history. *Alltagsgeschichte* understands historical continuity and change as a result of the actions of individuals and groups. It does not regard 'structural determinants' either superior to action or as its preconditions, but considers these as their parts. Hidden structures can only be glimpsed, it is argued, in human practices (Lüdtke 1995: 16–21).

Brad S. Gregory compares *Alltagsgeschichte* with Levi's *microstoria* and not with that of Ginzburg. Their common features are the stress on agency, the criticism of determining structures and big processes, as well as their reliance on anthropology. But the subject of *microstoria* is first of all early modern history while *Alltagsgeschichte* concentrates on the twentieth century. It seeks to grasp experience while Levi's *microstoria* is trying to reconstruct social relationships. But they both place individuals and their interactions at the centre of historical processes (Gregory 1999: 102–10).

Microhistory as a little brother of *Alltagsgeschichte*

Although it could be, and we have seen that in fact it was, argued that *Alltagsgeschichte* is the German equivalent of *microstoria*, in German historiography, microhistory has emerged as self-designated too, replacing historical anthropology among historians who studied periods other than the twentieth century, mainly the early modern age.[5] Hans Medick has refused the focus on historical change and the groups that favoured this change. He advocates instead a concentration on losers and marginals. According to Medick, historical anthropology has made 'the primary modes of human behavior and basic situations in human life' into the object of study. These efforts appeared on the margins of German historiography, in work that ranges from folk culture through women's history to working-class history (Medick 1995: 41–47, quotation 46).

In 1993, when the representatives of German microhistory launched a periodical, it was still called *Historical Anthropology* (*Historische Anthropologie*), but its editors later came to describe their own work more and more as microhistory.[6] In doing so, Medick or Jürgen Schlumbohm have arrived at a place different from their original destination. Members of the Proto-Industrialization Workgroup at the Max Planck Historical Institute in Göttingen originally investigated the early phase of industrialization in rural Germany, but by the time their bulky monographs had been written, they interpreted their own work as microhistory – under a strong influence of *microstoria*. These big books are two-sided: their authors went over to microhistory while conserving certain features of the traditional quantitative social history. Medick claims that the advantages of both approaches can be preserved: grasping 'lived experience' and also retaining the advantages of a statistical approach (Medick 1996: 25).

Medick thinks that the interconnections of universal history can only be revealed through a local history that is a result of a microhistorical analysis. He claims that his research on the weavers' village of Laichingen is a local history that is a problem-oriented part of universal history. Investigating small local societies with details of their everyday life does not bar us from asking general questions, and even opens new ways of answering them. Medick's micro-analysis reveals how Pietism assisted proto-industrialization in Württenberg. He interprets the high infant mortality as a 'normal exception'. Just like Fredrik Barth, he favours a microhistory that does not gloss over exceptions but asks questions on the basis of them. His view of microhistory is close to that of Levi, but Medick agrees with Kracauer and Lepetit that microhistory does not suit every purpose so he advocates a multi-perspectivity (Medick 1994: 44–50, 1996: 48).

Schlumbohm's microhistory is about agrarian change from the seventeenth to the nineteenth century, similarly based on the usual source material. He claims that microhistory challenges macro-history to a 'fruitful dialogue', gives a new dimension to the historical process and demonstrates agency. Case studies reveal finer interconnections than quantification and they take readers closer to lived experience (Schlumbohm 1994: 19–29). According to Ulbricht, these books make it clear that the Göttingen microhistorians are partly still held captive by social science history (Ulbricht 2009: 45–46).

The presence of microhistory in German historiography is not exclusively marked by the reception of *microstoria* and certain results of *Alltagsgeschichte*. The work of researchers coming from different directions can also display characteristics of microhistory. These should also be mentioned briefly.

The peasant, the shaman and the pope

The historical demographer, Arthur E. Imhof reconstructed the 'life world' (*Lebenswelt*) of Johannes Hoos who was a peasant from Hesse living from 1670 to 1755. This was determined by geographic factors, the ownership of land, and religious–political affiliation. Imhof claims that these small 'life worlds' were completely heterogeneous, that it is pointless to look for representativity. Still, there were formative experiences in this age, too: plague, famine and war. The uncertainties induced people to look for long-term points of reference: it was not worthwhile to make an investment in personal lives that were of very uncertain length, only in more solid objects, such as undivided family property. Johannes Hoos's home, the Välte farm had survived intact for more than 400 years. Wealth and prestige resulted in advantageous marriages from which non-heirs could also profit.

When contrasted with our world, Imhof underlines the advantages of Johannes Hoos's life world: instead of Hoos's three palpable dangers we have now many uncertain fears; our life on earth is longer, but we have lost eternity; and finally when the individual person stands at the centre, then human life is bound to degrade into concealment of the deterioration of the physical condition of our bodies and trying to forget about our inevitable death (Imhof 1984). This book combines micro-investigation and interest in 'the great historical question' just as microhistory does. What is problematic – the relationship of these two – is the already well-known representativity problem of microhistory. How can we get to know early modern peasant life from Johannes Hoos's single case? Or is Menocchio an authentic representative of popular culture? What we may miss in Imhof's book, is agency: individuals are more puppets in the hands of great historical forces than active agents who form history.

We have already briefly mentioned Wolfgang Behringer's book, originally published in 1998 (see above, p. 4). It tries to uncover the roots of a popular belief through the detailed analysis of a single case. One winter evening in 1578, when drinking and talking about the afterlife, the shepherds Chonrad Stoeckhlin and Jacob Welch make a pledge to each other that the one who dies first will appear to the other and tell him what the other world is like. Eight days later Welch dies and keeps his promise, bringing horrid news and exhorting his friend to lead a godly life. Stoeckhlin changes his ways and enters into regular contact with the other world: four times a year an angel appears to him. He becomes a charismatic healer in contact with supernatural forces: the phantoms of the night. Finally he ends up standing before the court of the bishop of Augsburg and is subsequently executed as a witch. His confessions induced the most bloody witch hunt ever between the Danube and the Alps, claiming 68 lives.

Similarly to Ginzburg's book about the *benandanti*, Behringer is revealing elements of the popular beliefs of the Alps pertaining to white magic: the belief in the phantoms of the night that fly and amuse themselves at night accompanied by beautiful music. They are well-intentioned and help humans, embodying a peasants' utopia. But in Christian theology there was no place for such beliefs, the 'phantoms of the night' were classified as demons, and those who believed in them risked being charged with witchcraft. In his personal version, Stoeckhlin tried to reconcile myth, Tridentine Catholicism and popular demand, but he proved unsuccessful: he was executed and the belief in the phantoms of the night was merged into the idea of the witches' Sabbath (Behringer 1998).

Wolfgang Reinhard wrote a 'micro-political' study of one of the Borgia popes, Paul V. He concentrates on personal and institutional networks. Micro-political action means that individuals do not pursue the interests of the organizations of which they are members, but their own. While Pope Paul V wanted to keep his neutrality in the conflict of Catholic powers at a macro-political level, in micro-politics he favoured the Spanish because of his family interests. At the same time the French gained a success in micro-politics, building up a client network in Rome that later served as a foundation for their macro-political dominance in Catholic Europe (Reinhard 2009: 4–5, 681–82). Reinhard does not call his book microhistory, but it is justifiable to ask if his very detailed analysis, the method of network-analysis, advocated by several microhistorians, and his attention to individual decisions might support a claim that this book is microhistory.[7] The question, do Pope Paul V's politics qualify as a 'great historical question' is debatable, as is the status of all historical problems, as a matter of fact, since it is always decided by cultural factors. As we shall see in the next chapter, a strict application of this definition criterion of microhistory might result in the removal of several works from the category of microhistory. Such, for example, is Ulbricht's approach to microhistory.

Ulbricht's book, *Microhistory: People and Conflicts in the Early Modern Period* is one of the few comprehensive works on microhistory. It is historiographic in its nature in the first chapter, presenting to the reader microhistory, its past and its possibilities. Ulbricht then gives seven microhistorical studies based on his research on particular moments from everyday people's lives in early modern Schleswig-Holstein. These enable him to come back to theoretical problems in the closing part of his book. Ulbricht defines microhistory as an amplification of the scale of research, i.e. a reduction of the area under investigation, which enables the historian to grasp the totality of sources and to combine these in the analysis. He stresses that it does not make sense to contrast microhistory with macro-history, for the former is often macro-history in itself, one that has not been cut off from its roots (Ulbricht 2009: 14–15, 33–36). He concludes:

> Microhistorians try to research the relationships between people (and their groups) in different areas of life with a greater scale – and this way more precisely, with a lower rate of mistake and without deductionism. Microhistory can therefore be unquestionably understood as general history.
>
> (Ulbricht 2009: 35)

Ulbricht is a very strict representative of a certain idea of microhistory, and with unyielding severity he is evicting many Anglo-Saxon works that claim to be microhistory from the paradise of microhistory. He is certainly right to some extent: it is reasonable to apply a looser definition of microhistory when we take a look at the output of English and American microhistory. That is what we shall do in the following chapter. When sketching a broad overview of precursors, the microhistory of communities and the different attempts to apply the approach of microhistory to English and American history, evoking the scholarship of Davis and those historians that follow the Italian example more closely, two theoretical questions will be addressed: the relationship of historical anthropology and microhistory on one hand and the nature of 'incident analysis' on the other.

Notes

1 Palle Ove Christiansen claimed that it was a social historical application of the 'social drama' that enabled Le Roy Ladurie to reintroduce the event into French historical tradition (Christiansen 1988: 15).

2 Lepetit argues that maps with different scales are suitable for different purposes, but are otherwise completely equal. I find András Kulcsár's argument convincing that from detailed maps, we can produce survey maps, but never *vice versa*.

3 On that issue, several *Annales* historians are divided. Revel claims in the introduction of *Jeux d'échelles*, that some of the authors argue for multiscopic history (Marc Abelès, Alban Bensa, Lepetit and himself) while others (Gribaudi, Cerutti and Rosental) claim that the micro-level should be preferred, because it generates macro-phenomena (Revel 1996b: 13, cf. Cerutti 2004: 18–19).

4 This book can also be regarded as an attempt to realize the plan outlined by the author five years earlier: to find an adequate form of expression to link in their

adverse effects the small and the large, the social and the cultural (Davis 1990, quoted by Schulze 1994: 12).

5 The term 'microhistory' is not exclusively used by early modern historians in Germany, Lüdtke also employed it when presenting *Alltagsgeschichte* (Lüdtke 1995: 14).

6 Consequently, the terms *Alltagsgeschichte*, historical anthropology and microhistory are considerably merged into one another in German usage.

7 According to Ulbricht, Reinhard claims that microhistory is an expression of a negation of all values, so, in fact, he identifies it with postmodernism, and judges it severely – although his own work is quite close to it (Ulbricht 2009: 51–52).

3 Microhistory in a broader sense
The Anglo-Saxon landscape

Geertz and the cats

As we have seen, much of the theory and practice of microhistory rests on anthropology, and this makes it similar to historical anthropology, which can be defined as an application of the approach and methods of twentieth-century British social and American cultural anthropology to historical sources. It is therefore worth having a closer look at the relationship between microhistory and historical anthropology, especially that flourishing branch of the latter that rests on Clifford Geertz's symbolic – or interpretive – anthropology. He treats culture as text, as the aggregate of systems of interpretable signs. According to Geertz, human behaviour is mostly symbolic, therefore the meaning is to be discovered (Geertz 1973: 3–31).

Italian microhistory has never denied its close ties to anthropology. Ginzburg and Poni advocated 'a finely focused ethnographic history' that is based on the 'assumption that the past is utterly alien to the present, that the citizens of sixteenth-century Rome or Bologna were as different from us as are the tribes of the New Guinean highlands' (Muir 1991a: ix, xi). Grendi claimed that by radically changing the scale of observation, microhistory has put into practice the lessons of social anthropology (Grendi 1996: 234). As we have seen, Ginzburg drew a parallel between the historian and the doctor whose knowledge is rooted in specific experience (Ginzburg 1989a), and this idea is very close to what Geertz suggested, namely that we should generalize as in a clinical diagnosis; not abstracting from the cases but generalizing within them. We should not fit observed cases to an existing law, but place the observed significant signs into an intelligible framework (quoted by Levi 1991: 99, cf. Geertz 1973: 3–31).

Levi, however, argues against the historical application of Geertz's anthropology in his study *The Dangers of Geertzism*. According to Jacques Revel, the core of this criticism is that there is no 'unified homogenous context'; what we can find is just 'multiple experiences and social representations, partly contradictory, at any rate ambiguous, through which people construct their world and their actions' (Revel 1996a: 26, cf. Levi 1985). According to Angelo Torre, Geertz regards the context as given and does not investigate its origins. Since we have no direct access to the context itself, just its individual manifestations, the reasoning turns into a tautology, and the relationship between society and individuals remains unresolved (Torre 1987: 206–39). Lepetit similarly concludes that the argument of Geertzian anthropology enters a false circle: the text mirrors the context, and the context gives meaning to the text (Lepetit 1993: 124). It is clear that Italian microhistorians and their followers are hostile to Geertzian anthropology[1] mainly because of its outlook concerning agency: in its perspective, the only real agent is culture, which acts through individuals, just as discourse acts through individuals in Michel Foucault's views, while microhistorians insist that past people should be seen as autonomous actors. Cerutti remarks that historical anthropology inspired by Geertz supposes the existence of a cultural universe embracing everyone (Cerutti 1990: 13–14). It is exactly this that stands at the centre of Roger Chartier's critique of Darnton's classical essay, 'The Great Cat Massacre'.

This is probably the most famous example of the application of interpretive anthropology to historical sources. Darnton evokes this episode on the basis of an eighteenth-century French printer, Nicolas Contat's memoires. In the 'great cat massacre' journeymen and apprentices lived out their emotions against their master and his family. These feelings were fed by the tension between the capitalist conditions of printing shops and the patriarchal image of the past, according to which masters, journeymen and apprentices used to work together as members of a friendly community. But – and this is Darnton's main question – what made the pursuit and killings of cats so hilarious for them?

Two apprentices, Jérôme, Contat's alterego, and Léveillé cannot sleep because of the night concert of stray cats on the rooftops. When Léveillé imitates cat calls above the master's bedroom so that he can have no wink of sleep, he gives an order to the apprentices to get rid of the demonic cats. Maiming was reputed to be effective against them – though calling a priest was also considered by the superstitious master. The printer journeymen and apprentices kill the pet of their master's wife first, accusing her of witchcraft. Also, claims Darnton, she was symbolically raped in this way. Then a *charivari* was staged for the master, allegedly cuckolded by his wife with her confessor. When killing alley cats, the atmosphere of the carnival is in the air, Jérôme and Léveillé appear as kings of the Carnival, and just like a carnival, the massacre of cats in the Rue Saint-Séverin also concludes in a mock trial and an execution: a judgment is passed on the master printer as employer. The joke was conveyed by symbols, not by the mere killing of cats – just for us, readers, all this has to be explained: what was an insult and why. Darnton writes that the master himself, in contrast to his wife, did not fully grasp the meaning, which only increased the apprentices' and journeymen's merriment (Darnton 1985: 75–101).

This essay was seriously attacked both for its alleged defects in research and presentation and its symbolic anthropological approach. Roger Chartier is arguing convincingly that Darnton was wrong in identifying the genre of Contat's work; that there was neither witchcraft, nor *charivari*, nor carnival in this episode. Symbols, wrote Chartier, were not freely available for everyone like air; they did not form a unified symbolic universe, for the society of France under the *ancien régime* was not unified but fragmented and the use of symbols conformed to this fact. The urban artisan culture of the printer apprentices could not play 'with the full repertory of diabolical and carnival motifs that Darnton attributes to it' – provided that this case took place at all (Chartier 1985: 682–95, quotation 694).

Before considering Darnton's reply, it is worth taking another famous example of the historical application of anthropological theory into consideration. Marshall Sahlins's famous case study about James Cook's death on Hawaii in 1779 will further highlight the difference between the approaches of historical anthropology and microhistory.

Killing a god

Captain Cook landed on Hawaii for the first time during the New Year festival, the Makahiki on 17 January 1779: the English ships were welcomed by ten thousand Polynesians, gifts were brought to them and the captain was identified with the god Lono. Three weeks later, the English sailed out of Kealakekua Bay, but due to a broken foremast, they had to return. When a cutter was stolen, Cook wanted to take the Hawaiian king on board as a hostage. Going towards the King's quarters, Cook was still the object of veneration. Coming back, however, he was met by increasing hostility and finally, he was killed on the shore. 'Cook was transformed from the divine beneficiary of the sacrifice to its victim – a change never really radical in Polynesian thought, and in the royal combats always possible', writes Sahlins, quoting Valerio Valeri (Sahlins 1985: 106).

The god Lono and the winter rains bring fertility to Hawaii, and for this period, the rites in the temples of Ku, the warrior god, are suspended. When Lono leaves, these are re-consecrated with human sacrifice. Lono's arrival is a great feast. His image goes round the island, is greeted everywhere with offerings, but then local people fight the members of the god's entourage and defeat them in a ritual combat, taking the fertilized land from them. At the end of this circuit, there is a main ritual combat between the image of Lono and the King, fighting for the well-being of his people as well as his sovereignty. The King arrives from the sea in a canoe, dies symbolically when touched by a spear, but then resurrects and beats the god, who plays the role of the sacrifice for two days: ritually, fertility is taken from the god for the humans, and finally, the image of Lono is set adrift in a canoe which is filled with offerings.

'Cook was making the same circuit as the Makahiki image, at just the same time' (Sahlins 1985: 121); his circumnavigation of Hawaii and embarkation at Kealakekua corresponded exactly with the myth, argues the anthropologist. Cook accepted the role of Lono. We should not think that all Hawaiians considered him the living god, but the priests had the means to press this interpretation on the population. The Makahiki festival would have ended on 1 February, and Cook's ships left the island on the night of 3 February – so his timing was almost perfect. It was his unexpected return in a week that caused trouble. For the Hawaiian king and chiefs, the return of Lono in the period of the King's victory was not only inexplicable, but also dangerous: the ritual crisis meant political threat, the question of sovereignty was re-opened. When the cutter was stolen, events might have seemed the inversion of the final ritual combat: Lono landed with his armed men, who killed a chief, and they wanted to take away the King in a canoe.

For a European mind, it is hardly understandable that someone venerated as a god in one moment can be killed in another. But Hawaiian gods are different from European, claims Sahlins. In Hawaiian mythology, humans sometimes defeat gods. This is the only way to take fertility from them (for example that of women and that of the land). But this is so in a more general sense, too: in Polynesia life is a killing of gods. Plants and animals are the gods' descendants, too. They are deprived of their divine element, the power to reproduce, by cooking. In the last analysis, life is to be taken by force from the gods: men are warriors. Therefore, Cook's status as Lono did not shelter him as much as a European might think: he was regarded instead as a god whose necessary defeat by men was an integral part of the culture (Sahlins 1985: 104–35).

The interpreter's knowledge versus the uncertainty of microhistory

Returning to the case of the cat massacre, in his reply to Chartier, Darnton maintained that the genre of his source is, in fact, a worker's autobiography. He also claimed that if historians do not intend to reveal what actually happened, the subjectivity of a source is not disadvantageous but positively beneficial. As for the main issue of contention, he wrote:

> Symbols work not merely because of their metaphorical power but also by virtue of their position within a cultural frame [...] the joke worked because the boys were able to play so many variations on standard cultural themes. [...] They turned the roundup of cats into a witch hunt, a carnivalesque festival, a trial, and a bawdy variety of street theater.
>
> (Darnton 1986: 227, 230–31)

That is, Darnton has maintained his original interpretation of the great cat massacre, moreover, he has rounded it up with a structural analysis centred on liminality (Darnton 1986). At the same time, Dominick LaCapra questioned the legitimacy of Chartier's questions and criticized Darnton: the concepts of marginality and liminality, central to his reply, were not yet really present in the original essay. Although Darnton's starting point is the alleged radical difference between past and present, his reading seems to uncover the past, despite its alleged polisemity, writes LaCapra. Since Darnton concentrates on message and world view, he does not pay attention to the composition and working of the texts themselves (LaCapra 1988: 102–5).

The historical anthropological reading of Cook's death has also been seriously challenged. Gananath Obeyesekere was involved in a long discussion with Sahlins. The Sri Lankan anthropologist claimed that there was almost certainly no

Makahiki festival in 1778. His main point was, however, that even if there had been, the Hawaiians would have been able to regard Cook's arrival as a mere coincidence: just because of arriving during the Makahiki, he would not have been automatically called Lono. Obeyesekere pointed to the fact that there were others, for example chiefs that were also called Lono – so this might have had different reasons. In the afterword of the second edition of his book, he reacted to Sahlins's reply, also written in the form of a complete book. Obeyesekere maintained that the Western anthropologist failed to show convincingly that Hawaiians had seen Lono in Cook and that he had fallen victim to a ritual murder. According to Obeyesekere, Sahlins just tried to demonstrate that other members of his crew were also regarded as gods, and that this happened in other Melanesian cultures, too. He argues that Hawaiians lacked common sense and practical rationality (Obeyesekere 1997: xiii–iv, 95–97, 187, 194, cf. Sahlins 1995).

From the point of view of microhistory, what is interesting here is not the – fully justified – indignation of the third world intellectual, but the fact that interpretation is dominant in anthropological, consequently also historical anthropological, works. If we try to measure Sahlins's essay against the definition of microhistory given in the Introduction, we can identify both the microscopic analysis of a historical case and the 'great historical question' concerning the Polynesians' way of thinking. We do not, however, find agency. Even if Sahlins's interpretation is correct and it is not too far from that of the contemporary Hawaiians, the case is still that in it culture prescribes action and leaves no room for the individual.

As for Darnton's essay, not only can a similar absence of agency be detected that makes the actors' deeds mere manifestations of culture, but the presence of micro-analysis is also doubtful – while it is debatable to what extent the symbolism of cats in Western culture could be regarded as a 'great historical question'. Darnton's essay is based on a few pages of Contat's memoirs, and he does not aim at a full reconstruction of the event – in fact, he does not even attribute importance to proving that the 'great cat massacre' took place at all. He does not think that he could give an answer to his 'great historical question' through a micro-investigation. His approach is basically hermeneutical: he is in search of meaning and strives to establish an interpretation. Historical research is therefore clearly driven into the background.

The rhetorical-textual turn in anthropology pointed to the constructed nature of cultural texts on the one hand and (in the wake of Foucault, we could add) to the context of power relations on the other (Clifford and Marcus (eds) 1986). These insights may be referred not only to historical anthropology, but also to microhistory. In the case of *Montaillou* or *The Cheese and the Worms* for example, anti-clericalism served as a point of departure. We have also seen how Ginzburg's works were marked by the thinking dominating the 1960s and '70s according to which popular culture was a counter-culture which appeared in a clearly positive light.

When analysing Geertz's classical essay on the Balinese cockfight, Vincent Crapanzano claims that the author's real goal is not understanding the natives' point of view, but an interpretation of cultural data. Moreover, Geertz places himself, and thus also the reader, at the top of the hierarchy of understanding (Crapanzano 1986: 51–76, cf. Geertz 1973: 412–53), just like Claude Lévi-Strauss, in fact. Microhistory, quite the opposite, not only relies on its sources to a much larger extent, but also gives the reader the experience of a partial and uncertain knowledge: we shall never be able to understand the source analysed as well as its author.

This seems to be the most significant difference between historical anthropology and microhistory. This section should, however, be closed by stressing their similarities: generalizing in the case observed, revealing the systems of contexts of the observed particular case – this may be the common platform. When events are dissected and subjected to a close analysis, they may be used as a lens that gives us a clearer picture of reality – that of deeper and more general structures, claims the microhistorian Osvaldo Raggio (quoted by Szekeres 1999: 15). As quoted, Lepetit also thinks that the goal of 'changing the scale' is to identify the system of contexts that form the framework of social action' (Lepetit 1993: 126). According to Geertz, the point of doing 'thick description' is very similar: 'to draw large conclusions from small, but very densely textured facts' (Geertz 1973: 28). Due to the determining influence of anthropology, the ties of historical anthropology and microhistory are undoubtedly stronger than their differences.

From an (early) modern personality to the Neckarhausen version of European history

The closeness of historical anthropology and microhistory is clearly demonstrated by Alan Macfarlane's great book on Ralph Josselin, a seventeenth-century Puritan clergyman. This is one of the first products of the effect of anthropology on history, and – in contrast to the books mentioned earlier – it is usually ranked by microhistorians as a predecessor. Josselin's exceptionally detailed diary recorded both his incomes, expenses and the important events of his life, while it also served as a religious diary, thus mirroring the totality of a family's life. As a yeoman, Josselin personified Weberian protestant ethic: he was hard-working and thrifty, he took out loans only exceptionally, planned very cautiously and recycled the profits, investing into land or the education of his children.

According to the English anthropologist, Ralph Josselin's 'family life corresponded closely to that of mobile modern urban families.' Marriage was decided by the young and not their parents. That of the clergyman himself was based on personal affection, too, and the most important relationship in his life was to his wife. They had a 'joint role relationship'. Their relationship with their children was based on love, too. Despite their early separation and the distance between them, they remained in a close relationship with each other. His kin, however, was not close to Josselin: in case of need, he turned to friends and neighbours for help. He was, moreover, certainly not a 'contented, adjusted personality, free from the strains and conflicts of modern life', rather 'as anxiety-ridden, as insecure, as many of his modern counterparts. His fierce introspective battles against temptation might well help to label him as a "neurotic" by modern standards'. In his life, God was omnipresent, the only stable point in an insecure world (Macfarlane 1977, quotations 110, 159, 192–93).

Josselin's personality is explained on the basis of a microscopic investigation and not from the author's general knowledge of eighteenth-century (or Hawaiian) culture. There is no doubt that the Puritan clergyman possessed agency, and his example demonstrates – just like *The Cheese and the Worms* – something unexpected. Although Macfarlane cannot be classified among the English followers of *microstoria* for chronological reasons, he occupies an important place among its predecessors.

We have already met Scribner's suggestion that historians should give up the illusion of revealing the past and should concentrate instead on the dialogue as a determining context (Scribner 1997: 31). As if following this advice, it is the relationship of community and domination (*Herrschaft*) that stands at the centre of David Warren Sabean's six case studies about early modern German popular culture (Sabean 1984). He investigates the 'dynamics of power'. Culture in Sabean's interpretation is an attempt to exercise power.

Hans Weis did not attend communion in Neckartailfingen in 1587. When analysing his case, Sabean concentrates on two aspects of domination: how religious institutions were used to reinforce power on one hand and how villagers tried to fill these institutions and rituals with their own interpretations, and how they fought for these with the authorities on the other (Sabean 1984: 37–60). Creating the general atmosphere of terror, office holder and large landholder peasants dominated Zell unter Aichelberg. Investigating the death of the pastor, who died in suspicious circumstances, Sabean declares that 'the village was determined by a matrix of fear'. As the new pastor was afraid of meeting a similar fate, he appealed to the villagers' conscience to counterbalance fear, using anxieties about the afterlife to counterbalance worldly terror. The call to their conscience made it possible for the poor to open their mouths, to make a stand against power (Sabean 1984: 144–73, quotation: 164). Sabean used a witchcraft case to analyse 'the metaphorical structure of language, and how metaphors can be understood to provide a grammar of social relations' (Sabean 1984: 94–112, quotation: 95). In the volume *Power in the Blood*, the backbone of the essays is the analysis of concepts. The details of the micro-event, however, are not interesting for Sabean; he does not strive for a microscopic analysis, but stresses his interpretations instead: his reading of culture, power relations and the importance of communication.

These essays can be regarded as preliminary studies to his two Neckarhausen books (Sabean 1990, 1998). These exceptionally detailed monographs reveal the history of this Southern German village between 1700 and 1870. The first volume is about the material conditions of life. Sabean weaves the texture of his book from threads of the development of agricultural prices, demographic processes and life stories. He integrates marriages, household relations and self-sufficiency into one structure. Sabean's main thesis is that changes in demography, agrarian technology and the economic system led to significant modifications in the working of the family as far as the transfer of properties and mutual economic assistance was concerned. From the 1740s, when agrarian production got more intensive and population pressure more significant, marriages appeared that were endogamous from the point of view of income. These prevailed from the early nineteenth century, and this phenomenon produced and maintained social class (Sabean 1990; Gray 2001).

These conclusions were reinforced by the analysis of five cohorts of Neckarhausen villagers, born in five different decades of the period under investigation. Sabean concluded that it was through affinal kinship that modern social class was born. Marion Gray thinks that this double analysis of a single village might change the way in which historians see the transformation of Europe from agrarian communities to modern class society (Sabean 1998; Gray 2001: 430–31). Weighty reasons can be found for including Sabean's scholarship in microhistory: not only *Power in the Blood*, but also the Neckarhausen volumes are built on detailed case studies; agency is always present: the dominance of the interpreter does not mean that culture acts through individuals, leaving them no room for action. Therefore, Lene Wul also regards Sabean's work as microhistory, even microhistory at its best (Wul 2000: 23–27). On the other hand, while the essays of *Power in the Blood* do not try to deepen micro-analysis, the Neckarhausen monographs concentrate on the investigation of a community in the long run – so their microhistorical character can be called into question. This latter concentration on community takes us to the next stage of our survey of Anglo-Saxon historiography.

The microhistory of the community

It was relatively early that American historians wrote microhistorical works which had a social historical outlook. Paul Boyer's and Stephen Nissenbaum's magnificent book about Salem witchcraft was published in 1974. It concerns not the persecution itself but the divided community of Salem Village. The authors depart from economic factors: the amount of the tax paid clearly divided the settlement into a flourishing eastern part, having closer ties with Salem Town, and a western part, isolated from the markets. It was the inhabitants of the latter half of the settlement who advocated the independence of Salem Village from Salem Town. The opposition culminated in the hostility of two leading families, the Porters and the Putnams. The arrival of a new pastor put a spark into the powder keg of the chronic conflicts: he presented the internal division of Salem Village as the opposition of good and evil. In 1692, his followers, partisans of the independence, unable to find a political solution for their frustration, accused their opponents of witchcraft.

Unlike in Macfarlane's classical study about Tudor Essex, according to which the rich ruling faction of the community usually accused the poor of witchcraft (Macfarlane 1970), Boyer and Nissenbaum claim that the Salem case was a desperate counter-attack of a social force in retreat, bound for final defeat: using witchcraft accusations the 'Puritans' tried to overpower the 'capitalists', or 'individualists'[2] (Boyer and Nissenbaum 1974: 106–7). Boyer's and Nissenbaum's microhistory has a distinct social historical character. Their microscopic investigation boils down to an economic explanation. As we have seen, they formulate their conclusion rather as an exception than a historical rule.

If we step out from the Anglo-Saxon historiography for a minute, we can find a close parallel to *Salem Possessed*. At the heart of Jaime Contreras's book stands the fight between two clans, the Soto and the Riquelme (Contreras 1997). The scene is sixteenth-century Spain, where, half a century after the Jews' mass conversion to Christianity, the inquisition charged five hundred 'new Christians' in Lorca and Murcia with secretly following Jewish rites. One hundred and seventy-five of them were executed at the stake within two decades. Contreras claims that social tension stands in the background of the events: the new elite using the economic possibilities conquered the leading positions of the urban self-government, and many of their ranks also bought themselves into the nobility. The old Christian elite started to demand 'purity of blood' in the mid-sixteenth century to get rid of this dangerous rival and to prevent its social ascent. This discourse of exclusion created a difference between old and new Christians that had not existed earlier, although their rivalry had long been embodied by the opposition of the Riquelme and Soto clans.

When the inquisitor Cristóbal de Salazar attacked the recently risen members of the local bourgeoisie, he could count on the support of the Riquelmes. But when protestations induced the pope to order a revision of the case, and subsequently the King of Spain intervened, the inquisitors had to stop. Contreras argues that this was due to a loss of support by the Riquelme clan, proving the limited scope of the inquisition: it was impossible to uproot the 'new Christians' from Spanish society. But, we can ask, why did this became evident just at the moment of the papal-royal intervention? Can it be just taken as a manifestation of the Riquelmes' changing sides? There is some contradiction, too, in that the inquisition is said to have revealed latent divisions in the society, while the author also claims that it suffered a defeat finally through not being able to break the unity of the oligarchy; when charges of heresy threatened the whole patriciate their solidarity was revived (Contreras 1997: 25, 282). How many people should have died at the stake for Contreras to declare the inquisitors' action as successful and the losses of the local elite as grave?

In John Demos's multi-disciplinary approach to New-England's witchcraft cases, he applied four distinct approaches: biographical (about the witches themselves); psychological (about their accusers); sociological (linking witchcraft to social forms and structures) and historical (investigating change). In each of the four parts of his book, Demos had two detailed case studies and a summary with a social science history outlook. In *Entertaining Satan* the macro-approach as originally envisaged remained dominant, though, as the author writes, micro-historical case studies acquired more importance as his work proceeded (Demos 1982: ix).

The above-mentioned Anglo-Saxon historians do not stand alone: other colleagues of theirs have also concentrated on 'little communities' (cf. Redfield

1955). Margaret Spufford's *Contrasting Communities* is about three English villages in the period between 1525 and 1700. Comparing Chippenham, Orwell and Willingham, she concludes that 'no determinism, economic, social, educational or geographical, will fully account for the existence of religious conviction: which is as it should be' (Spufford 1974: 352). In 1979, Keith Wrightson and David Levine investigated the history of the Essex village of Terling during the same period. They found that new cultural divisions in society strengthened the old ones, based on property, etc. (Wrightson and Levine 1995: 172). Recently, Barry Reay has ventured to understand social change in the western world through the history of three Kent villages, focusing on the nineteenth century. He tried to follow in the footsteps of Sabean, and understood his work not as local but as microhistory (Reay 1996).[3]

These books usually put the stress on the determining influence of the structures and hardly leave space for an active individual to shape history. We now proceed in another direction, to Anglo-Saxon microhistorical works in which individuals come to the foreground, and micro-analysis dominates, but what is questionable is whether these micro-analyses are performed in order to find the answer to a 'great historical question'. If we understand microhistory standing with one foot in social and another in cultural history, then the books that we have just looked at are closer to the former, and those books about to be surveyed, are closer to the latter.

English microhistories

Sir James Holt's *Robin Hood* demonstrates that micro-analysis was already present in English historiography prior to any influence of *microstoria*. He tried to reconstruct the oldest version of the Robin Hood story, its geographical origins and social context. In Duby's *The Legend of Bouvines*, the memory of the battle was the subject of the last part of the book. In Holt's book, the stress is on the legend all along. Paradoxically, he still makes great efforts to establish the identity of the original Robin Hood (Holt 1982) just as Le Roy Ladurie did in his charming book about Françouneto, a witch featuring in a local legend around Agen in the south of France (Le Roy Ladurie 1987).

An interesting book opens a window on the life of a medieval community in the south of France, similarly to *Montaillou*. The merchant Peyre Marques hid his gold during a dangerous phase of the Hundred Years' War, but forgot where. No wonder that finding a hoard of coins when a drain-pipe was unblocked created a hefty controversy. Since everyone was interested in having the treasure, or a part of it, the sources of the case reveal the everyday life of Rodez, a town divided into a *bourg* ruled by the count and a *cité* under the bishop's jurisdiction. Each chapter of Ann Wroe's book has a person and his life at its centre advancing the story of the gold by a step or two, while also adding new colour and detail to the picture of the local community. Little stories make the everyday existence of Rodez come to life. Wroe also includes her own story, that of the research into the narrative (Wroe 1995).

James Shapiro's arresting read, *1599: A Year in the Life of William Shakespeare* takes the months of the year 1599, the year of the opening of the Globe and the birth of *Hamlet*, one after the other 'to locate the wellspring of Shakespeare's genius in his formative experiences', to link his plays to the context of their birth and enrich their interpretation with relevant new ideas, since 'Shakespeare's work emerged from an engagement with his times' (Shapiro 2005: xviii, xxii). It can be argued that the work of one of the greatest figures of world literature qualifies in itself as a 'great historical question', but Shapiro also claims that the object of his micro-investigation, the year 1599, represented not only a fresh start in Shakespeare's art but also the death of chivalry and the birth of the British Empire, represented by the failure of Essex's Irish campaign and the foundation of the East India Company – and both found their way into Shakespeare's plays, too (Shapiro 2005).

Also questions concerning Robin Hood, an icon of present-day Western culture, might be qualified as 'great historical questions', but other works on early modern English history certainly fail to do so, and being interesting remains the only *raison d'être* of micro-analysis. In a recent book, Chris Skidmore asks if Robert Dudley's wife fell victim to an accident or a murder on 8 September 1560. In his book, the author tries to accomplish a minute reconstruction of the death of the wife of Queen Elizabeth's favourite, including a reconstruction of the fatal staircase where she allegedly fell, accompanied by the statistics and pathology of staircase accidents. Skidmore concludes that the two deep head wounds mentioned in the coroner's newly found report are suspicious and he points to a possible individual initiative of Dudley's armed retinue to get rid of their master's burdensome wife. He thinks that the scandal destroyed Dudley's chance of marrying Elizabeth. The importance of this episode is, however, significantly reduced by hindsight: for contemporaries the question of Protestant succession was vital, but we cannot escape our knowledge that Elizabeth's long rule was a flourishing period of English history, and Protestant succession was brought about without any problem in spite of the fact that she had no son. Moreover, Skidmore himself devalues the importance of Amy Robsart's death and its micro-analysis by proving that Elizabeth did not want to marry either Dudley or anyone else; the question of marriage was just raised by her from time to time for foreign political considerations. It was, therefore, not because of this episode that Elizabeth became the 'Virgin Queen' (Skidmore 2010).

The 'strange death' of Edmund Godfrey was similarly a *cause célèbre* in 1678, leading to hysteria about the 'Popish Plot'. The Westminster Justice of the Peace, found strangled and pierced with his own sword in a ditch, became a Protestant martyr. Alan Marshall's book explores not only the case itself but tries to explain Godfrey's death by reference to his little known life and recently discovered personal letters. Thus, he eliminates all earlier theories of murder, both improbable and more plausible ones, and points to suicide as the most probable solution of the mystery.[4] The family had ample reason to find a cover-up for the case: thus not only were Edmund Godfrey's estates not forfeited but they were also able to use his death as political capital (Marshall 1999).

Penelope Hughes-Hallett in her book uses the dinner given by the painter Benjamin Robert Haydon for Wordsworth, Keats, Charles Lamb and others in London on 28 December 1817 to give a sweeping overview of the social life of the cultural elite. The micro-analysis is made possible by letters and diaries commemorating the event itself, but most of the book is about the participants' lives on one hand and the London of the age on the other (Hughes-Hallett 2002). Finally, Paul Chambers' book on the Cock Lane ghost appearance in 1761–62 is a good example of works that can hardly be called microhistory because their micro-analysis is not complemented by any effort to reach a general conclusion (Chambers 2006).

John Brewer's book is on the verge of microhistory: James Hackman, a former officer, a clergyman in love, shot Martha Ray in front of Covent Garden Opera House in London in 1779. She had been a lover of the First Lord of the Admiralty, Lord Sandwich, for sixteen years and was mother of his nine children. Brewer's goal was not to reconstruct 'past reality', but to analyse contemporary and later representations of this case: to discover which meanings this case assumed and how the eighteenth century has been seen ever since (Brewer 2004). Similar both to Duby's and to a lesser extent Holt's book, the case serves as a pretext to think about its afterlife, its representations, so it is certainly not clear-cut microhistory.

Incident analysis and microhistory

It was in connection with Brewer's book, that Darnton coined the term 'incident analysis' to denote the books which have been located on the periphery of microhistory in the previous section. By 'incident analysis' Darnton denotes works that do not try to arrive at macro-level conclusions from analysing events, but concentrate upon the ways people interpret their experiences, upon the meanings given to events by actors, contemporaries or others (Darnton 2004: 60–64).

We might compare these works with those of historical anthropology, both being somewhat similar to and also different from microhistory. In the latter case the dominance of culture reduces, even annihilates the historical actors' range of action. Consequently historians have no reason to deepen their analysis to microscopic detail. In the case of 'incident analyses', microscopic investigation focuses on the individual, and social and cultural factors tend to be neglected. So much so that Thomas Kuehn even claims that microhistorical narratives 'exalt the sameness between past and present' (Kuehn 1989: 533).

Anglo-Saxon historiography usually defines microhistory very loosely; its lists of microhistorical works may be very different from those in this book, works mentioned here can be classified there under different headings, and quite different books from those listed here qualify as microhistory (see e.g. Evans 2002: 8–9; Cartledge 2002: 27–29; Burke 2008: 44–47; Curthoys and Docker 2006: 202). There are but a few who call their own work microhistory in the title of their books. One of these is Paul Kléber Monod, who maps the history of a small English town in the eighteenth century using a murder case as a point of entry to get closer to the 'individual level of experience'. With a broad sweep, the author reveals the inner conflicts of the community starting from the sixteenth century: Puritans against Anglicans; the rich against the poor. In the murder case, Monod sees resistance to the emergence of a local Whig elite. He claims that the development of Rye is typical: while the town wanted to be the castle of God in Tudor and Stuart times, by the end of the seventeenth century this confessional logic was abandoned, having led Rye – and England – into a series of conflicts. In the eighteenth century, Rye lived its cultural revolution: 'Like the rest of England, then, Rye experienced first the failed revolution of the godly, then the successful revolution of the polite' (Monod 2003, quotations: 4, 238). The micro-analysis of the murder of Mr Grebell rather serves as a pretext for this thesis: it could not possibly have given birth to it in itself.

The stern critique, Ulbricht, asserts that no theoretical or practical effect of microhistory can be felt in Eamon Duffy's book on Morebath either. But Ulbricht appreciates the look into the world of Puritanism, allowed in Peter Lake's book, *The Boxmaker's Revenge* (Ulbricht 2009: 23, 26, cf. Duffy 2001, Lake 2001). If we cross the Atlantic, such uncertainties will be stronger, even if we can meet a few classics of the microhistorical approach.

We should start our survey by briefly mentioning the first book that has called itself microhistory in 1959: George R. Stewart's *Pickett's Charge: A Microhistory of the Final Attack at Gettysburg, July 3, 1863*. Decades before the birth of *microstoria*, Stewart stated very clearly its goal:

> Let us approach the charge, then, as a microcosm. Thus we may be able to see the war as clearly by looking minutely and carefully at a period of a few hours as by looking extensively and dimly throughout four years.
>
> (Stewart 1987 [1959]: xii)

The author used a microscope to analyse the fifteen hours of the decisive failed attack of the Confederate troops led by General Pickett to learn about the experience of the whole of the American civil war.

The best-known representative of American microhistory is Natalie Zemon Davis. Her most famous book, *The Return of Martin Guerre* is based on a famous case in sixteenth-century France: a young Basque peasant leaves his family, and eight years later his place in the family and the marital bed is occupied by another in the village. Later, a law-case is initiated against the impostor who is on the verge of winning the case when the real Martin Guerre appears in the court-room. As Davis recalls, it was this case that led her to microhistory. She was the historical adviser on Daniel Vigne's film *Le Retour de Martin Guerre* (1982), then she wrote a book about it (Daniel 2004: 278–79, cf. Davis 1983). This case will be treated in detail in Chapter 6, here only a critical voice will be given some room.

The starting point of the book is that 'we still know rather little about the peasants' hopes and feelings: the ways in which they experienced the relation between husband and wife, parent and child: the way in which they experienced the constraints and possibilities in their lives'. Although Martin Guerre's marriage with Bertrande de Rols was in no way typical, this does not pose a problem, argues Davis, because the 'unusual case can sometimes uncover motivation and values that are lost in the welter of the everyday' (Davis 1983: 1, 4). So her goal was not just to present an atypical case but through its minute contextualization to present a general picture.[5] Christiansen criticizes Davis for concentrating on individual motivation, which makes her book depart from its preordained course:

> Her otherwise meticulous work comes to stand in glaring contrast to whole and half suppositions and intuitive 'explanations' at the popular magazine level. The most interesting thing, however, is that she in fact had no need at all to pose these theoretically problematic and empirically unnecessary, person-fixated 'Why?' questions.
>
> (Christiansen 1988: 18)

For it is not the motivation of the actors of the story that is important, but the character of French agrarian society. But Davis 'let the means, Martin's life story, become a central thing', and instead of the 'collective history' originally envisaged, she ends up with writing the 'individual history' of Bertrande, Martin and Arnaud (Christiansen 1988: 18).[6]

For Jean de Coras, judge of the court of appeal in the case, and the chronicler on whose first-hand account much of Davis's book is built, it was the intelligent impostor, Arnaud du Tilh, who was the protagonist of the case. For the twentieth-century feminist historian, it was the wife, Bertrande de Rols who took the main role. Albert Finlay criticizes Davis for making an anachronistic figure of Bertrande (Finlay 1988: 570).[7] This is problematic for it sows the seeds of some contradictions demonstrated by the fact that the original French film omitted the detail according to which it was Bertrande who was the plaintiff in the legal case against Arnaud du Tilh, while into the Hollywood version (*Sommersby*, John Amiel, 1993) a new element was introduced in order to make the audience believe that Bertrande was in love with Arnaud. In that film, she claims that he is not her real husband to save him from an impending death sentence for a murder committed by the real Martin Guerre.

Palle Ove Christiansen is critical of microhistory in general, represented for him by *The Cheese and the Worms*, *Montaillou* and *The Return of Martin Guerre*, and seen as a new, culturalist history heavily influenced by postmodern scepticism (Christiansen 1988: 5, 15–16, 21–22). He asserts that microhistorians falsely assume that structural studies are incompatible with an interest in lived experience, and, opting for the latter, they deprive their research of the possibility of accumulating knowledge. Christiansen believes that these two can be reconciled and evokes Umberto Eco's first novel, *The Name of the Rose*, as a proof that 'it is possible not only to write at the same time about structures and living people, but also to write about the living through the structures' (Christiansen 1995: 10). It is surprising that a novel is set as an example, but Christiansen's general idea is far from unique. The challenge is 'how to sound like a pilgrim and a cartographer at the same time' – as Geertz puts it (Geertz 1988: 10). Medick similarly thinks that historians should proceed in a way in which they do not lose either 'lived experience' or the advantages of a statistical approach (Medick 1996: 25).

Christiansen's criticism comes from the side of social history against a microhistory that leans towards cultural history. An overview of Anglo-Saxon microhistory, especially in the forthcoming sections, seems to justify his challenge. For the original Italian school, microscopic investigation was never a purpose in itself, but represented an attempt to answer 'great historical questions'. The same cannot be said about Anglo-Saxon microhistory. Davis's book on the Martin Guerre's story reveals that such questions may be pushed to the background by something that has also been central in *microstoria*: the focus on the agency of past people. Anglo-Saxon microhistory, as we shall see, focuses more and more on the case: investigating it for itself, for its own interest and for the sake of the people involved – but no longer with the ambition of learning about a 'great historical question'. It seems, therefore, more and more justified to call these works 'incident analyses'.

Prostitutes, nuns and other scandals

Laurel Thatcher Ulrich's book presents the life of a hitherto unknown woman and a community in the middle of nowhere. John Lewis Gaddis calls it 'historical palaeontology' (Gaddis 2002: 42). The midwife Martha Ballard lived in Hallowell, Maine, the territory from which Augusta was later split, and wrote a diary from 1785 to her death in 1812. In this, she recorded the events of 9,965 days, but mainly incomes, expenses and the deliveries where she assisted. The diary reveals the women's world unknown from the sources produced by men. Like Shapiro's later book about Shakespeare, each chapter of Ulrich's book takes a month's diary entries as its point of departure, but – unlike Shapiro's book, which is about a single year – here November 1792 is followed by December 1793 and January 1796, etc. This way, we get a chronological overview of Martha's life and at the same time a picture of the yearly cycle of the community's life (Ulrich 1990, cf. Shapiro 2005).

We learn from Ulrich that, up to about 1800, premarital sex was frequent in New England. Half the daughters of Augusta's select men had premarital pregnancy (quoted by Cohen 1999: 226). This tolerant attitude was, however, soon altered; and in the 1830s it was generally accepted that fallen girls had no other future than in the brothels of the big cities. At the same time, the young people flooded to New York. They were trained in commerce and trades, but they no longer lived in their masters' households, following the old custom of apprenticeship, but in hostels – without barriers and oversight, enjoying sudden freedom. What happened to these young men and women in the metropolis? How did these clerks and fallen girls create the world of brothels in New York? This could have been the 'great historical question' of Patricia Cline Cohen.

Instead, she reconstructs the life of the prostitute Helen Jewett, arriving in New York from Augusta, as well as the details of the news coverage of her murder case. The author concentrates on her correspondence with her former lover and future murderer. She convinces the reader that, though acquitted by the jury, he was indeed the culprit, and she gives interesting details about the romantic garnish of early nineteenth-century prostitution (Cohen 1999).[8]

Irene Quenzler Brown and Richard D. Brown's *The Hanging of Ephraim Wheeler*, who raped his own daughter in 1805, is similarly rather incident analysis than microhistory. Although the authors tried to learn as much as possible about the protagonists, this was, in fact, only possible in the case of the murderer, who told his story on the night before his execution. So the Browns were forced to build many detours into their text, for example about the life stories of the judges, that do not take it forward. What we can really learn about from the book, is the trial itself (Brown, I. Q. and Brown, R. D. 2003).

Another book, frequently mentioned as microhistory, is Alan Taylor's work about William and James Fenimore Cooper. Although the micro-analysis is less pronounced, its conclusions are the most wide-ranging – and this is hardly a coincidence. In Taylor's microhistory, it is agency that is central – as everywhere in American microhistory, concentrating on events and individuals – but he also draws important conclusions about the development of American society after the Revolution: how quickly big fortunes were amassed using the wide channels of upward social mobility, and how quickly these could be lost. William Cooper had worked and fought all his life to achieve gentility, but even his son, already brought up as a gentleman, noticed in him the moral and cultural imperfection of the nouveau riche (Taylor, A. 1995). It is paradoxical that the upstarts of a more dynamic and competitive society aspired to the position of the old hierarchical elite which they replaced. Their failure was unavoidable in the long run.

As so many representatives of American microhistory, Richard L. Kagan chose a European subject for his book. His protagonist is a poor woman from Madrid, Lucrecia de Leon, whose more than 400 dreams were recorded between 1587 and 1590. These represented political and social criticism of Philip II's rule. He featured in the dreams as the source of all evil, and the failure of his policies and the fall of his dynasty was foretold by Lucrecia. She was the mouth-piece of the courtiers dissatisfied with Philip II's rule. When the political situation became too dangerous for the king, he himself ordered Lucrecia's arrest. During her ten-year long investigation by the inquisition, however, Lucrecia played the simple-minded woman, just as Bertrande de Rols had done (at least according to Davis), denied authorship of her dreams, and finally escaped execution (Kagan 1990, cf. Davis 1983).

Peter Linehan's microhistory is more successful than Kagan's. His 'great historical question' may not be more than a particular question of ecclesiastical history, but it is directly through his micro-analysis that he can give a surprising answer to it. In the thirteenth century, the papacy usually sided with the mendicant orders against the bishops. In this respect, the bull *Super cathedram*, issued in

1300 against the Dominicans, represented a change. Linehan renders it probable that in its background, we can find a scandal in Zamora, Spain, where nuns and Dominican friars maintained scandalous relationships (Linehan 1997).

In another investigation into the affairs of a religious community, and with a very different authorial attitude, Judith C. Brown claims to have found lesbianism in the seventeenth-century Italian convent of Pescia (Brown, J. C. 1986). It is evident that for contemporaries it was rather fake sainthood that stood at the centre of the story, but Brown wanted to address an issue that was major by the standards of the late twentieth century. Thus she ran the risk of missing the point of her story; it is still doubtful whether she could really address the question of lesbianism through her micro-investigation of the Abbess Benedetta Carlini.[9] If we survey other Anglo-Saxon microhistorical works based on Italian sources, instead of a 'great question' the centre stage will be occupied by whatever raises the interest of the general reader.

The American microhistory of Italy

According to Tolstoy, 'happy families are all alike; every unhappy family is unhappy in its own way'. As for Giovanni and Lusanna, heroes of Gene Brucker's book, published in the book series *Microstorie*, we cannot claim that their marriage was similar to all other marriages in its happy phase, at least, since it was the very existence of this legal bond between them that was called into question. It was the subject of a major legal case in Renaissance Florence, whether Giovanni, a member of the elite, was secretly married to Lusanna, a beautiful, poor widow. Brucker describes her as a special woman who risked everything for her passion, challenging the social and political order (Brucker 1986). Thomas Kuehn's convincing review makes the point that Brucker's book is effacing the difference between past and present, and 'Lusanna emerges as an Americanized heroine' (Kuehn 1989: 514, 533, quotation 514). Although she won the case in the first instance,

> it is equally important to remember that she lost in the end and that, throughout, the language of the sources portrayed her with gender stereotypes. [...] Brucker's Lusanna, for example, may have moved against prevailing views and asserted her prerogatives by suing her lover (especially if she took monetary settlement to drop the matter, as Giovanni accused her of doing at one point), but she also accepted those views when she acceded to a secret wedding ceremony without notarial record and dowry. The entire issue of what it was she would have 'won' from the conflict confronts us with the sort of limits a woman faced.
>
> (Kuehn 1991: 14–15)

Kuehn thinks that the sources of the case are not suitable for reconstructing Giovanni's relationship with Lusanna, but just to write a trial narrative, for example in the form of an extended case study of legal anthropology (Kuehn

1989: 534). If he is right, hardly any microhistory is possible. If the sources of the trial are only suitable to inform about the trial itself – as really seemed to be the case in the Wheeler book – Ginzburg should never have set out to learn about a popular culture taking Menocchio's trial as his starting point (cf. Brown, I. Q. and Brown, R. D. 2003; Ginzburg 1980).

The northern, German parallel to Giovanni's and Lusanna's case is that of the aristocrat Erasmus Limpurg Schenk and Anna, daughter of Hermann Büschler, the richest burgher and five times mayor of Schwäbisch Hall. From Steven Ozment's book we learn not only about their secret affair and the evicted and disinherited Anna's legal conflict with her family, but also about southern Germany in the sixteenth century. In this book, the agency of the historical actors is stressed; though constrained by their social positions and culture, they carved out for themselves a space for action – for example as a prisoner first of her father, later of Schwäbisch Hall, Anna was kept on a chain, but she escaped both times (Ozment 1996).

Each chapter in Ulrich's book starts with a full quotation of one month's entries from the diary of Martha Ballard (Ulrich 1990). One of Ozment's main sources is the correspondence between the two lovers. His two other books, which also qualify as microhistory, are similarly built on letters. Thirty per cent of the text of Ozment's book about a Nuremberg couple, Magdalena and Balthasar Paumgartner, is made up of their correspondence: 20 per cent in the form of full quotations from letters and 10 per cent of sentences or paragraphs built into the historian's thematically organized text (Ozment 1986). Four years later, he published a book based on the letters of three sons of a famous Nuremberg merchant family, aged between 15 and 25, students and apprentices far from home. Ozment published in full all the 207 letters which make up 85 per cent of his book, and he limited himself to writing introductions to chapters, that follow each other in chronological sequence (Ozment 1990). We can observe a clear tendency towards an increasing respect for the voices of past historical actors, at least in the form of respecting the autonomy of texts from the past. Returning to Italy, for example Thomas V. Cohen's and Elizabeth S. Cohen's book comprises the complete documentation of nine trials from late Renaissance Rome followed by commentaries (Cohen and Cohen 1993).

It was unfortunately not Jacques Fournier who led the interrogations in Trent in 1475, so R. Po-Chia Hsia's book focuses narrowly on the blood libel itself: how most members of the local Jewish community fell victim to a legal procedure launched against them after a little Christian boy died, and how the papal investigation to review the case ended in failure (Hsia 1992). Hugh Bicheno's *Vendetta* narrates the antagonism of two aristocratic families in Central Italy from the thirteenth century in alarming detail, culminating in the rivalry of Federico da Montefeltro and Sigismondo Pandolfo Malatesta, both outstanding *condottieri* of the mid-fifteenth century. The author has a clear preference both for Malatesta, who enjoyed a bad reputation among his contemporaries and later historians, and for military history: tactics, armour and fortifications.

From his book, we can best learn about the world of Renaissance warfare (Bicheno 2008).

The unsuccessful Pazzi conspiracy in 1478 was a turning point in the Medicis' route to the domination of Florence. This stands at the focal point of Lauro Martines's book *April Blood*, that brings us close to the real nature of Renaissance politics, depicting the gradual weakening of political participation, the tightening grip of the Medici oligarchy on republican institutions and the growing dissatisfaction of many, such as the members of the wealthy Pazzi family, used to having a say in public affairs, but losing their former influence and often even threatened in their existence. Lorenzo Medici's cruel revenge for his assassinated brother taken on the conspirators' families demonstrates Martines's point about the cruelty of Renaissance politics: not even in Florence or Venice was there such a thing as a legitimate political opposition; in politics adversaries were annihilated (Martines 2003).

Ingrid D. Rowland wrote the history of a 'Renaissance forgery' in her interesting book, *The Scarith of Scornello*. In 1634, close to Volterra, Curzio Inghirami 'found' hundreds of Etruscan scrolls (*scarith*) and subsequently published them. Representatives of contemporary academic life usually regarded the scrolls as forgeries, especially because the alleged Etruscan writings were written on paper. They attacked Curzio's sensational discoveries, according to which Prospero de Fiesole foretold the birth of Jesus Christ and also gave arguments to the Catholic party in the theological disputes of the seventeenth century. It was, however, not noticed until 1700, that the 'Etruscan' paper bore the watermark of the paper works of Colle di Val d'Elsa.

Rowland points out that Etruscan traditions were very important for the Grand Duchy of Tuscany and were used to cement its cultural unity. As Curzio was more and more attacked outside Tuscany, he was defended by more and more important personalities in Tuscany itself. Curzio's discoveries can be interpreted as an element of the intellectual fight between Rome and Florence (Rowland 2004). Early modern academic life is the scene of *St. Augustine's Bones*, too. The earthly remains of Pavia's patron saint were found on 1 October 1695 during renovation works in the cathedral. The debate on their authenticity is the subject of Harold Samuel Stone's book, pamphlets, other polemical academic works and their reception (Stone 2002).

Though these microhistories bring unknown worlds closer to their readers, it is an open question whether their micro-analyses primarily serve to answer 'great historical questions'. No wonder Otto Ulbricht takes a strict stance against American microhistorians, claiming that they have given up the original goals of microhistory and just concentrate on the story itself. For him, the stories of Lusanna, Anna Büschler and Benedetta Carlini are not microhistories (Ulbricht 2009: 22–23). Although ideal microhistory takes a middle road between Duby's history, in which the battle of Bouvines serves merely as a pretext to tell us what the author knows about peace, war and battle in the Middle Ages, and many American works that in their analysis do not move towards the general, and although in ideal microhistory the historian finds the answer to the 'great historical question' in the micro-analysis itself, it still seems justifiable to apply a looser, more lenient definition of microhistory, for there is no narrow case study that does not result in more general implications. As Johann Wolfgang Goethe remarked to Eckermann on 29 October 1823, 'Each character, however peculiar it may be, and each object you can represent, from the stone up to the man, has generality' (Moorhead (ed.) 1930: 17). James Sharpe's book about an alleged possession investigated by King James I concentrates on a single case but it gives an idea about witchcraft accusations in general (Sharpe 1999). Although Alan Marshall did not solve any great historical problem by suggesting that Edmund Godfrey committed suicide in 1678, his analysis of the case gives a vivid overview of politics in Restoration England (Marshall 1999). Eric Jager's interesting book about the alleged rape of a knight's wife and the ensuing trial, ending with the last duel ordered by a court in France in 1386, allows a rare insight into this world (Jager 2004). Even the story of the Cock Lane ghost paints a colourful picture of eighteenth-century London, presenting a wide range of situations and characters from Doctor Johnson through emerging Methodism to the two African boys who were the first to hear the ghost knocking on the wall (Chambers 2006).

The *quasi-microstoria*

American historians, however, also write microhistory that is closer to the Italian original. Muir and Guido Ruggiero, who have presented *microstoria* to the English-speaking public through three collected volumes in selections from the *Quaderni Storici* can be mentioned as such (Muir and Ruggiero (eds) 1990, 1991, 1994). The north-eastern Italian province of Friuli was in a state of war at the end of February 1511. Peasant militias stood in arms expecting the attack of imperial forces. Their commander, Antonio Savorgnan, head of the Zambarlano faction of the local nobility, used this tense atmosphere to let artisans and peasants massacre members of the rival Strumiero faction in Udine. Muir's analysis of the case uses social history as well as anthropological theories to explain the possible causes and bloody rituals of this massacre. He stresses the importance of the *vendetta*, the shared culture of vengeance murder, and brings together in his analysis the traditional modes of killing: that of men (*vendetta*), of wild animals (the hunt) and of domesticated animals (of which the festival context is the carnival). According to Muir, there was a 'peculiar bond between the body-centred nature of carnival imagery and the style of vendetta murder. In revenge as in carnival, the human body and its parts produced the vocabulary and syntax for symbolic communications' (Muir 1998: 97).

If the Giovanni and Lusanna marriage was unusual, that of the scion of one of the most famous Venetian families, Marco Dandolo, to Andriana Savorgnan was even more so – for the latter was not a member of the Friulan aristocracy, but a famous courtesan. In his volume *Binding Passions*, Ruggiero tries to map out how passion was controlled in late Renaissance Venice. Passions not only demanded a free outlet during the carnival, but a complete counter-society was built on them and he consecrates this volume to that. For Andriana's marriage had defied all conventions: she lost her influential supporters – who otherwise helped famous courtesans escape the increasingly strict state control of prostitution – and she was immediately referred to as a common tart. Although charged with love magic by the inquisition, she managed to escape to the *Terra Firma*, the territory belonging to the Venetian Republic, where the couple could live undisturbed, contradicting the logic of the overall context sketched by Ruggiero himself (Ruggiero 1993: 24–56). His knowledge of the period and these problems does not derive directly from Marco and Andriana's case, but from a set of similar cases. In his micro-analyses we can always glimpse a surprisingly multifaceted system of relations. Ruggiero does not arrive at a general conclusion at the end of his book, it is rather through the texture of his overlapping case studies that the face of the age is sketched (Ruggiero 1993: 223–24).

In his *Machiavelli in Love*, a series of studies analysing both a literary text and archival sources, we can learn about the greatest political thinker of the Renaissance from a special angle. Arguing against Michel Foucault, Ruggiero claims that sexual identity, as identity in general, was a consensual reality in the Renaissance, a reality shared by a group. For his family, the ageing Machiavelli's love for a young singer was a scandal, but his friends were well disposed to it. Similarly, his friend Casavecchia could admit his homosexuality in this circle, while he denied it vigorously in front of the general public of the masculine world of Florence (Ruggiero 2007: 6–8, 138–39). Ruggiero's books are both characterized by a 'great question' and by micro-analysis, we can only ask if he can always find a clear answer in the latter to the former.

Tommaso Astarita chose judicial sources for his microhistory about early eighteenth-century rural southern Italy. At the centre of his attention stands a case in which it is not the woman poisoning her husband, nor her lover who is sentenced to fifteen years in prison but the neighbour, who obtained the arsenic – the murderer herself escaped. The village of Pentidattilo is used to represent typical poor and isolated communities, its social and cultural history is said therefore to be representative of a significant portion of the con-temporary population. Village hierarchy, gender relations, views on reputation and honour are the main themes of the book. Anna de Amico seems to have been sentenced because she was not well connected locally; she fell victim to her marginality (Astarita 1999).

Mentioning these books, we seem to have accomplished a full circle and have arrived back at *microstoria*. The main objective of Chapter 4 is to find answers to the still open questions. We shall therefore address first the representativity problem of microhistory or, in other words, the micro–macro link, then the problem of multiscopic versus microhistory, and finally the difference between 'incident analysis' and microhistory. On one hand, attempts have been made to find answers to these questions on the peripheries not discussed earlier, on the other we can try to give answers to these questions taking microhistorical works about the peripheries as our points of departure. Some theoretical considerations seem to come together into a compact theory of microhistory, while others will feature as rivals to this concept.

In contrast to the first three chapters, which have been organized on a geographical basis, Chapter 4 is problem-centred. We shall not only see solutions to old questions being outlined, but also new problems will emerge when discussing the microhistory of recent years. Debates on postmodernism having somewhat abated, we should also confront the challenges of the present, looking for a place for microhistory in the historiography of the future. The relation of microhistory to experimental history and global history will be addressed.

This book is not intended to be a balanced overview of microhistory; not just because objectivity is an illusion, one that – as opposed to other illusions – is not worth pursuing, but because of a conscious advocacy of microhistory. This lends this book a subjectivity that will become more pronounced in Chapter 4, and which will be further increased in Part II. Meanwhile, hopefully, the nature of microhistorical knowledge will be better understood.

Notes

1 This is not necessary. András Lugosi argues that the holistic Ginzburgian branch of Italian microhistory (as opposed to the branch that is preparing reductive models of reality) has ties of affinity with symbolic anthropology: both want to observe the 'inscrutably perplexed world in its complexity'. But Lugosi suggests – differently from Ginzburg – that microhistory should not be imagined on the model of medical diagnostics but rather on that of homeopathy: this knowledge is possible without aspiring to generality (Lugosi 2001: 24–42, quotation 27–28).

2 As the authors stress, this is an oversimplification: for us the two groups would seem more similar than different. Also, 'the pro-Parris Villagers, for their part, must have felt deeply the lure of the forces which were transforming the Town: the very forces they feared and despised. [...] Villagers were not only at war with each other; they were also at war with themselves' (Boyer and Nissenbaum 1974: 107).

3 Medick's monograph has demonstrated the possibility of another outlook: local history and microhistory not being positioned against each other (Medick 1996).

4 He quotes Conan Doyle in the epigraph of the book: 'How often have I said to you that when you have eliminated the impossible, whatever remains, however improbable, must be the truth'. Marshall refers to nineteenth-century court evidence that death by self-strangulation was indeed possible (Marshall 1999: 181–82).

5 While there was no uncertainty in the film, in the book Davis could share her doubts with the readers. Where there was a hole in the fabric of her direct sources, she tried to patch it up by using archival material of a time or area that at least touched on hers (Ginzburg 1988: 116).

6 While the French film version capitalized on the dramatic qualities of the case that lent it instant notoriety, leaving the question of Arnaud's real identity open to the moment the real Martin returns, Davis summed the story up in the first two sentences of the introduction, and tried to reveal instead the motivation of the actors: why did they do what they did – building her narrative exactly on the 'Why?' questions heavily criticised by Christiansen.

7 His overall criticism is thorough and to me it seems convincing: 'Unfortunately, none of the central points of the book – the knowing Bertrande, the devious court strategy, the tragic romance, the Protestant justification, the self-fashioning peasants, the

conflicted judge, the "multivalent" text – depend on the documentary record' (Finlay 1988: 569–70). Sigurður Gylfi Magnússon will present a different view.

8 Sigurður Gylfi Magnússon is going to give this book a different evaluation in Part II.

9 Intimacy in an early modern convent is probably best shown by Craig Harline's book about Sister Margaret, thanks to his very detailed sources, partly the denunciations of this nun from Leuven addressed to the archbishop of Mechelen (Harline 1994).

4   The periphery and the new millennium
Answers and new questions

The longest road to Ithaca

We have seen Darnton advising historians to stop when they do not understand something: if they dig deep here this site could serve as their point of entry into an alien system of meanings, an unknown world-view (Darnton 1985: 5). The first significant result of Hungarian microhistory can serve as an example for this: why did one landlord beat another half-dead on 23 May 1784, in the village of Bercel in Eastern Hungary, when allocating the plots for the peasants to cultivate water-melon? Lajos Für departs from this event, not understandable at first glance, and in order to find the answer, he explores a hitherto hardly known world. On reaching the end of his book, his reader's sympathies are turned: we find out that the victim of slight build, Lajos Olasz was a ruthless exploiter, while the strong assailant, Boldizsár Bessenyei appears to be an impoverished representative of a patriarchal approach, defending villagers from Olasz (Für 2000).

'When you sail for Ithaka, / Wish that your trip be long, / Full of adventures, full of knowledge' – advises Konstaninidos P. Kavafis in one of his poems. He may be thinking about the microhistorians, who should not hurry writing their *opus magnum*, because they will only be able to see in their microhistorical case what their preliminary experience allows them to:

> Forever Ithaka must be in your mind.
> To get there is the goal of your trip.
> But do not hurry your journey at all.
> It is better if it were to take many years;
> And you an old man to finally anchor there,
> Rich with what you gathered from this trip,
> Expecting no wealth that Ithaka will give you.
>   (K. P. Kavafis, *Ithaka*.
>   Translated by Alex Moskios)

Für's long experience as a historian of the eighteenth century made it possible for him to see larger historical processes behind the conflict on the melon field, and present a fresh view of the agriculture and society of tidal lands lying in the flats of the Tisza river. A less experienced historian would have 'anchored' in a Bercel less 'rich' in experience then Für.

The most interesting find Für has made is a contradiction which he does not reflect upon; the landlord who was beaten, Lajos Olasz, was clearly a representative of progress in agriculture, while members of the impoverished Bessenyei family represented outdated forms – just like those making witchcraft allegations in Salem Village. But Boldizsár's brother, György Bessenyei, also active in the series of attacks on Lajos Olasz though not present on 23 May 1784, was a playwright, the iconic figure of literary history whose first play marks the beginning of the Enlightenment in Hungary in 1772. He was a former member of Empress Maria Theresa's Hungarian Noble Guard in Vienna – just like his brother Boldizsár himself. The Bercel case reveals that the forces of past and present did not face each other as black and white figures on a chessboard; instead they merged into one personality: a traditional noble mentality and a certain kind of Enlightenment were fully compatible. It is Für's book that forces this admission on researchers of the period, raises questions and thus opens new directions for research. Microhistory seems to be the best medicine against the 'simple truths' of history.

Fractals and history

If we insist that microhistorians arrive at an important conclusion at a general level, there are two possible ways – unless, of course, we think that it is purely by chance that the micro-analysis gives us the answer for a 'great historical question'. The first possibility is that the answer sought for can be found in any odd detail, just as the sea is said to be present in each drop of water. As we have seen, Auerbach says so in his *Mimesis*, and Matti Peltonen has also evoked Leibniz's monads to this effect – as we shall shortly see. The other possibility presupposes a selection mechanism at work in microhistory, and this line of thought can be traced further when considering Für's microhistory and we evoke fractals.[1]

Fractals are central to chaos theory.[2] They are 'systems with an intricate geometrical structure. When magnified, they reveal a finer and finer structure in different enlargements, and each of these is similar to the original structure.' (Muraközy 1997: 54). This self-similarity is, 'a symmetry in the scales. It is about repetition, pattern inside pattern' (Gleick 1999: 122). We can find this characteristic not only in mathematics or in lifeless nature, but also in the living world. Benoît Mandelbrot has moreover found recurring patterns at every scale in data of cotton prices: charts of daily and monthly changes in cotton prices fit perfectly (Muraközy 1997: 58–59; Gleick: 1999: 104, 122–23). The railway network of Europe is clearly a fractal, too. Bach's music or Picasso's drawings have also been analysed as fractals (Fokasz, Kopper, Maródi and Szedenics 1997: 266–67; Nyikos, Balázs and Schiller 1997: 244–45; Hsü and Hsü 1989). We can often observe self-similarity without having a clear idea of its cause. Could we find this phenomenon in history, too?

The obvious problem is that in the case of the cotton prices, to remain within the sphere of human society, self-similarity is found between two sets of homogeneous data. If we try to find self-similarity between the infinite complexity of the past on one hand and a microhistorical book on some minor detail on the other, reality on one hand and written representation, paper and ink, on the other, the effort seems to be clearly hopeless. If, however, we think about Für's microhistory, a solution to this problem begins to emerge.

Having worked for several decades as an agrarian historian, Für had an overall view of the agriculture and rural society of eighteenth-century Hungary. Studying archival sources, he came across the incident at Bercel and recognized an overall pattern in that single case. The microhistorian imagines a general picture, and suddenly recognizes its pattern when meeting a particular case. The decisive moment is that of selection. Microhistorians work long decades in archives and they meet scores of individual cases, and in one of these, the only one that they write up as microhistory, they recognize the features of a whole age or the complete problem they are studying. There is self-similarity between 'History' on one hand – as an imagined, only latent and unrealized representation – and microhistory on the other – as a limited therefore realizable representation. So, self-similarity here does not exist between reality on one hand and a book on the other, but between two representations, two discursive entities, which exist in the historian's mind only. In this approach the fractal-like nature of microhistory is not chance or unbelievable coincidence, but reasonable necessity.

This idea about recognition is clearly platonic. Plato thinks that cognition is the soul's recollection of eternal ideas. As he writes in *Phaedo*: 'we remember afterwards the things which we knew previous to our birth' (Plato: *Phaedo*: xxi, 76a, transl. B. Jowett). But when microhistorians recognize the whole in a part, we need not suppose this to be due to the experience of their souls earned before their births, rather the sudden crystallization of their experience earned as a researcher, the realization of something hitherto obscure, the flame of intuition lit suddenly following a long preparatory phase. This is the same phenomenon which we have met earlier, described by Peirce as 'abduction' and connected to microhistory by Muir. Abduction is the sudden regrouping of hitherto unconscious information into a new form (Muir 1991a: viii, xvi–ix; Sebeok and Umiker-Sebeok 1980). So, we may say that microhistory is born by way of abduction, based on the phenomenon of self-similarity.

The contextual knowledge of the microhistorian and the 'singularization of history'

Like Ginzburg, microhistorians try to answer one of the 'great historical questions' on the basis of their micro-investigations, perhaps finding an Indo-European oral popular culture in Menocchio's confessions made before the inquisition, or, as Levi has done, finding cooperating extended families in the anomalies of land prices in Santena. But, as we have seen in Für's case, the prerequisite of this 'finding' is the previous macro-level knowledge of the historian. Strengthened by the lessons of Gyula Benda's book, this line of thought also brings us back to the difference between microhistory and 'incident analysis'.

We can most easily decipher an encrypted document, or actually a handwritten page found in the archives, if we have an idea what it might be about. Benda's book about the society of Keszthely, a small Hungarian town between 1740 and 1849, is much like Medick's and Schlumbohm's voluminous work (Benda 2008, cf. Medick 1996, Schlumbohm 1994). It supplies ample evidence that when making a statement, the historians' well-founded contextual knowledge is dominant: it empowers them to dismiss or correct and interpret their sources. In the relationship between a particular source document (a written representation of the past) and historical context (a comprehensive mental representation of the given problem or age), the latter is dominant. But in order to have such a contextual knowledge, historians need the previous experience which has confronted them with hundreds of individual source documents. Therefore, while a detailed document is needed for a micro-investigation, not even the richest sources make microhistory in themselves. At best, they might result in an 'incident analysis'. In order for microhistory to furnish the answer to a 'great historical question', a microhistorian with comprehensive contextual knowledge is also necessary.

At this point, we might reconsider Auerbach's case. He claims that any detail of the *Odyssey* or Virginia Wolf's *To the Lighthouse* would have been suitable for him to characterize the whole work, or, in fact, a complete period of European literature (Auerbach 1959). Still, the main factor in his case, too, seems to have been his wide contextual knowledge that made deep analysis possible. Thus, the sea may be there in every drop of water after all, but certainly not for everyone. Probably there is no other way for microhistory than to rely on the microhistorian's contextual knowledge.

Auerbach's literary history seems to be similar to Duby's microhistory in which the author was already in possession of the answer to his 'great historical question' when beginning his micro-investigation. Their background knowledge of European literature or the Middle Ages also permitted them to pick out the most characteristic texts or battle for microscopic investigation. But microhistory may rely on its fractal-like character even more than that. What Peirce calls abduction is a sudden crystallization of previously unconscious information. It is not that microhistorians recognize an already familiar general pattern of a particular age or problem when they meet a particularly well-documented case in the archives, it is rather that they actually create this pattern through the micro-investigation. It is through writing microhistory that the hitherto hazy general picture becomes clear for them and its previously disordered elements fall into place. It is through micro-investigation that they actually find the answer to their 'great historical question'.

This is certainly not the only way to see microhistory. Scandinavian microhistory, like that of Hungary, also contributes important theoretical considerations to the debate about the nature of microhistory. The latest book of the author of Part II of this book addresses the history of Iceland with a combination of social and microhistory approaches (Magnússon 2010). In contrast to the view outlined earlier that perceives microhistory as straddling the fence between social and cultural history, Sigurður Gylfi Magnússon locates microhistory clearly on the side of social history and firmly believes that it has the capacity to renew it. He advocates the 'singularization of history' focusing on the object itself and using only the directly relevant analytical tools to put ordinary human beings at the centre of research.[3] Magnússon makes a stand for postmodernism and – in opposition to Levi and his followers – rejects metanarratives (Magnússon 2003, 2006). It is important to notice that the hostility of many Italian microhistorians towards postmodernism is not the only possible theoretical stance.

Matti Peltonen from Helsinki links Ginzburg's theory about clues and Walter Benjamin's about monads to the thoughts of Michel de Certeau about marginal phenomena. Peltonen argues that these can be more easily analysed than central phenomena, and that these analyses reveal much more: Benjamin for example saw the whole of nineteenth-century modernity in the shops of the arcades of Paris (Peltonen 2001). Chuanfei Chin also tries to address the well-known problem of microhistory by doing research about marginal groups and still aspiring to arrive at macro-level conclusions. He claims that it is the identification of the marginal group by the majority of society and the way it interacts with it that can serve as a basis for these macro-conclusions (Chin 2011). When we turn our attention to Russian and Russia's microhistory, other theoretical considerations will emerge.

Russia's microhistory

Even a superficial glance at the volumes of *Casus*, the almanac of Russian microhistory, reveals that a central concern of the articles about Russian history published in them is the relationship between the oppressive state and the individual. Olga Kosheleva's study about Ivan Ribnikov shows Peter the Great's state being characterized by humiliation, detention and torture. Ribnikov was more guilty of bad business calculations than larceny in his venture to deliver firewood for the Admiralty, but he was still sent to prison several times and to do forced labour. As a Russian counterpart to the *microstoria*'s 'active individual', Ribnikov is an example of the 'enduring individual': he resisted when he was able to, he endured torture, he fled several times. Kosheleva claims that through Ribnikov, readers can get an experience of Peter the Great's time (Kosheleva 2002).

Yevgeniy Anisimov writes about the gruesome system of denunciation that came into being in early modern Muscovy. Russian subjects were obliged by law to denounce those who infringed the laws in the eighteenth century. If they neglected this duty, they became punishable themselves. Moreover, the whole society lived in the shadow of corporal punishment: anyone was subject to this from the peasant to the colonel of the Imperial Guard. The telling expression 'the redistribution of pain' is still in use. A general atmosphere of fear formed the Russian mentality. This is demonstrated through the cases of Mikhail

Kosmin, who went to the authorities to make his dutiful denunciation but was so much afraid that he fainted in front of General Ushakov, and of Pavel Mikhalkin, who spent half a year in custody following his denunciation and emerged as an invalid. When the accused and the denouncer both stuck to their statements, they were both tortured in turns to find out who was lying – or who would break first (Anisimov 2003).

The English historian, Orlando Figes demonstrated in his *Whisperers* (2007) how this system developed under Stalin. With the help of a group of Russian researchers, he built on the memories and written sources of 450 people born between 1917 and 1925. His magnificent book is most successful in conveying ordinary people's experience in Russia under Stalin.

> It was a warm summer evening, 28 July 1938, and Nelly's grandmother had gone to pick the raspberries in the garden, leaving her in charge of her sister Angelina while her mother, Zinaida Bushueva, nursed her baby brother and prepared the meal. Since the arrest of her father, nine months earlier, Nelly had grown used to helping in the house, although she was only four years old. Zinaida was breast-feeding Slava when the front door opened and two NKVD soldiers appeared. They told her to get dressed, and took with her the children to the NKVD headquarters in the centre of Perm. A few minutes later Nelly's grandmother returned with the raspberries: the house was empty, her family had gone.
>
> (Figes 2008: 316)

This book is definitely microhistorical in its basic character, though not based on one single, deep micro-investigation, but on dozens of elaborately presented cases. However, it can be argued that Figes's narrative goes against one of the main principles of microhistory: agency. It is not just that in his chapters, micro-level cases follow the macro-level thesis as illustrations, but also that, in *Whisperers*, Stalin is the only autonomous agent; everyone else is suffering rather than shaping history. As in Ribnikov's case, we can witness an oppressive system at work which allows individuals to be human and decent only in the few open fissures, in the gaps in the structure which otherwise determines their behaviour. We do not see ordinary Russians forming these structures by their decisions and deeds, although the work of, for example, the German *Alltagsgeschichte* school gives plenty of examples showing that it is possible to see individuals as autonomous actors even in a twentieth-century dictatorship.

The same lesson can be drawn from Adam Zamoyski's book about Napoleon's unsuccessful Russian campaign, which links agency directly to responsibility. Similar in outlook to Figes's book, Zamoyski first enumerates the structural causes of Napoleon's failure, then proceeds to those decisions that later solidified into structures, limiting later actions, for example Napoleon's belated decision to withdraw his troops from Moscow. But his account conserves a microhistorical character in so far as it stresses the agency of the officers and individual soldiers in shaping their fate. Like Colonel Marbot, each commander could have followed the example of the Poles who put clawed horseshoes on their mounts. Most of them did not, which resulted in the near annihilation of the French cavalry. Or the writer presents the example of Albert de Muralt who carried a little iron pot that saved his life: he loaned it to those who had food but no pot to cook in, so they shared their food with him (Zamoyski 2004).

Thus, in Zamoyski's narrative, responsibility for the failure of Napoleon's campaign and the death of most of his troops falls not only on the Russian winter or on Napoleon and his marshals but – proportionately – on all his soldiers. We might say that microhistory is advantageous in uniting a cultural and a social historical outlook: a unilaterally social historical outlook with the focus on structures would not allow these perspectives to enter the picture.

The responsibilities of the historical actor and the historian

The classic microhistorical treatment of 'Napoleon's fatal march on Moscow' or Stalinism would be a narrative built on the experience of a single army unit or family. The dozens of micro-analyses of Zamoyski's and Figes' books are not so well elaborated. Moreover, their micro-analyses do not serve as a direct basis for their answer for a 'great historical question', so their status as micro-history is dubious. But as we have seen, both address agency in different but equally significant ways. Both Figes' negative and Zamoyski's positive examples highlight the point that the individual's freedom of action is not restricted to questions such as how a sixteenth-century Friulan miller can imagine the birth of angels or whether or not the *podestà* of a seventeenth-century village in Piedmont is able to handle local conflict. Agency is also to be explored in areas where individual decisions concern matters of life and death. It is fully justifiable for a historian to apply a microhistorical approach, just as social and cultural history do in general, to the area of politics.

The famous 'butterfly effect' of chaos theory, according to which a single movement of a butterfly's wing in Brazil may result in a hurricane in North America, alludes to a promising application of microhistory, in which micro-analysis is concentrated on those moments which are 'chaotic' in the sense that minor changes result in events taking quite different historical tracks.[4] Military history, as we have seen in the cases of Stewart's and Zamoyski's works, is a promising candidate for this type of microhistory. Agency and responsibility, too, are almost naturally stressed in these books.

One further example is Peter Englund's celebrated book about the battle of Poltava (1709), signifying the end of the early modern Swedish military great power and the rise of Russia (Englund 1992). Englund's analysis reveals a host of lower-level causes for Charles XII's defeat; we still cannot claim that any of these was solely responsible for it, since there is a clear over-determination in history. Picking out a single point from the chain of causes does not take us anywhere nearer to historical understanding. Zamoyski rightly claims that clawed horseshoes could have been used by the French during their retreat from Moscow or that Napoleon should have sent his cavalry that had lost their mounts to safety back from Moscow earlier instead of forming them into useless infantry units. Still, this single move could hardly have given him victory at Leipzig, even less prevent the return of the Bourbons to France in 1814. Bearing over-determination in mind can help microhistorians not to be too quick to give answers to their 'great historical questions' on the basis of their particular micro-analyses.

Microhistory still seems the best means to point to the fact that structures – at a given moment those unalterable conditions that limit the historical actors' freedom of action – are to a large extent the product of individual decisions that point to the responsibility of the actor. Johann Gustav Droysen claimed more than one and half centuries ago that the field of history is the moral world (Droysen 1868: 11). Both historians' and readers' judgements are basically of a moral character. This moral dimension of history gives microhistory an additional advantage over other ways of writing history: the enhanced closeness to the past may reduce the chance that history declines into pure hagiography.[5]

Not only do historical actors have responsibility: if texts, including historical texts not only mirror but form our world, then historians, including microhistorians, are historical actors and have responsibility. When, instead of pointing out oppressive structures that cripple and kill people, microhistorians highlight how people build, maintain, erode or eventually destroy structures, they emphasize agency and responsibility, and advocate an enhanced responsibility for the future.[6]

While some microhistorians claim that microhistory has long been dead, and its direct influence for example on the *Annales* or some German historians was, in fact, strongest in the 1990s, the approach of microhistory is clearly in the ascendant. This is probably due to the fact that as postmodernism has, if not changed, at least modified the intellectual milieu, the use of history as a reading was significantly reinforced. Micro-investigations have come to the fore as several historians have moved towards satisfying this public demand.

As we have seen, military history gives ample scope for the microhistorian. At first glance, *microstoria* does not seem to work together with the other best-selling branch of history, biography,[7] but Renata Ago argues that the biographical approach perfectly fits the aspirations of microhistory: it can present both the goals and the uncertainties. According to Ago, in order to understand what an action meant to the historical actor, it is not biographical studies that are needed, but the kind of investigation Levi was pursuing about the land market in Santena (Ago 2004: 43–44). Sabina Loriga, however, has turned towards biography. Instead of writing someone's biography, characteristically for her Parisian intellectual environment, she has written a theoretical book about biography, also reflecting on the relationship between microhistory and biography. She thinks that two dangers should be avoided: a search for the statistical average, in which case biography serves generalization, and the intention to present every particular case, to write everybody's biography (Loriga 2010: 260–63).

The new millennium has brought more recent modifications. We have to investigate how, if at all, microhistory can adapt itself to these changes. How do representatives of recent approaches use microhistory? What is microhistory like today, and, even more, what potential does it have for the future? At the beginning of the twenty-first century, history might still to some extent be pre-occupied with the history of memory, the problems of space and time, maybe also with probing the limits of historical representation, as the so called experimental history is doing. History may, however, be better characterized by the postcolonial and, in general, global historical approach, while non-human history has also appeared, ranging from climate history to that of animals. In the rest of Chapter 4, these will be briefly evoked.

Experimental history and microhistory

Twelve years after *Entertaining Satan*, Demos published *The Unredeemed Captive*. In 1703, Indians descended on a small town in Massachusetts, abducted more than 100 Englishmen and took them to Canada. Most were released after a couple of years, but the minister's seven-year old daughter, who had been adopted by an Iroquois family, refused to return home. She claimed she had become an Indian, and even married an Indian husband. The book has alternative beginnings and endings, but its most striking feature is the openly fictive text built into the narrative at its dramatic climax when an English delegate, who recorded the story, and two Jesuit missionaries try to persuade the girl to return home – but in vain. She utters one single word: 'No.' On her reasons, writes Demos, 'we can only speculate – only imagine – but that much, at least, we must try.' And he opens Eunice's thoughts to the reader in one and half pages, typeset in italics (Demos 1996: 108).

Openly fictive elements play an even larger part in the English historian Simon Schama's book *Dead Certainties (Unwarranted Speculations)* (1991), in which we can read a private soldier's first person singular account about the battle of Québec on 13 September 1759. Furthermore, readers can also be present at the police interrogation of the Harvard University janitor who discovered the remains of the victim in the murderer Professor Webster's laboratory. In the book's epilogue, Schama admits that these episodes are fictive in their entirety. Concerning his writing, he says that it is 'a work of the imagination that chronicles historical events', and he also adds that 'the narratives are based on primary sources' (Schama 1992: 327). Yet, since all this is revealed only at the very end of the book, his readers are, more or less, left in uncertainty as to what it is that they are actually reading. For the book contains admittedly fictive descriptions and details that, as it later turns out, can evidently not be based on sources; the reader might also deem those parts fictive that are later mentioned as being based on primary sources. Such texts are the letters written to the governor of Massachusetts in Professor Webster's favour. For the reader, the strongest feature of Schama's book is the deliberate juxtaposition of real and fictitious elements.

The same merger of fiction and reality stands at the centre of the American Robin Bisha's study, 'Reconstructing the voice of a noblewoman of the time of Peter the Great: Daria Mikhailovna Menshikova. An exercise in (pseudo) autobiographical writing'. After two paragraphs of introduction, we can read the first person singular narrative of Princess Menshikova, who is about to join her husband in exile in Siberia. She relates her life in this narrative, on the last day of her life (Bisha 1998). This article is a result of a serious historical research, but is clearly fictitious. So is the fascinating book of Russell McCormmach about an invented German theoretical physicist, into whose figure and life those of real-life scientists are merged (McCormmach 1982). Approaching history with a post-modern epistemology and trying out new fashions of historical narration walk hand-in-hand. This is clearly demonstrated in a collection of essays from the journal *Rethinking History* (Munslow and Rosenstone (eds) 2004), in which Bisha's study was republished, or in the classical work of one of its editors, Robert A. Rosenstone about the way in which three Americans experienced nineteenth-century Japan (Rosenstone 1988), which has a distinct literary character.

If we agree with Reinhard Koselleck, according to whom historical sources do not direct, but rather tie the hands of the historian – they must not be contradicted, but they never prescribe for him what he should say (Koselleck 2004: 111) – then the narrative techniques applied by Demos, Schama or Bisha do not disqualify their works as history. All historical narratives contain fictitious binding elements, so the difference between an average historical work and those quoted above is just in quantity and not in quality. If we interpret them as microhistory, we might argue that their 'great historical question' is the definition of history as a literary genre, of probing its limits. They are labelled postmodernists for they deliberately merge real and fictitious or they provocatively apply fiction as an independent element or even the organizing principle of the narrative, while historians usually reduce this to a minimum and cautiously mark the fictitious elements of their narratives.

The above examples demonstrate that a – loosely defined – microhistorical approach is fully compatible with the experiment with historical narratives. In all these experiments with historical narration, micro-analysis has a significant place, and indeed, as we have already seen, Peter Burke, among others, has suggested the approach of microhistory to his colleagues in 1991 (Burke 1991: 241–42). This should call our attention again to the fact that although *microstoria* was clearly hostile towards postmodernism, this controversy does not seem to be unavoidable. We could perhaps say that the more cultural historical the outlook of the microhistorians, the better their chances of embracing postmodernism. While postmodernism too is clearly on the way out, there are more recent trends which should also be considered here.

From experience and global microhistory

Social sciences and history approach the territories outside Europe with a typical European thinking. Dipesh Chakrabarty's *Provincializing Europe* addresses the problematic nature of this fact using the study of India as an example. The historical study of modernization involves using European concepts. The transition to capitalism entails a transformation of both the reality and the self-reflection of a certain country: a transition to the use of the Western language of modernity (Chakrabarty 2000). In light of the global climate change, he argues for a uni-fication of the studies of human history and natural history (Chakrabarty 2009). For Ewa Domanska, the changing focus of his attention signifies a tendency: 'theoretically oriented scholars are becoming more and more aware that, after the postmodernist turn to fragmented reality, micronarrative (microhistory) and local histories, there is a need to reconsider "big picture questions"' (Domanska 2010: 120). In her reasoning, microhistory belongs to the past postmodern period. But there are examples that show that new ways of thinking do not disqualify the microhistory approach.

Frank Ankersmit uses the concept of 'historical experience', a sudden impression of direct 'authentic' contact with the past (Ankersmit 2003), and Hans Gumbrecht employs that of 'presence' to break with the hermeneutical outlook of postmodernism that traps knowledge into the language and isolates it from the outside world – in the case of history, from the past. Gumbrecht opposes 'presence' to 'meaning' defining their 'cultures' in opposition to each other; the 'culture of meaning' dominates our world, in which the 'culture of presence' can only appear in momentary aesthetic manifestations. This is par-allel to the de-contextualized nature of Ankersmit's 'historical experience', a result of the momentary disappearance of the barrier between the historian and the past. Both Ankersmit's historical and Gumbrecht's aesthetical experiences are sudden, intensive and precede linguistic conceptualization (Simon 2013).

Microhistory is not very far from these theoretical considerations. Conveying the feeling of 'historical experience' to the readers, or at least its illusion, has been a central aspiration of cultural history in general and many microhistorical works in particular.[8] As we have seen, it was exactly this point that was the object of serious criticism formulated by Christiansen, representing a more traditional social history, addressed to microhistory (Christiansen 1995: 9). And as for Gumbrecht's ideas, his *In 1926* was an early example to realize them. This historical work is somewhat similar in its fragmentation to Auerbach's *Mimésis*, the resurrection of the year 1926 realized by 51 mosaic stones, alpha-betically ordered essays from one on bullfighting to one on Heidegger, each presenting a different aspect of the pivotal year of 1926 (Gumbrecht 1997).

But of all hitherto mentioned trends, global history is the most pronounced, whether its works heed Chakrabarty's advice or not, and it is exactly in global history that the role of the microhistorical approach seems to be best secured. Namely, if we do not take microhistory as being the opposite of macro-oriented history but rather regard it as one of its versions,[9] intending to answer a 'great historical question', we shall see no reason to regard the victorious march of global history as a funeral march for microhistory.

Auerbach argued in 1952, that Goethe's concept of world history is outdated: we cannot judge everything on the basis of the same cultural tradition, we need different 'starting points, [...] concrete details from which the global process can be inductively reconstructed.' This thought has prompted Ginzburg to understand the processes of eighteenth-century colonization through one single case, the figure of Jean-Pierre Purry (Ginzburg 2005: 666). In her essay, Lara Putnam explores the links between microhistory and Atlantic history which address the intercontinental interconnectedness of the sixteenth and twentieth centuries, usually focusing on the time of the slave trade. Although micro-history is fully capable of undermining orthodoxies also in an Atlantic context, she advocates that Atlantic historians should aspire for more; setting the spatial limits of their investigation on the basis of an initial micro-analysis, they should contextualize their microhistory with the help of prosopography (Putnam 2006). Dale Tomich argues that historians should write microhistory as world history seen through the perspective of an individual. Microhistorians should follow Braudel's advice and turn the hour-glass again; having accomplished a micro-investigation, they should go back to the *longue durée*, to structural time, and recreate world history in the light of the lessons of microhistory (Tomich 2008).

Early examples of microhistory include Jonathan D. Spence's book about the impoverished Chinese province of T'an-ch'eng between 1668 and 1672. Based both on memoires and literary sources, Spence presents and analyses four cases to draw a picture of famine and violence in rural China with unusually sharp lines (Spence 1978). More recent works of microhistory, however, not only address remote countries and exotic situations, but focus on cross-cultural ties, sometimes even on a global scale. In a successful attempt, Tonio Andrade wrote a full-fledged global microhistory about seventeenth-century Taiwan. In 1661, a Chinese warlord invaded the Dutch colony of Taiwan. Only one fortress could resist, helped with the unexpected arrival of a Dutch fleet. The Chinese set a siege, but they were starving and ravaging the countryside, quickly losing the sympathy of the local population. Sait, a Chinese peasant, a former beneficiary of Dutch colonial rule, sneaked into the fortress and advised the Dutch to blockade the Strait of Taiwan and thus starve the warlord Koxinga's troops. Instead of following his advice and winning the war, the Dutch did not trust Sait. The Chinese soon received supplies and took the fortress with the help of a German, a former sergeant in the Dutch army, who helped them to construct the siege works that allowed Koxinga to capture the fortress. 'When war came, the intercultural cooperation that had allowed Taiwan to thrive dissolved. Friendship across cultural lines became harder to maintain', writes Andrade. The different treatment of defectors by the two warring parties proved to be decisive. Sait paid with his life for his effort to help the Dutch (Andrade 2010: 590).

One of Natalie Zemon Davis's exciting books is about al-Hasan al-Wazzan, alias Leo Africanus. A sixteenth-century Arab geographer, born in Granada and raised in Morocco, he spent nine years in Rome as a prisoner of the Pope. He wrote the first description of Africa. The real subject of the book is cross-cultural connections (Davis 2006). Alexandra Parma Cook's and Noble David Cook's microhistory is about Francisco Noguerol de Ulloa, a sixteenth-century Spanish conquistador who returned to Spain from Peru with his second wife only to learn that, contrary to what his sister had written him in order to bring him home, his first wife, from whom he had practically fled to the New World, was still alive. The book is built on source documents produced by the ensuing litigation. The authors want to present the experiences of the 'hundreds and thousands of other young men of his generation, who had rushed overseas, full of expectations and illusions'. They claim that apart from his accidental bigamy, Francisco's experiences were typical. The authors follow in Natalie Zemon Davis's footsteps in the sense that they do not try to look into the souls of their heroes: they restrict themselves to reporting their heroes' deeds as reflected in the written sources (Cook, A.P. and Cook, N.D. 1991). Trans-Atlantic connections are at the core of the book, due to its subject, but not really at the centre of the authors' attention. The transcontinental flow of information, a decisive element of the bigamy case, both in oral and written forms, could have been explored much more deeply.

Just as in the case of Chambers' book about the Cock Lane ghost, two African boys and Methodists are central to Randy J. Sparks' microhistory, which is, however, basically about trans-Atlantic and cross-cultural connections. Two princes of one of the slave trader towns of the Bight of Biafra were taken prisoner by a British guineaman as a result of the conflict with another slave trader town. Sold first in Dominica then in Virginia as slaves, the princes escaped to Britain where the business partners of their family and Methodists helped them to avoid being enslaved again and finally to return to Africa. 'A microhistory of the eighteenth-century Anglo-Atlantic World', the princes' experiences open a window to the amazing world of the slave trader elite of this West African area, in which cultivating British customs and corresponding in English with their business partners was the rule (Sparks 2004, quotation: 3, cf. Chambers 2006). It seems to be clear that while a microhistorical approach can significantly enhance our understanding, the global approach is not just compatible with microhistory, but microhistory directly demands exploring among others the global implications of the case under the historian's microscope.

The benefits of microhistory

In this overview of the history of microhistory from *microstoria* through its direct impact on French and German historians and Anglo-Saxon microhistory to that on the periphery, we have concentrated on the three elements of its definition. The microhistory of Russia exposed agency and the related issue of responsibility while Anglo-Saxon historical works highlighted the 'great historical question' – or rather how it faded in works that can instead be called 'incident analyses'. Theories of 'changing the scale' and 'multiscopic history' were mentioned, too, but here the priorities of agency, individual action and micro-level were rather accented, and the fractal-like character of microhistory was suggested to work as 'micro–macro link'. The insistence on agency seems to preclude the approach of historical anthropology, built on Clifford Geertz's anthropology, in which culture is predominant. The space given to agency in microhistory and the stress laid on the 'great historical question' for which micro-analysis tries to find an answer, might contradict each other. But since the microhistorians' overall contextual knowledge derives from the study of hundreds of cases, it is not impossible to find a balance, and an 'emic' approach might be the solution: questions regarded as important by contemporaries should be picked, if possible, as subject-matter for microhistory. We have also seen that although *microstoria* was originally hostile to postmodernism, it does not have to be: the aversion felt by social microhistorians is counterbalanced by cultural microhistorians' sympathies.

As a result, the picture of a microhistory has emerged in which microhistorians are enabled to recognize the whole in a single case by their preliminary contextual knowledge. When conducting a micro-investigation, due to the fractal-like character of microhistory, they recognize the pattern they have in their heads about a certain age or general problem in the particular case when studying its sources in the archives. A fully fledged self-similarity will emerge when writing about the micro-level phenomenon; they continue to think about the general. In an ideal case, micro-analysis is not just a pretext for microhistorians to present an already formulated answer to a 'great historical question'; it is the study of the single case itself that allows the crystallization of this answer in the microhistorian's mind.

Micro-analyses are suitable for unveiling the agency of past individuals, and the justification for concentrating historical research at the micro-level and giving answers to 'great historical questions' on the basis of individual agency is given by the conviction that structures of history are built, upheld and demolished by the actions of individuals. Microhistory reveals this connection, always true but with other methods often left in the shadow. This, in turn, brings with itself the questions of responsibility, put finally to microhistorians themselves, too.

Microhistory is able to apply the approaches of both social and cultural history: to grasp the meanings of the latter and provide the explanations of the former and, within the frames of a very circumscribed investigation, show the historical actors' experiences, how they saw their lives and what meanings they attributed to the things that happened to them on one hand and on the other give explanations with references to historical structures, long-lived mentalities and global processes using a retrospective analysis, all of which were absent from the actors' own horizons of interpretation. As argued, this complexity can only be presented without over-simplification when investigating a very narrowly defined object.

When seen from the point of view of the reader, microhistory has four assets: it is appealing to a general public, it is realistic, it conveys personal experience and the lines branching out from its focus reach very far. The story about Martin Guerre or Menocchio is interesting in itself, and this can bring microhistory to a wider audience, which makes it enjoyable for the professional historian, too. Then, the closeness of microhistory to the soil of reality is evident, too. Roland Barthes's 'reality effect' has a better chance of being felt here (Barthes 1968). Since the works of microhistory usually address issues at the level of the individual, they are best placed to convey 'lived experience' to the reader, however vague, as written words always are, in contrast to a vivid reality. Other ways of writing history can hardly surpass microhistory in this. Finally, microhistory is able to present a diversity of contexts within the frame of a relatively limited investigation, thus presenting the fabric of the society and culture to its readers. It seems to be important to balance these attempts so that the table of microhistory may be solidly and evenly supported on its four legs.[10] In this way historians using a microscope can work effectively against oversimplification and superficial historical judgement. These ideas might be corroborated by or checked against the cases presented in Part II of this book, in which Sigurður Gylfi Magnússon will present a rival interpretation.

Notes

1 In his overview of the historian's craft, Gaddis also invokes chaos theory and refers to fractals (Gaddis 2002: 71–89).

2 Chaos theory describes those areas of nature that can be characterized by simple non-linear differential equations (Muraközy 1997: 58).

3 The concept will, of course, be given detailed treatment in Part II.

4 Donald McCloskey explores the applicability of the thinking of chaos theory in history, building on the characteristic of sensitive dependence on initial conditions (McCloskey 1991). This is different from the line of thought from the previous application of the idea of fractals, stressing self-similarity.

5 This danger is certainly not fully eliminated. Nathan Wachtel's series of Marrano portraits from sixteenth–eighteenth-century Latin America of Jews who were forced to accept Christianity but exercised their old religion in secret, or at least kept a memory of it, underlines their self-sacrifice – similarly to Weis's book on Cathar heresy, already discussed (Weis 2000). Wachtel's book, based on exceptional sources such as the notes of an informer concerning the night conversations of Francisco Botello and Juan de Leon, or the minutes of Manuel Bautista Perez's torture, is very efficient in conveying lived experience to the reader. But the ways in which one of the richest men of Peru, the slave trader Perez, acquired his wealth or Botello's racism towards his mestizo son who wanted to marry Botello's niece, remain unconsidered. Martyrs cannot be criticised (Wachtel 2001).

6 If we believe with Figes that individuals can only be humanistic and decent in the fissures, the gaps in oppressive structures, then we, in fact, give primacy to structures. Building historical narratives on the micro-analysis of individual behaviour is only justified if we assert that historical structures are the results of earlier individual actions. The theoretical coherence of a consequent microhistorical point of view therefore requires a rejection of Lepetit's concept of multiscopic history and an acceptance of Rosental's views that claim priority for the micro-level.

7 Possible common points of microhistory and biography, even autobiography, will be addressed in detail in Part II. Here only the relevant work of two Italian microhistorians is briefly mentioned.

8 I do not claim that in Ankersmit's eyes these are all successful attempts. But he too thinks it possible to bridge the gap between historical experience and the historian's text: see his views on Huizinga's *The Waning of the Middle Ages* (Ankersmit 1997).

9 See also Ulbricht's arguments (Ulbricht 2009: 33–36, 341).

10 For an exploration of these characteristics of microhistory see Szijártó 2002.

Part II

In Part I we have seen how István M. Szijártó has brought out diverse manifestations of microhistory in different countries, how the methods of microhistory have developed in various ways in the western world, and what kind of dialogue this ideology engages in with other disciplines and other cultural trends within the humanities and social sciences. The emphasis has been primarily upon three important concepts within the scholarship of micro-history: micro-analysis, agency, and the intention of each author to answer a 'great historical question'. By exploring the role of such concepts in individual studies, he has succeeded in formulating a working definition of microhistory as a scholarly approach to history.

The reader will quickly notice that the authors of this book often differ in their views of various important aspects of microhistory. We make no attempt to gloss over our differences, but vigorously maintain our own arguments, and leave it to the reader to make up his/her own mind about individual aspects of the book, taking account of the differing views expressed here. And that is precisely the approach used by many microhistorians in their work: they do not seek to fill in the gaps in their knowledge, but stress that the reader should be aware of the limitations of the study, and hence of the conclusions reached.

In Part II we broaden the focus from the historiographical approach in Part I to a more wide-ranging consideration of contemporary ideas on the practice and significance of microhistory. For the purposes of this discussion I shall now in Part II take two empirical examples: one illustrating the methods available to microhistorians in shaping their research, the other a test case that I use to present and evaluate certain theoretical issues relating to (micro)historical research. Finally, I present myself as a subject for enquiry and provide a critical review of the current position of microhistory in the world of historical ideas and the methods that appear to point to the most promising ways forward to the future.

5   The doctor's tale
The living and the dead

Halldór Jónsson and the brothers from Strandir

The scene is Strandasýsla, the region of cramped inlets and narrow valleys along the rugged east coast of the Westfjord peninsula in the north-west of Iceland. The time is the last decades of the nineteenth century. At the farm of Tindur in the parish and commune of Kirkjuból live a tenant farmer Jón Jónsson and his wife Halldóra Halldórsdóttir, parents to nine sons. Five of these boys die young. Four – Níels, Halldór, Ísleifur and Magnús – survive to adulthood.[1]

From the short unpublished autobiography that the second of these brothers, Halldór (1871–1912), wrote in 1906 covering the first twenty years of his life, we find that his was a happy childhood that he looked back on with a degree of fondness and nostalgia: 'Life in my parents' home was Christian and good, so far as I best remember, and we children were constantly exhorted to adopt good practices and keep God's word at our fingertips'.[2] It seems that there was a strict order to all life in the household: everyone was up by six in the morning and in bed by ten. Halldór also notes how the family put considerably more effort into keeping the place clean and tidy than on most other farms (though not as punctiliously as in later years, at the time when he was writing his autobiography):

> The living room and the whole farm were swept out daily, though the living room loft was only washed twice or so a year. By then a thick coat of filth had built up there and snow was often brought in to dampen it, then most of the dung would be shovelled out and the place washed down. Tables, shelves and bed frames were washed much oftener and the bedding aired. In my parents' later years on the farm this changed considerably, after the new living room was built (1883), much brighter and roomier than the old one. Then the loft was washed every Saturday evening, and the whole living room from top to bottom in spring.

The food, in Halldór's opinion, was wholesome and of excellent quality and every care was taken in its handling to ensure that it was free from contamination. The boys were not given coffee 'before we were six or older, and then just coloured milk to start off with'. Later, coffee was consumed without stint.

> The dogs were allowed to remain unmolested up in the living room loft except at night, and at mealtimes they would go round from man to man, getting themselves scraps of food. No one then realized the danger of infection that this can lead to, as in the recent outbreak of hydatids.

Halldór mentions that he himself was a rather fussy eater, but the brothers generally had enough to eat, except principally in spring when supplies began to run low. 'But we always had everything we needed when it was available, and we never showed any sign of stunted growth even if good food ran low for a while.'

Halldór describes the games the brothers played and the tasks they were expected to perform in their younger years, and it is clear that they were well content with their lot. It seems to have been a close-knit family, held together in common purpose. As with almost all Icelandic autobiographers of the period, the *kvöldvaka* left a lasting impression on his memory – the 'evening gatherings' when the household came together to work (carding and spinning wool, for instance) and entertained each other by readings from books, singing hymns, practising their lessons and the like. The autobiography provides a wealth of images from everyday life on Icelandic farms. For instance, Halldór tells about how visitors were treated – how the family always went out of its way to make them welcome, how rare it was for complete strangers to turn up at their door. He remembers being shy and self-effacing, how tongue-tied he became in front of people he did not know, how difficult he found it trying to make a favourable impression on them.

Halldór describes his parents with a clear but affectionate eye:

> My parents' marriage was good and loving, and it struck me how thoughtful and attentive my father was to his wife and children, and to the household in general, whether at home or away. This was less evident with my mother, that was just the way she was, but there is no doubt that she loved him dearly. Her mind was not as strong as it might have been and this sometimes made life less happy than it might otherwise have been, along with various other vexations.

The brothers were set to work from an early age, though, as Halldór saw it, without their ever being exploited. He especially enjoyed watching over the sheep so long as the brothers could do it together. But when he was lent to the minister of the church at Fell to do some shepherding on his own he suffered horribly and generally felt uncomfortable anywhere away from the bosom of his family. Even his confirmation classes were a trial for him because of his shyness and he felt he had not done himself justice, though the parish register shows that all the brothers performed well in the short time they were under formal instruction at the minister's hand.

The descriptions of the boys' home life in this chapter and the incident related in its final section are presented through the eyes of Halldór and his elder brother Níels, as recorded in their diaries and letters some years later when they were nearly fully grown. The farm of Tindur where they grew up was considered an excellent sheep holding, with enough land to support the family fairly comfortably. Their income was supplemented by seasonal fishing from the fishing stations on the Steingrímsfjörður fjord, and on occasions the same purpose took father and sons all the way west to Ísafjörður, the largest settlement in their part of the country.

Just as elsewhere in the traditional farming community, working patterns in rural Strandasýsla were very much bound to the seasons. In general, one task followed fast on another with seldom much slack time in between. Very often at times of heavy demand the jobs mounted up and it was necessary to keep working night and day so that years of effort might not go to waste. For this reason there was close co-operation between the local farms on jobs both great and small. People lent each other their labour and materials and banded together in groups to attend to particular tasks and projects. As well as fostering a sense of common purpose and encouraging lively communication between the farms, this sharing of labour created a basis for a degree of specialization within the district: men and women became known for their skill in certain tasks – building walls, teaching or slaughtering, for example – and were called upon in case of need. In addition, whole households took on work for agents from outside, processing wool from farms other than their own.

Working practices on Strandir consisted chiefly of the traditional tasks of the Icelandic rural economy. But we also glimpse distinct signs of changes similar to those that were going on in various other farming communities in Europe at the time, a move away from autarky (self-sufficiency) towards what has been termed 'proto-industry'. Icelandic historians have generally tended to downplay this development in their country. There are, however, descriptions of these kinds of practices from various parts of the country. The writer Þórbergur Þórðarson, for example, mentions households in Reykjavík in the nineteenth century where the people took on work from outside making and mending nets, this work being organized in one of two ways:

> Either the people bought all the materials in the shops and chandleries, wove it into nets, and sold them on to dealers with the edges unweighted, or the dealers themselves provided the materials and paid a fixed tariff for weaving the nets. The dealers then put the nets in their shops for sale to fishermen.
> (Þórðarson 1936–40: 149)

Another instance of this early form of domestic industrialization appears in an article written by the member of parliament Þorkell Bjarnason in the last years of the nineteenth century. He describes a poor farmer of his acquaintance who provided for his family over the winter by taking on wool work for people from outside:

He was a penniless man with many children, but he provided what he needed for himself and his large family by taking wool on credit from traders in autumn and producing knitwear, paying for the wool with the knitwear and buying food with the money left over. He worked this way for himself and his family year after year, without him, his wife, or the children ever being empty-handed.

(Bjarnason 1892: 208)

In fact, a fair amount of this kind of proto-industrial activity went on, entirely separate from the self-sufficiency farming of the rural areas as it is customarily portrayed by Icelandic historians. This kind of nascent specialization is significant for the conditions under which Halldór and Níels lived their lives, both in their parental home and after Níels had set up on his own at the farm of Gjögur, also in Standir. The society in which they grew up was in fact significantly more complex than historians have generally allowed for, and the interplay of its different strands in all probability served as an incentive for people seeking to improve their conditions and encouraged them to keep their eyes open for new solutions to the tasks they had to face.

The economy of Iceland being almost entirely pastoral, settlement was in farms rather than villages. Each farm supported a family, perhaps with other relatives and, depending on the size of the holding and means of the farmer, a number of contracted labourers and domestic servants. These farms were often scattered at long distances and communications between them could be difficult, especially in winter. Villages only start to develop in the late nineteenth century, always on the coast around fishing centres and trading posts. Despite the scattered nature of the settlement, Halldór describes a close-knit community, with a constant coming and going between the farms of people sharing work tasks or simply seeking each other's company. Organized gatherings and formal socialising were rare. The church was the focus for such social activity as existed in the parish; other entertainment was sporadic and occasional. Beyond this there were a number of the societies and associations operating in the district and their meetings were generally well attended, especially by men.

This is the environment in which the brothers grew up. In 1893 their father gave up his tenancy and he and his sons became *lausamenn* in the surrounding districts (wage-earning free labourers resident on other people's farms). Halldór supported himself by teaching and building work, mainly house construction and drystone walls, together with writing and whatever else fell his way. From this he managed to build up a decent living; we can follow how he got on during his time as a jobbing labourer in some detail since, at the end of each year, he compiled lists itemising all his possessions in scrupulous detail, including estimates of their value.

At the start of the new century Halldór married Elín Samúelsdóttir, the daughter of the farmer of Miðdalsgróf in the same district. At the time Halldór was 31 years old and his wife eighteen. Together they had five children. Halldór died in 1912, in the prime of his life, drowned while fishing out from Steingrímsfjörður.

Níels, his elder brother, married Guðrún Bjarnadóttir, the daughter of the farmer of Gjögur a little further north up the coast. They had one child. Níels died in 1934.

The reason it is possible to follow the life courses of Halldór and Níels Jónsson in such detail is because both left behind them enormous amounts of writing in the form of diaries, letters (including those between the two of them) and other material. In this the brothers were by no means unique: the peasantry of Iceland was by this time almost universally literate, and literary endeavour was highly regarded, in part to supply material for reading aloud at the winter evening gatherings. Halldór started his diary in 1888 at the age of seventeen. The diary was not his earliest literary undertaking: for two years prior to this he had been recording various bits of information relevant to the management of the farm. He kept his diary up to the day of his death in 1912.[3] Elsewhere, and alongside this, he set down various pieces documenting his ideas and ruminations, as well as practical material about himself and the running of the farm. Five large volumes of this type have been preserved: three he entitled *Samtiningsbækur* (miscellanies), one *Í tómstundum* ('In idle hours') and finally *Búkolla*.[4] Apart from this original material, we also have in his hand fifteen collections of verse containing poems copied out from both printed and manuscript sources, each of them of up to 400 pages (Lbs. 1870–84). Finally, we have copies of the local newspaper *Gestur* (The Visitor), which he edited and wrote out entirely by hand, as well as, along with his brother Ísleifur, composing the vast majority of the articles. The paper was circulated around about ten farms in the district, with each contributing a small sum to read it.[5] Together these records constitute a massive corpus, particularly when one takes into account that the writing and copying were done under trying conditions in old turf-built farms, often in extreme cold and with a lack of light, by a man who had to labour with his hands every day of the year. All Halldór's literary activities are characterized by great precision and accuracy, as well as being produced in an elegant and aesthetically pleasing hand.

Níels started keeping his diary in 1893 at the age of 23 and the entries span over 40 years, up to 1934.[6] As with Halldór's, Níels's diary appears to be a labour of love, carried out with great care and attention to detail. It is impressive in size and broad in scope, providing a detailed account of his day-to-day working life and those of the people around him. Both these men's writings constitute contemporary sources of the first order, not least in being authentic works from the hands of ordinary young men of the peasant working class.

From the personal effects of Níels and members of his family we have just under 100 letters, falling broadly into two groups. On one hand there are the letters, twenty-two in total, that Níels wrote to his betrothed (and later wife) during the years of their courtship from 1890 to 1895. These letters are highly unusual in both form and content: they are beautifully produced constructions, some of them ornately decorated with drawings in Níels's hand. They are more than simply love letters in which Níels opens up his innermost feelings and desires; they are also letters of encouragement and exhortation, holding up a revealing mirror to contemporary society. They express how the two parties visualized their future and can be seen as representative of the thoughts, hopes and aspirations of young people in general as the nineteenth century drew to its close.

Second, there is correspondence to or about Níels from his brothers and other family members. The greatest number are from Halldór (forty-five), followed by Ísleifur (twenty-one), with only seven from Magnús. Finally there is the heart-rending letter that Níels received in 1914 from Halldór's widow Elín with news of the death from diphtheria of their youngest son.

In the final part of this chapter I shall apply the methods of microhistory to a single incident from the lives of the brothers from Strandir, an incident centring on death, the grief it engendered, and the tactics used to cope with it. Before doing so, I shall need to consider death more generally as a phenomenon in Icelandic society. The particular example, it seems to me, opens up a new perspective on how death was perceived within this society – what it meant to the people involved. The insights that emerge from these personal responses I believe take us much deeper into the realities of people's lives than can be achieved through any amount of statistical data and so illustrate some of the strengths that the microhistorical approach has to offer.

Health, disease and mortality in nineteenth-century Iceland

Mortality rates remained stubbornly high among people of all ages in Icelandic rural society throughout the nineteenth and on into the early twentieth century. At different times, various parts of the country were ravaged by crippling outbreaks of disease. Statistical data show that death was not just pervasive but might appear from any of a wide variety of causes. The country was host to endemic diseases such as typhoid, tuberculosis (consumption), leprosy, tetanus, echinococcosis (hydatid disease) and diphtheria. Epidemics of all these recurred at frequent intervals in different parts of the country. Domestic conditions often exhibited a state of overwhelming squalor. For example, it was common practice to spit on the floor in the living quarters and the saliva then spread infection from man to man.[7] Jón Blöndal, the district medical officer for the Borgarfjörður region, western Iceland, writes as follows in his annual report to the surgeon general for 1901:

> It is as if even now people's dwellings have no right to exist freed from the expectoration. Most people simply spit wherever they happen to be, and even if there are spittoons provided people rarely use them, and the Icelander needs constant admonishment on this matter.
>
> (ÞÍ 1901)[8]

Lighting and ventilation were limited and baths were taken only irregularly. Lice were an unwelcome but persistent guest and scalps covered with sores and disfigured by rampant bacterial growth were a common sight.[9] Dogs and other domestic animals were allowed to roam freely around the houses, licking up left-over food from people's plates. Facilities for waste and sewerage disposal were at best basic, at worst non-existent. This, and much else besides, is taken up by Jón Blöndal in his report for 1902. On the cleanliness and hygiene of Icelandic homes he has this to say:

> For instance, far too little care is taken over the safety and cleanliness of domestic water supplies. Wells are often dug in the worst possible places, e.g. in rotten bogs where there is so much decay in the soil that that water in them is invariably foul. They are often poorly constructed, with no proper protection against rainwater seepage. Sometimes they are situated unhygienically close to the middens from the cattle sheds and other filth. People generally cannot be bothered to keep a special container to raise water with, or if there is one it is not used. Thus I have more than once seen cowmen lowering the water buckets from the cowshed or the farm into the well, covered with filth from the floor of the byre or the kitchen where the dogs sniff about and the men spit without restraint. – Bodily hygiene is woefully deficient, and it seems to me that those who slop anything at all from their bodies once a year reckon they are doing a good job. Heaven alone knows the state of the common people out in the country who not once in their lives once they have attained adulthood wash themselves over from head to foot! [...] In brief, the notion of cleanliness is more or less dormant, though with honourable exceptions and happily many of them, and it will take much time and effort to awaken it, should anyone ever take it upon themselves to improve matters. Domestic dwellings lack light and air. Stoves are a sadly rare sight and even where they exist they are little used, so that people have to huddle together in one or two rooms to keep themselves warm. Because of the lack of heating the dwellings decay rapidly and become insalubrious. They are destroyed by damp within a few years, if they are not dilapidated and leaking already, and then become uninhabitable in winter as a result of the cold.
>
> (ÞÍ 1902)

Similar comments can be found in many of the other district medical officers' reports of the period. The conditions they describe meant that Icelanders had little defence against disease of any kind. On top of this, care of the sick was almost invariably carried out inside the home, generally under extremely trying conditions. As an example we may quote Halldór Jónsson, who recounts in his autobiography an encounter with a mentally disturbed woman while he was tending sheep at the manse at Fell shortly after confirmation: 'I had to be in the cowshed and for a time there was a madwoman running loose in there. At first I was terribly afraid of her.' (Lbs. 1673). Often the only recourse was to isolate such people – 'shut them away', as it was usually expressed. Sigurður Sigurðsson, district medical office for the county of Dalasýsla, described conditions for the mentally ill in his own district in an unpublished report to the surgeon general:

> But as regards *the insane*, there have been and still remain the most intractable problems here: facilities for caring for them are woeful and

there is a total lack of accommodation for such people, especially if the condition is very pronounced. For this reason the mentally ill generally have to be consigned to outhouses and so have to suffer cold in winter, spending most of their time huddled up, with the result that they become bent double and deformed.

(ÞÍ 1907)

Conditions were often no better for patients with contagious diseases, or for those who tended them. Davíð Scheving Thorsteinsson, the district medical officer for the county of Snæfells- and Hnappadalssýsla, takes this up in his report to the surgeon general for 1899:

The residents of a household are reluctant give testimony against their masters and so it is difficult to show unequivocally that the provisions of the law are being followed in all respects. However, one may just imagine the state of filth you can find in hovels like those where there are a pair of lepers living. I measured these shacks and here for interest's sake I record the dimensions of one of them.

Height of walls c. 1¾ ells. 'Living room' 9 ells in length, 4 ells in breadth, 3½ ells from floor (dirt floor) to roof ridge. Roof laths and eaves boarding white with mould and wet with condensation, battens similarly with white patches of rot (this was August). 2 small window openings facing west, c. 8 × 12 inches. Inside this room there are 5 beds: one across the gable end, and 4 along the side walls, with c. 2½ feet = 1¼ ells between the beds. – There is also a fireplace and then a number of small chests. In this shack there were 8 – eight people [...] Both of these lepers are married and have children. They are not on poor relief and are *absolutely* determined not to go into the leper hospital.

(ÞÍ 1899)

Children born into nineteenth-century Icelandic society had an appallingly low expectation of reaching their first birthday. In the early part of the century the mortality rate for infants in their first year stood at around 35 per cent. This figure fell significantly in the second half of the century, to 20 per cent in the years 1881–90, 12 per cent in 1891–1900, and 11 per cent in the first decade of the twentieth century.[10] Davíð Scheving Thorsteinsson identifies some of the general reasons for the high incidence of infant mortality in his annual report to the surgeon general for 1898:

Space in houses is so cramped that there can only be a tiny fraction of the minimum we judge necessary for each individual. On top of this there is no ventilation. When we add to this the *downright squalor* on all sides which *poisons* what little air there is, it hardly comes as a surprise to hear of 23 infants out of 112 dying in their first year, even without there having been any outbreak of disease.

(ÞÍ 1998)

Earlier in the report infant mortality had been recorded as 20.4 per cent for the district for that year, and Davíð also provided figures for exactly when in their first year these children had died.

One reason often cited for the marked drop in infant mortality in the course of the nineteenth century is that as the century progressed breastfeeding became increasingly common. There is almost certainly some truth in this; but it should also be said that, when one examines the unpublished district medical officers' reports preserved in the archives, one finds frequent and repeated complaints about how difficult it is to persuade women in rural areas to breastfeed their infants, and these complaints continue well on into the second decade of the twentieth century.[11]

In his report for 1907, Guðmundur Scheving Bjarnason, district medical officer for Strandasýsla (whom we shall meet again at the birth of Halldór's children and as one of the protagonists in the events recounted in the final section of this chapter), writes as follows:

> *The treatment of infants* in this area, as in most other parts of the country, *leaves an enormous amount to be desired*. To be sure, people here nowadays generally take more care about keeping their babies clean than they used to, and they are more suitably clothed now, but there is still a long way to go. The problem really arises when we come to the nutrition of children. *With only a very few exceptions, all babies around here are brought up on the bottle.* The midwives have told me that it has become more or less impossible to get mothers to have their children on the breast. The mothers feel themselves tied too restrictively to the child and so unable to attend to the most essential jobs around the farm. The acute shortage of working women has a large part in this and means that farmers' wives have hardly a moment to spare from their most urgent domestic duties, and this is greatly to be lamented. Since, as things stand, children are generally nourished not on breast milk but on cows' milk mixed with water, and not always properly prepared, it is hardly surprising that *many of them are constantly subject to digestive complaints*, which are indeed *the commonest cause of death among children here*, followed by – at a considerable remove – *colds* and other chest ailments.
>
> (ÞÍ 1907)

Similar remarks – that the resistance to breastfeeding lay in a lack of appreciation of its importance among midwives, or at least their failure to impress this importance on their charges, along with the limited time available to mothers to attend to their children – occur repeatedly in the records of the Icelandic district medical officers.[12]

Sigurður Sigurðsson goes into even greater detail on the subject of child rearing and nutrition in his report to the surgeon general for 1907:

> It is only a very few infants that are reared entirely on the breast. In 1905 I obtained a document on this subject from a midwife, in which it appeared

that of 72 children born in the period November 1904 to November 1905, 9 were entirely breastfed, 31 on breast and bottle, 28 on the bottle alone, with 4 cases unknown. We can safely assume that the proportions have since changed little if at all. Children who are on the bottle are given cow's milk and water; the vast majority boil both beforehand, but there are times when this precaution is overlooked, and so it is a wonder that fatalities are not more frequent. Many fail to take sufficient care of the bottle and teat; some believe this a waste of time, others just turn a deaf ear to admonitions. In many homes I have seen bottle teats carved out of wood with a hole drilled through; these are seen as convenient in that they last a long time. But they are rarely boiled in water, maybe simply washed from time to time [...] Many lay great store by getting children to eat as much as possible of various grown-up foods, often before the child is ½ a year old. Digestive complaints in young children are common here and often contribute to their deaths when there is some other sickness to complicate matters.

(ÞÍ 1907)

Judging from these and similar accounts, it is easy to see why the chances of survival among young infants were as low as they were. What makes the passage above particularly interesting is its date, well into the first decade of the twentieth century. The situation was in all probability considerably better in urban areas, where cow's milk was not so readily available to the poor and so nursing mothers were often compelled to breastfeed their infants.

The mortality figures for children between the ages of one and four present a depressing picture. For instance, in the decade 1856–65, 4.5 per cent of children in this age group died each year. For 1876–85, the figure was 3.8 per cent.[13] Thus, though infant mortality (in this age range) was falling, the figures were still high by European standards. Throughout this period, and in fact well on into the twentieth century, the health system remained rudimentary and unstable. Since the middle of the eighteenth century, when the first qualified physician started operating in Iceland, the number of district medical officers (local doctors) had been increasing slowly and access to them might often be the difference between life and death. In most cases, though, people stood helpless before epidemics and other calamities, with no recourse but to put their faith in God or simple luck, as will be exemplified below.[14]

Epidemics raged unchecked at frequent intervals, often with catastrophic loss of life. For example, in 1894 Halldór Jónsson notes in his diary quite startling death rates (for such an unpopulated region) as a result of an influenza epidemic that had swept through the community: at least fifteen fatalities (and quite possibly more) from his immediate environment between April and the end of May, with many more incapacitated. During the same period, two boats went down at sea with the loss of twelve more lives.

Accidents, especially at sea, were another ever-present threat, as Halldór was later to find to his own cost. The small open rowing boats that fished the coastal waters of Iceland were generally manned by local farmers and young farm labourers (often the sons of local farmers), and when they went down it often left a great scar in the neighbouring communities with entire families having to face an uncertain future. The sea was only the most obvious of the dangers facing Icelanders in the normal course of their lives: all travel was fraught with peril, especially in winter or when it involved fording fast-flowing and unpredictable rivers. Many died when caught out by bad weather crossing the mountains from one district to another. Death by misadventure and death by exposure were abiding realities in the lives of all rural Icelanders.

At each man's door

The ubiquity of death in nineteenth-century society presumably had a profound influence on the character of those that survived – and in particular, it seems reasonable to suppose, on children. In their homes children frequently witnessed their family and friends passing from this life, often, it would seem, completely arbitrarily. They learned from an early age that disaster could strike at any time and, when it did, there was little else to do but to steel themselves and get on with their lives. We encounter this kind of reaction in countless later nineteenth-century autobiographies (Magnússon 1993: 90–114). For instance, in many of them accounts of diphtheria appear as a kind of recurrent motif. In one of his miscellanies Halldór Jónsson wrote:

> When I was in my first year I caught diphtheria, which most of our brothers died of, and was so far gone that María, who was with me at the time, believed me dead, for to all appearances I had stopped breathing. In a kind of fit of outrage, my father sucked hard on my nose and mouth, and with that the thing that had stuck in my windpipe became dislodged, and my breathing started to return and I gradually began to recover. But I was sickly for a long time afterwards and remained pale-complexioned for the rest of my days.
>
> (Lbs. 1673)

The statistics, to be sure, give us a certain picture of the connections between life and death in nineteenth-century Iceland. This picture, however, remains just an outline sketch until we fill in the details of how ordinary people perceived and came to terms with death and grief in their own lives. And the ideal place to conduct such an enquiry is in the personal diaries that so many Icelanders of the time used to keep records of their thoughts and activities.

One thing that strikes us as curious, initially at least, as we read Halldór's diary is the way in which he presents the deaths of close friends and relations. Over and over again he records such events simply as if in passing, seemingly in no way different to the manner he uses when describing everyday events like the weather or fishing catches.

We need here to turn back and consider exactly what diaries are and how they are put together. For reasons of economy, morality and even personal emotion, diary writers always have to set a limit to the events they record and be selective in what they talk about and what they reject – and it is precisely the last of these that seems to lie at the heart of Halldór's reticence in presenting death. Halldór quite obviously 'designed' his diary along certain lines, lines that precluded detailed discussion of the impact of individual deaths on his own personal existence. He chooses to describe events as they appear before his eyes, without bringing himself or his feelings into the account. This kind of diarist is well known in western countries at this period and historians of the emotions have concluded that it is in many cases a natural response at times of grief and mourning not to discuss the death of close friends and relatives in people's diaries, since the memory can simply be too painful (Rosenblatt 1983: 99–121). Instead, they attempt to cope with their grief through silence.

But in Halldór's case things are not quite so simple. When we look more closely at his diary entries various interesting features appear that shed some light on his attitude to death and grief, despite his self-imposed limitations on expressing them. Much as it may seem that Halldór's diary contains nothing of his opinions and attitudes, it would be quite wrong to maintain that it is some kind of objective 'logbook' of his life, stripped of all emotional response.

As mentioned, Halldór dutifully noted in his diary every death that occurred around him without attaching any personal emotional response to them. Instead, the accounts are 'neutral', apparently simple recordings of everyday events. Níels is if anything even less taken up with other people's deaths; at least, initially anyway, we hear less of them in his diary. When, later in life, he starts to record con-scientiously the names of those who have died he does so with very much the same lack of emotional input as his brother. It should be noted here, perhaps, that Gjögur, where Níels lived, was a sparsely populated district, which may in part explain why accounts of people's deaths feature less prominently in his diaries. As an example of how Níels goes about describing sudden death, we can quote from a letter he wrote to his fiancée when he was working at the fishing camp at Bolungarvík, concerning two men he had known at the camp:

> Four days after Þórarinn Benidiktsson's bones were found, as I mentioned in my previous letter, the men from Garðstaður fished up Benedikt Gapríel. His head and fingers were missing. There were two pairs of gloves on his chest with his name in them, which was how he was identified, and keys in his jacket pocket. Þórarinn was identified by other features. They were both put into the same coffin and interred by the dean on Saturday, 28 April. On Friday, and Saturday, he held services over more bodies that had been brought into the church.[15]

If Níels seems to show a marked detachment in his recording of people's deaths, then Halldór's indifference, as manifested in his diaries, at times seems absolute. In most cases he simply notes the death but gives few, if any, details of its cir-cumstances. Sometimes he goes a little further, i.e. beyond simply naming the disease responsible, particularly in the case of someone who was close to him.

On 2 June 1892 he announces the death of a neighbour in the following words: 'Recently deceased is the Rev. Guðmundur Gísli of Kleifar, who has long been insane' (Lbs. 1858).

Just occasionally over the long period of Halldór's diary we find more circumstantial accounts of individual deaths in the area:

> A tragic accident occurred at Kirkjuból on Monday, 27th *inst.* The 2 eldest children of Grímur and Sigríður, Benidikt and Guðmundur, drowned in the gully that runs round the hay meadow between the farmhouse and the outbuildings. Grímur was in the outhouses and they had been leaving him and going back to the farm. They are still unfound, nor any trace of them except for one of their caps in the gully, and no one knows for sure how it happened, but there is ice in the gully and the bodies are presumably under the ice. The gully has been thoroughly searched.
>
> (Lbs. 1859: 29 March 1893)

In the kind of language used this is the first time that Halldór shows anything approaching emotion over the death of his neighbours. But his composure seems to have reasserted itself fairly quickly: 'The Kirkjuból boys were found further down the gully the day after they drowned. The men who went north on the Smáhamrar ship got 12 barrels of liver.' (Lbs. 1859: 1 April 1893).

In a letter to his brother Níels, Halldór describes the death of the boys from Kirkjuból in rather more detail, and with an interesting difference in emphasis:

> On Monday, 27th *inst.* there was a tragic accident at Kirkjuból, in which the 2 eldest children of Grímur and Sigríður, Benidikt and Guðmundur, drowned in the gully that runs round the hay meadow there outside the farm. Their father was in the outbuildings and they had gone to him, or one of them had come to him in the buildings and was wet, complained he had cold feet and his father asked him how he had got across the gully. The boy said he had waded over. So Grímur told him to take the snow bridge across the gully but paid no heed to how he would go about getting over it. This was just recently in the thaw and the gully was extremely full. When Grímur had finished in the outbuildings he went home and the boys had not returned and nobody knew anything about them. So they started to search and one of their caps was found in the gully. Both the bodies were found the next day towards the bottom of the gully. There are many who blame Grímur for not having tried to break the ice at once and get men in when it was clear they had gone into the gully. Quite possibly, if they had been reached within two or so hours, it might have been possible to revive them. No accident like this has happened around here in living memory. The boys were, I recall, in their 5th and 6th years.
>
> (Lbs. uncatalogued: HJ to NJ, 31 March 1893)

What stands out about this later account as compared to the diary entry is that here Halldór takes a particular stance towards the event that occurred. What is more, it is a 'pragmatic' stance, aimed at the proper practical conduct in the situation that arose, rather than in any way an emotional one. Any censure of the part played by the father is directed not at his having sent the boys home alone but at how he set about the rescue. Halldór's attention is taken up by the operation itself and how it failed; anything else that might raise questions about the events he passes over in silence: this would have demanded an evaluation of people and events that would of necessity have had to be founded on emotional grounds.

These two accounts of this incident raise certain questions about Halldór's mode of expression in his diary and letters. The differences are in reality very small. The simple fact that a few days had elapsed between the diary entry and the letter may mean that Halldór had had time and space to think about things, as well as the chance to hear what people had to say about them, and in this lies perhaps the main difference between them – the added distance the letter writer had from the events he relates. The diary is dealing with things that have happened on the day they are recorded; in the letter, the events are becoming history.

It may be worth speculating that men like Halldór might perhaps be hesitant about using their diaries as a repository for their deepest feelings on matters that touch their psyche – in part because the diary has the function of being, as it were, their constant companion through life. Halldór may have taken the view that he did not want to be constantly reminded of events of this type when he looked something up in his diary – something that he did often. Letters are not personal in the same way; they are for other people and so do not become a part of a person's permanent self-image in the way that diaries do. Their composition is subject to various rules of expression, and once they have been sent the writer will usually never see them again. Thus we might suppose that they might allow for a greater expression of emotion in relating events such as those described above. In Halldór's case, however, the fact remains that, despite everything, the emotion displayed in both sources is very similar: it is held firmly in check.

Halldór's recording of deaths gives other cause for speculation. There are for instance, striking similarities between the way he describes the deaths of people and of animals. As one example of many, his diary entry for 12 November 1900 reads as follows: 'A woman died of exposure after setting out from Ólafsdalur last Thursday. Kristín Hannesdóttir lived at Svínadalssel. A lot of sheep that Torfi of Ólafsdalur had at Traðardalur in Saurbær were buried in snowdrifts and 1 horse'. Halldór's view of reality was deeply grounded in nature and based on powerful connections between people, animals and the landscape. In his writings these three elements appear almost inextricably linked: he devotes appreciably more time and space to men and animals, but when the landscape is mentioned it is always as something significant, with decisive power over people's lives. The reason, of course, was that all life was so intimately bound up with the vagaries of nature and the land that these things, in all his contact with them, demanded the kind of respect and consideration that we normally, at our best, reserve for living beings. This attitude to nature clearly influences everything in how Halldór thinks about things and expresses himself about them. It is revealed, for example, in diary entries where he describes the loss of horses or livestock. In recording such events, the distinction between animal and human deaths almost disappears. Two examples from his diary for May 1890 illustrate the point. The former records events for the 17 May: 'I heard today that a boy from Fell had drowned in the river Fellsá on the 14th *inst*. He was called Magnús Björnsson and was aged about 9'. The second comes four days later: 'My Sóley ['Buttercup', one of his ewes] today bore a white ram but he was still-born under her'. Halldór's method in presenting these two events is strikingly similar: the links between man and nature were simply too strong for it to be possible to drive hard distinctions between them. At times it seems he directs more thought, care and consideration to the sheep than the human: 'Botna cannot bear her lamb; these 3 female lambs that have been born are on the living-room floor' (Lbs. 1858: 18 May 1892).

Halldór's apparent detachment extends even to the birth of his own children. As his children come into the world one after another, the event is noted along the following lines: 'This morning Ella was unwell. I went to Hrófá to fetch Margrét the midwife. Got horses at Heiðarbær. It is now well into the night and the baby is still not born. I am going to go and fetch Dr Scheving' (Lbs. 1675: 21 May 1902). His first child was in the process of being born, something that must have been a major landmark in his life. But, to judge from the diary, this event had no precursor, nothing leading up to it, and it is presented in the same matter-of-fact tone that Halldór used for the most mundane episodes in his life. He continues the following day: 'This morning at 9½ of the clock Ella had the baby. It is a boy. I went out there with Scheving today. His call here cost 5 kr, including a glass of cough drops I got from him'. We hear no more of mother or child before 28 May: 'Ella has been in a bad way today, from pains, probably from constipation. It is now 1 o'clock and everyone is asleep except me. I am sitting over Ella. But will soon go to bed'. His accounts of the births of all his other children over the next years are similar: when Elín goes into labour he notes that the midwife has been sought, the child has been born, and the midwife paid a certain fee. Thereafter we hear almost nothing of these children until they reach the age where they can put their hands to work and he starts to teach them to read, write and do sums.

We can compare the diary entry with a letter to his brother Níels in the same year in which Halldór describes the birth of his first-born thus:

> The animals have turned out well for me this spring, except that the fox had one lamb that I had, but then there were 3 pairs of twins. I now have 6 ewes with lambs and one infertile, and then I am getting 4 ewes from brother Ísleifur. I also have 9 yearlings, with 4 born of them and suckling well from them. I have also received a heifer from Samúel. Then, last but not least, I want to tell you that I became the father of a little boy on 22 May. The birth was very difficult because he was big, born 16 marks [*c*. 3.5 kilos].

I have not had him baptized yet. He has been pretty healthy, more or less, and Ella has been back to full health long since.

(Lbs. uncatalogued: HJ to NJ, 13 June 1902)

Here Halldór permits himself a slightly greater expression of emotion than in his diary, though still curbed within strict limits. His announcements of the births of his other children over the next years are in similar vein: 'I must not forget to mention that on Easter morning I acquired a little workman. I still cannot tell you what he is called because the minister has not yet come to see him, but there is every likelihood that this is another Jón to add to the many there are already' (Lbs. uncatalogued: HJ to NJ, 4 May 1905).

We may again note, both in the text and in Halldór's thinking, a clear correspondence between the birth of his lambs and that of his children – though it would be wrong, I think, to see them as being entirely parallel. The emotions that stirred within Halldór's breast with regard to men and beasts were not identical, though there were palpable connections between them. It all sprang from one and the same perception: life and death were so inextricably linked within human experience that, whether things went well or badly, there was good reason to avoid indulgence in any kind of emotionalism. In the parallelism between men and beasts we can see, in part at least, an explanation for Halldór's apparent detachment in the face of death as we find it in the diaries. The slaughtering of animals was part of the ordinary working round of every person in the society in which Halldór lived and one of the most significant jobs of the year on many farms. At the slaughtering the ground lay covered with the bodies of dumb animals with whom many of those present had formed bonds of trust, even of affection. In his autobiography Halldór recounts his very earliest memory:

> The first time I remember having had my attention taken by what was going on was when a black-flecked cow that my parents owned was led up the gap between the cattle byre and the house and shot on the flat patch of land above the farm. I remember well how extraordinary it seemed to me. According to what I have been told I would then have been in my third year and was carried on up there on the arm when the cow was slaughtered.
>
> (Lbs. 1673)

The slaughter of animals was generally accepted like any other law of nature and thus without comment or complaint. The same applied to the deaths of family and friends.

Halldór's accounts of gruesome and unsettling incidents are invariably expressed in measured and dispassionate language, as in this, from a letter to his brother:

> We have recently heard that Hildur, the wife of Eggert Magnússon who used to live at Brekka, was not able to deliver her baby. First, the midwife and Magnús Guðlaugsson were fetched in but they could do nothing. So

they called in Dr Sigurður of Hrappsstaðir and he dismembered the child limb from limb. The woman is now well on her way to recovery.

(Lbs. uncatalogued: HJ to NJ, 10 January 1903)

Such traumas were to be taken with equanimity: the only thing that mattered, the only thing that paid, was to face up to whatever life threw at one with single-mindedness and imperturbability. We can view the flat, factual tone that Halldór (and others in his position) adopts as an emotional defence mechanism that he used as a shield against the horrors that were a repeated and inevitable part of daily life. There seems every reason to believe that Halldór lived in a state of constant grief, or at least the constant prospect of grief: he needed to keep himself always ready for the loss of people and animals that were dear to him. Grief was a part of his daily pattern of interaction with everything that lived and breathed. What is unusual about Halldór's behaviour, when viewed against received theories of grief, is that his reactions to and preparations for grief were focused not on a single specific individual or event, but rather on *all* life around him. Seen in this light, Halldór's refusal to allow himself emotional reaction becomes comprehensible.

The thin line between life and death

Doctors in nineteenth- and early twentieth-century Iceland were few and far between, often serving large areas with poor communications. The dearth of medical provision could often have harrowing consequences. The diaries we have been looking at present a graphic image of people's everyday lives and how they faced up to sickness, death and grief. In the story related in the remainder of this chapter we encounter a response to life and death among ordinary people that may strike us as unexpected given the time, place and social status of the people involved, suggesting attitudes that can hardly be captured through the application of statistical demography alone.

The victim in these events was a close friend of Halldór's, Grímur Ormsson of Gestsstaðir. Late in 1902 he fell seriously ill and took to his bed. The relevant entries in Halldór's diary begin as follows:[16]

> 28 December 1902: Grímur contracted cholera and started to have cramps on the evening of Christmas Eve, so they sent for Dr Scheving and he came over, then went home and sent some medicine. By this time he was considerably improved. It is said that Grímur has now slept for more than a day, so deeply that it has been impossible to wake him, except once, just for a moment, and then he went back to sleep. There is a danger that something is not right. Samúel went over there.

This Scheving, full name Guðmundur Scheving Bjarnason, was the local doctor and district medical officer for Strandasýsla; we have meet him before, both reporting on the state of healthcare in the country and at the birth of Halldór's first-born son. The Samúel who 'went over there' was Halldór's father-in-law, Samúel Alfreðsson. Halldór continues in his diary the next day:

> 29 December 1902: Grímur of Gestsstaðir died late last night (10½ by the clock). When Samúel got up there he was awake and semi-conscious but he slipped away further and further until he died. My namesake has started making a coffin for him up there, Samúel with him.
>
> 5 January 1903: Today the late Grímur of Gestsstaðir was moved to the church. The coffin bearers are Samúel, Finnbogi, Grímur of Kirkjuból, Halldór of Heiðarbær, brother Ísleifur and myself. We drew the body on a sledge behind a horse.
>
> 6 January 1903: I went down to Tangi with Ella [his wife] and Tryggvi for saltfish. This evening Benedikt from Smáhamrar and Sigurgeir came round. They had a petition from several men to Jón of Tunga to get a doctor (Oddur of Reykhólar) to examine the body of the deceased Grímur of Gestsstaðir. It seems that many people are afraid that the medicines from Scheving hastened his death. I took this petition over to Tunga in the evening. Jón is going to send it south [to Reykjavík]. This is however hardly his responsibility, it ought much rather to be brought before the county sheriff.

Jón of Tunga was the local government officer (*hreppstjóri*) for the district and Oddur Jónsson was the medical officer for the Reykhólar district, which bounded Strandir to the south.[17] He soon found himself embroiled in the case:

> 10 January 1903: Dr Oddur could not be got to come north, claiming that he could only go on the orders of a sheriff. He also wants to have another doctor with him. Benedikt and Guðmundur of Kollafjarðarnes went straight away today to the sheriff.
>
> 13 January 1903: Dr Oddur was sent for yesterday.

Matters were finally brought to a conclusion:

> 15 January 1903: I worked in the outbuildings because Samúel went over to Tunga. There Dr Oddur performed a post mortem on the late Grímur. Witnesses were Jón of Tunga and Halldór from Heiðarbær. Scheving was there and present at the time. No others. The sheriff was there. Oddur expressed no opinion on what had caused Grímur's death. Oddur began the post mortem by sawing the head apart and examining it. Then he opened the chest and finally the abdominal cavity. This is presumably the first post mortem that has ever been conducted here in Strandasýsla.

The operation was, naturally enough, carried out in the living room at Tunga! What is notable here is that the local farmers seem to have felt no qualms about having, and expressing, their opinions on the performance of the district medical officer in the conduct of his duties, and in going to the lengths they did in pursuing their case. At the end of the year 1903 Halldór refers back to the contretemps with Dr Scheving:

> There has been considerable legal wrangling as a result of the post mortem carried out on Grímur of Gestsstaðir and other matters. Enormous dissatisfaction with the district medical officer, and a complaint has been sent to the authorities. There has been nothing but indictments and litigation over this.

The official records of the sheriff of Strandasýsla report that Dr Scheving came under concerted attack from local residents with the aim of having him removed from his post. The local government officer Jón Jónsson and a farmer called Guðmar G. Bárðarson, acting on behalf of a large group of farmers of the Kirkjuból district, entered a plaint against the medical officer for persistent dereliction of duty. The litigation dragged on for some years, with many people being summoned before the court to make depositions. The case was finally settled towards the end of 1905 with the district medical officer cleared of all charges and all comments as to his unfitness for office declared null and void.[18]

The dispassionate tone in which he relates the entire incident is all the more remarkable when we consider that Grímur of Gestsstaðir was very much one of Halldór's nearest and dearest.[19] Despite this, Halldór seems never to have seen reason to adopt a heightened style or display his feelings in any other way. His response, and that of his neighbours, is channelled into institutional protest. As in the case of the drowning of the Kirkjuból boys, it is a 'practical' response, acted out on a public and external level and expressed in terms appropriate to that level. This, it seems, gave those affected some kind of outlet for their grief, an outlet they were denied internally through their self-imposed avoidance of explicit expression of personal emotion. Halldór subsequently describes Grímur's second funeral, which took place on 22 January:

> Today the late Grímur of Gestsstaðir was laid to rest. The funeral was rather well attended as these things go. (The pall-bearers were Samúel, myself, brother Ísleifur, Finnbogi and Halldór.) We went out to Gestsstaðir when we came away from the church, got home at 2 o'clock. All the pall-bearers gave their time for free (I am not sure about Halldór).

Halldór goes into these events in a little more detail in a letter to Níels. He describes the onset of Grímur's illness and how Scheving was summoned:

> and he naturally responded immediately and came up there. He gave the late Grímur, it is said, 3 shots of opium, after which he felt no suffering. Then after he got home Scheving sent 3 doses that Grímur was supposed to take and this he did. These doses had the effect that he fell asleep and lay in a kind of stupor for most of the time until he died. He came to on the Saturday morning and seemed fairly cheerful and said, 'Sleep is all the

better now! I think I should now be sleeping myself to death'. Then he fell asleep for good that evening, for a whole day until he died.

(Lbs. uncatalogued: HJ to NJ, 10 January 1903)

A little later Halldór adds: 'This swift and distressing death day of Grímur's has sent a chill through many people and some are even willing to hold our doctor to account on the grounds that the medicine he provided was rather too powerful'. Halldór then indicates that people are intending finally to put their foot down so far as Scheving is concerned. The correspondence is in many ways similar to what he expresses in the diary entries, though here perhaps somewhat more forcefully stated and taking a more determined stance on the affair. In both, however, the narrative remains remarkably restrained.

Halldór said no more about the matter until the end of 1909. In his round-up for that year he noted:

This year death has finally relieved us of our pathetic, inept little doctor, who we have for many years longed would somehow disappear, namely G.B. Scheving. He shuffled off finally after a long and difficult illness on 24 January. His body could not lie in 'Strandir' soil and so was moved south to Reykjavík.

(Lbs. 1677: 31 December 1909)

Life went on, and with the loss of its breadwinner the fate of the Gestsstaðir family had to be decided: 'Samúel went with Bjargey of Gestsstaðir [Grímur's widow] up to Ljúfustaðir. She is sending her youngest child, Daði, there to be fostered'.[20] It is not long before we hear more of Bjargey's circumstances: in his diary for 16 May 1903 Halldór writes: 'A child was born to Bjargey of Gestsstaðir today at 2 o'clock. It is a boy'. This posthumous son of Grímur's was baptized in his father's name. A few years later, on 18 October 1906, Halldór records the following in his diary: 'A child died at Gestsstaðir the night before last, Daði, aged 4'. This is Daði Guðmundur Grímsson, the boy who was put out to foster on the death of his father.

Grímur's death had a profound and lasting effect on all aspects of his surviving family's external circumstances. These circumstances become all the more heart-rending when viewed against what had preceded them.[21] Early in 1902, i.e. a year before Grímur's death, Halldór records the following in his diary for 12 January: 'Today a child died at Gestsstaðir, Guðmundur Daði, the son of Sigurður V. Magnússon. Had been ill a long time'. The next day we read: 'A child died at Gestsstaðir last night, Daði, youngest child of Grímur and Bjargey, after a short illness'. Halldór does not mention these events again until four days later, on 17 January: 'Samúel and Grímur took the children's bodies to the church'. On 20 January we read:

I went with Grímur of Gestsstaðir, Samúel and Halldór of Heiðarbær over to Tunga, where they were supposed to be having the funerals of the

Gestsstaðir children. We dug the grave, solid ice down to near on an ell. We waited for the minister until evening but in vain. By then it was so late and the weather so bad that we stayed at Tunga over night.

The next day Halldór continues: 'We went home today without managing to see the minister. Since I got home I have done nothing of any note'. A few days later, on 25 January, he had further dealings with the Gestsstaðir household: 'I borrowed the *A-Division Parliamentary Gazette* at Gestsstaðir and read from it this evening'. Halldór read the *Parliamentary Gazette* a lot over the next days and had to make a quick trip to the trading post. Then, on 27 January, he writes: 'I was expecting them to have the funeral today, which is why I was so quick about the journey'. Nothing happened until the first week of February. Then, on 6 February:

> Samúel and I went down to Heiðarbær early this morning and my namesake went with us, and the children were finally buried. We got back at 3 ½ o'clock. Since I got home I have spent most of the time doing woodwork. Grímur paid me the pall-bearers' fee, 6.00 krónur.

The factual, apparently dispassionate nature of Halldór's diary comes out strikingly in his note about the financial transaction with one of the mourning fathers, viz. that at the end of the proceedings his close friend Grímur of Gestsstaðir has settled his part of the funeral expenses.

Grímur and Bjargey were married in 1886. Their first child was born the same year. This child died in 1887, aged one. Altogether they had twelve children, five of whom died young: in addition to those already mentioned, they lost a four-month-old child in 1891 and another in 1895 at two months.[22] In the same years at the start of the twentieth century that saw the deaths of Grímur and the two Daðis, two of Grímur's sisters also died. Þuríður, the mother of Halldór's wife Elín, died in 1901, aged 42, having produced eleven children. Four of these children were to die before reaching adulthood, including two within a few years of their mother.[23] Júlíana, Grímur's youngest sister, died in 1904, aged 43. She had produced seven children, five of whom died young, including a three-year-old son who died a few months before his mother. Two of her other children died in 1909.[24]

Of the history of Bjargey after this litany of tribulation not much is known except that she stayed on for a while at Gestsstaðir, presumably with the help and support of her oldest son, who was fourteen when his father died. According to the census records, Bjargey held the lease of Gestsstaðir until 1906, by which time, now aged 37, she had remarried. Her new husband, Kristmundur Jónsson, had been a workman on the farm and was thirteen years her junior. Together they had two daughters while they were still living in the parish of Tröllatunga, one of whom died young (Guðmundsson 1990: 50). In 1906 they moved away and settled in Gufudalssveit in Barðastrandarsýsla on the west side of the Westfjord peninsula. Bjargey Símonardóttir died in 1951, 86 years of age.[25]

The story of the family of Gestsstaðir, their eventual fates and their dealings, and those of their neighbours, with the district medical officer, can be taken as illustrative of the conditions that people in areas like the parishes of Strandir had to put up with and get used to. In the light of all that happened, we can hear the note of bitter sarcasm in Halldór's comment on the local doctor in a letter to his brother Níels in 1897: 'Everyone in good health, and to quote Dr Scheving, there is no point having a doctor here: everyone around here is as strong as an ox, nobody gets ill!!!' (Lbs. uncatalogued: HJ to NJ, 6 December 1897).

Notes

1 The Jónsson brothers played a central part in my research for a few years in the 1990s and the discussion here is based on this earlier work: see particularly the two book-length studies (Magnússon 1997, 1998). The name of the Icelandic printed sources will be given in English in brackets in the bibliography in the back of the book.

2 Lbs. 1673 4to: Halldór Jónsson: Í tómstundum ['In idle hours': notebook of Halldór Jónsson]. The abbreviation Lbs. denotes the the Landsbókasafn Íslands manuscript archive of the National and University Library of Iceland. All the manuscripts used in this chapter from the manuscript archive will be cited in the text as Lbs. with its appropriate serial number and the date when it was written (when possible). A full citation will be given at the first mention.

3 Halldór's diaries, preserved in the manuscript collection of the National and University Library of Iceland, comprise altogether 3,050 pages: Lbs. 1857–66 8vo (2,304 pages) and Lbs. 1675–78 4to (746 pages).

4 Lbs. 1867–69 8vo, Halldór Jónsson: Samtíningsbækur I, II and IV [Miscellanies I, II and IV]; Lbs. 1673 4to: Halldór Jónsson: Í tómstundum [Notebook: 'In idle hours']; Lbs. 1674 4to: Halldór Jónsson: Búkolla [Notebook. The name comes from a magical cow in a well-known folktale]. [All these manuscripts will be cited in the text as Lbs. with their appropriate serial number]. We know of two more volumes compiled by Halldór, now in the possession of his descendants, that he named *Rusl og moð* [Rubbish and scraps] and *Uppdrættir 1890–1895* [Drafts 1890–95].

5 Lbs. 1672 4to: Sveitarblaðið Gestur [handwritten local newspaper, 'The Visitor']. The paper appeared for two years, 1907–8, 14 sheets in the former year, 23 in the latter. To my knowledge, one of Halldór's descendants also possesses some copies of another local paper, Dalbúinn [the Dalesman], that the brothers Halldór and Níels wrote while they were still living with their parents in 1891–93. Initially they edited the paper together; then, after the first year, Halldór took over on his own. The paper was not distributed widely, according to what Halldór says in his autobiography.

6 Lbs. 2503–50 4to: Dagbækur Níelsar Jónssonar [Diaries of Níels Jónsson].

7 This habit is denounced, for instance, in an unattributed article ('Hættulegir ósiðir' 1897: 147). For an overview of various factors relevant to the external conditions of people's lives in nineteenth-century rural society, see (Magnússon 1993: 74–89). See also (Magnússon 1995: 295–323).

8 *Þjóðskjalasafn Íslands*, Skjalasafn landlæknis: Ársskýrslur lækna DI & II, 1901: Reykjavík-Siglufjarðar: Jón Blöndal: Borgarfjarðarhérað, 1901 [National Archives of Iceland, Archive of the surgeon general of Iceland: Annual doctors' reports DI & II, 1901: Reykjavík-Siglufjörður: Jón Blöndal: Borgarfjörður district, 1901]. All of the manuscripts used in this chapter from the National Archives come from the archive of the surgeon general and will be cited in the text as ÞÍ with the year of creation. The name of the author will appear in the main text.

9 The perennial problem of lice infestation was treated in an excellent article by the doctor Mattíasson (Mattíasson 1906: 161–75).

10 (Magnússon 2010: 99–111; Jónsson and Magnússon (eds) 1997: 264–65).

11 Comments on the increase in breastfeeding, and complaints that it was not proceeding fast enough, appear recurrently in the district medical officers' annual reports between 1880 and 1920: see *Þjóðskjalasafn Íslands*, Skjalasafn landlæknis 1760–1946 [National Archives of Iceland, Archive of the surgeon-general of Iceland 1760–1946].

12 In her doctoral thesis Ólöf Garðarsdóttir (Garðarsdóttir 2002) argues that the fall in infant mortality between 1870 and the early years of the twentieth century can be largely put down to the better education of Icelandic midwives. This seems rather at odds with the picture that emerges from the medical officers' reports, and it seems altogether more likely that the gradual increase in breastfeeding, with the resultant marked decline in infant mortality, is best explained by general changes in social, cultural and economic conditions.

13 (Jónsson and Magnússon (eds) 1997: 264–65). Infant mortality and mortality rates in Iceland in general are discussed in Magnússon's book *Education, love and grief* (Magnússon 1997: 90–92).

14 By far the best general survey of the field is the study by Jón Ólafur Ísberg, called in English, *Life and medicine: a health history of Iceland*. (Ísberg 2005).

15 Lbs. *óskráð* [uncatalogued letter]: Níels Jónsson to Guðrún Bjarnadóttir, inscribed 'pro tempore Bolungarvík, Sunday 6 May 1894'. The brothers were in the habit of inscribing their letters 'pro tempore', or just 'pt', to indicate 'temporarily resident'. At the same time as these drownings, Níels also records, both in his letters to Guðrún and in his diaries, that there was a serious outbreak of disease at Bolungarvík that claimed many lives – which explains the demands on the dean and church for conducting funerals. All of the letters are uncatalogued and here after they will be cited as *Lbs.* uncatalogued, the initials of the one who wrote the letter and the recipient and then the date it was written.

16 The events from Halldór Jónsson's diary (Lbs. 1675) are presented in the order in which he set them down.

17 According to the records of the sheriff's office of Strandasýsla, an application was made to the sheriff at the start of 1903 for another doctor to examine Grímur's body. The official records include brief details of the case and how it was pursued which tally in all important respects with Halldór's account in his diary. See *Þjóðskjalasafn Íslands*: Skjalasafn sýslu-og sveitastjórna [Archives of county and local district administrations]: Strandasýsla III, 23: Bréfabækur [Correspondence], 1899–1908.

18 *Þjóðskjalasafn Íslands*: Skjalasafn sýslu-og sveitastjórna: Strandasýsla V, 7: Dóma-og þingabók [Court records], 1892–1906.

19 Grímur was, for example, the uncle of Halldór's wife Elín and acted as Halldór's 'sponsor' (witness) at their wedding. He took over the lease at Tindur when the brothers' father Jón Jónsson gave up the tenancy and was always ready to welcome them back there in times of need. See *Þjóðskjalasafn Íslands*: Strandasýsla: Prestsþjónustubækur Tröllatungu [Parish registers of the church at Tröllatunga], 1889–1940; and the book called in English, *Icelandic genealogy* (Jónsson (ed.) 1994: 735–835).

20 *Lbs.* 1675 4to: Dagbók Halldórs Jónssonar [Diary of Halldór Jónsson]: 17 March 1903. It is maybe worth noting that this Daði, the son of Grímur and Bjargey, was born on 11 March 1902 and was thus barely a year old when he was sent away, temporarily at least, for fostering.

21 Death in Icelandic peasant society and its impact on those left alive is discussed in two of my books (Magnússon 1993: 90–114; Magnússon 2010: 99–111).

22 The role-call of death at Gestsstaðir, as at other farms, was frequent and unrelenting: for example, 'Daði of Gestsstaðir died this morning after 5 days in bed with pneumonia' (*Lbs.* 1864 8vo: Dagbók Halldórs Jónssonar [Diary of Halldór Jónsson], 3 July 1898) – in this case the tenant of the farm, Daði Bjarnason, aged 67.

23 (Jónsson (ed.) 1994: 761–99). See also: *Þjóðskjalasafn Íslands*: Strandasýsla: Prestsþjónust-ubækur Tröllatungu [Parish registers of the church at Tröllatunga], 1889–1940. Elín's brothers and sisters were to a large extent brought up and provided for by Halldór and Elín after the death of Þuríður, and her widower Samúel became a permanent resident in their home.

24 (Jónsson (ed.) 1994: 836–61). See also: *Þjóðskjalasafn Íslands*: Strandasýsla: Prestsþjónust-ubækur Tröllatungu [Parish registers of the church at Tröllatunga], 1889–1940.

25 *Þjóðskjalasafn Íslands*: Strandasýsla X, 7: Manntalsbækur [census records] 1904–15: Tröllatunga, Húsvitjunarbók [Record of pastoral visits], 1887–1938.

6   Refashioning a famous French peasant

The story

In the village of Artigat in the Pyrenees of southwestern France, over 400 years ago (in the sixteenth century), a wedding had recently taken place. The couple were mere children – the groom probably about 14 years old, the bride even younger – and the union had been arranged between their fathers. Both men saw the marriage as serving their interests well. Before long, the villagers felt that the couple ought to be blessed with progeny; but for eight years they remained childless, until a son, Sanxi, was born, following intervention by an enchantress to enable conception. Subsequently the young husband, Martin Guerre found himself at the centre of a family dispute, accused of stealing grain from his own father. This offence was taken seriously in the Guerre family, which originated from the Basque town of Hendaye. After that Martin Guerre vanished without trace; widespread searches yielded no result. For many years after Guerre's disappearance, his young wife Bertrande de Rols lived as a protégée of her relatives, alone yet unable to remarry, with no place of her own in society.

One day in 1556, eight years after the disappearance of her husband, a man turned up at Artigat, where the family were still living, claiming to be Martin Guerre. The initial response was reserved, as the villagers felt that he was much changed. But he gradually managed to convince all the villagers that he was indeed Martin Guerre. His wife too soon accepted him, concluding that, upon closer acquaintance, he was like himself. He won the villagers' credence mostly by demonstrating extensive knowledge of people and events in the past which could only have been known to those involved. But Guerre was certainly a changed man, both in appearance and in behaviour. He was a lively, sociable man; the vanished Martin Guerre, a skinny, shy boy, had developed into an interesting person. And in the end the village welcomed him with open arms, dismissing the changes as natural: Guerre had gone away a boy and come back a man. And perhaps it was not easy to keep in one's mind's eye an image of someone who had not been seen for eight years, in those days before visual media such as portraiture. Before long Martin Guerre and his wife started having children. Over the next three years two children were born to them, one of whom died in infancy. Things appeared to be going well in the Guerre family, until Martin's uncle, who had been guardian of his assets during his absence, refused to hand them over (or the account of how he had managed the property). Martin claimed his full inheritance, his father having died during his absence; his uncle maintained that Martin, since he had abandoned his family, had no right to reclaim his full previous assets. After all, it was the uncle who had taken care of the property, and supported Sanxi and Bertrande. The husband concluded that he had no option but to take legal action against his uncle, Pierre Guerre; the uncle and those around him now started to express doubts that the claimant was indeed Martin Guerre – and this was part of Pierre's defence in the case. People also recalled an event which was hard to reconcile with the claimant's story: the village cobbler had a last (mould) of Martin Guerre's foot, but his feet now appeared to be several sizes smaller than before he disappeared! A passing soldier reported that Martin Guerre had lost a leg in the war, so the claimant must be an imposter. More and more evidence was adduced.

Allegations and counter-allegations were exchanged, culminating in Pierre Guerre taking legal action against his supposed nephew. Both cases went to court, leading to long and complicated proceedings. Pierre Guerre, who had married Bertrande's mother, tried to convince his foster-daughter that her husband was not what he seemed. But Bertrande stood by her man, and he went on to win his case, that came to an end in 1560.

But that was not the end of the story. Pierre Guerre set out to investigate further, and find out who the imposter claiming to be Martin Guerre might be. He discovered that the man was in truth Arnaud du Tilh, nicknamed Pansette; he had a distinctly shady past, and was from a village not far from Artigat. The uncle renewed his accusations, now in the name of his foster-daughter Bertrande, but initially without her knowledge. She alone had standing to have the case re-opened; she was eventually persuaded by her mother to agree to the legal action. When the case came to court in the town of Rieux about 150 witnesses were called. Among them was Bertrande who, when it came to the point, could not state unconditionally that her husband was not who he claimed to be. Opinion was divided in the village, but the judge ultimately ruled that the husband should be condemned to death, as he was guilty of imposture.

The convicted man immediately appealed the verdict to the Parliament of Toulouse. Both Bertrande and Pierre Guerre were arrested, accused of making false allegations, and Pierre also of perjury. The husband maintained that his wife had been under pressure from his uncle (her foster-father), and had been party to the case only for that reason. The case had been principally motivated by the uncle's greed. The judge in the case, the learned Jean de Coras, who became keenly interested in all the facts, and handled the matter decisively, concluded that the husband was innocent after all: he was the real Martin Guerre.

Just before the verdict was to be handed down, the unexpected happened: the courtroom door opened, and in limped a man with a wooden leg. He said he was Martin Guerre. Seeing the two men side by side, there was no room for doubt: the one-legged man was certainly the true Martin. Pansette was unceremoniously found guilty, and executed soon afterwards. Before his death Pansette explained that, after being mistaken twice for Martin Guerre, he had decided to assume his place in the village. With the assistance of two local men, he gathered enough information to present himself convincingly as Guerre. He had seen this as an opportunity to start a new life, in comfortable circumstances.

The wife fell at her true husband's feet and begged for mercy, but he spurned her. She must, he maintained, have known the truth when she agreed to accept the imposter as her husband. It is clear that the learned and merciful Judge Jean de Coras was far from happy with the conclusion of the case, and found it hard to understand the reasoning of the one-legged Martin Guerre. Thus ends this dramatic tale, which has survived in French folk tradition over the centuries, into our own times.

The sources and the tale

There are two sources for this interesting story: first the court documents penned by Judge Jean de Coras – *Arrest Memorable* – and second *Histoire Admirable* by Guillaume Le Sueur, based on notes made by another judge in the case. Le Sueur may even have played some part in the proceedings himself. The two documents led to the Martin Guerre case acquiring the status of a folk legend in France, passed down from person to person as a gripping and shocking tale. Such folk traditions were used by American historian Natalie Zemon Davis when she wrote her famous *The Return of Martin Guerre* – along with all other available documents relating to the case, the region where it took place, and that period of history (Davis 1983). One of the sources used by Davis was the correspondence of Judge de Coras: this remarkable man was a true humanist, who influenced the development of the French legal system. His actions in the Martin Guerre case indicate his interest in the people involved, and his efforts to uncover the dogmatic context of Roman law.

As stated above, the story survived in French folk tradition. In due course the story was reworked by professional writers, inspiring novels, musicals, film and TV versions. Alexandre Dumas *père*, for instance, used the Guerre case in his novel *Les Deux Dianes* (*The Two Dianas*) and in the series *Crimes Célèbres* (*Celebrated or Famous Crimes*) (1841). A century later, in 1941, American author Janet Lewis wrote a historical novel focusing on Bertrande's viewpoint, *The Wife of Martin Guerre*. In 1982 *Le Retour de Martin Guerre* (*The Return of Martin Guerre*), a film directed by Daniel Vigne, was released, starring Gérard Depardieu and Nathalie Baye. Just as in the previous, literary, versions of the story, the film was naturally coloured by its director's ideas, and this led to the project's consultant, Princeton professor Natalie Zemon Davis, deciding to publish her own version, based primarily on the historical sources. As will be discussed further below, not everyone was pleased with her interpretation and the approach in her book, *The Return of Martin Guerre*.

Before long the American public had an opportunity to see their own version of the tale on screen in *Sommersby*, in which the events are relocated to the southern United States during the Civil War in the mid-nineteenth century. Released in 1993, *Sommersby* starred box-office giants Jodie Foster and Richard Gere. In that same year a musical, *The House of Martin Guerre* by Leslie Arden and Anna Theresa Cascio, was premiered in Toronto, Canada. After further development, it was staged on various occasions in the following years, including productions in the USA. Another musical, *Martin Guerre* by Laura Harrington and Roger Ames, was staged successfully in Connecticut in 1993. Yet another musical version was produced in 1996 on the London stage (Prince Edward Theatre): *Martin Guerre* by Claude-Michel Schönberg and Alain Boublil. Most recently, in 2010, a TV film of the story was set in the Black Forest in Germany after World War II: *Wiedersehen mit einem Fremden* (*The Return of a Stranger*), directed by Niki Stein.

In all these many versions of the story, the authors and directors have told it in their own way – selecting the aspects they found most interesting and developing them, often regardless of the true course of events. This is no surprise in fiction and film, of course; but historian Natalie Zemon Davis was accused of doing the same, i.e. telling the story as she saw it, without basing her account on extant empirical sources.

The classical approach to history versus the methods of microhistory

In the last chapter, a detailed account was given of the case of two Icelandic brothers, Halldór and Níels Jónsson. The objective of that discussion was *inter alia* to highlight how two different scholarly approaches often yield different conclusions – the macro and the micro approach. By viewing the subject of health in Iceland via statistical evidence, it was easy to reach the happy conclusion that the latter half of the nineteenth century and the first part of the twentieth had been a period of constant and steady progress. When the opportunity arose, however, to examine the same subject from the viewpoint of an individual, and how it affected his life and that of those around him, a quite different picture emerged. The strengths of microhistory were displayed here, in a rather simple but credible manner. The sources used certainly told their own story, but it was still necessary to examine the details. And it is precisely this last point which can give rise to highly divergent views. When a specific subject is explored minutely, in the manner of many microhistorians, the opportunity will often arise to connect individual aspects which are not reliably documented, and to consider the gaps in knowledge, gaps which are an unavoidable aspect of the work of historians. Macro-scholars tend to try to plaster over such gaps while microhistorians make the gaps in knowledge a subject in itself. The strength of the microhistorical approach is precisely that each subject addressed is discussed both with respect to known facts and to what is not known. The latter is, in other words, no less important to the historian's research than the former.

But discussion of the unknown naturally requires research methods and approaches which are quite different from those used by historians whose narrative is broad-brush – those who work with the 'grand narrative.'

In short, microhistorians have repeatedly pointed out that when researching a subject on a small scale a different approach is needed to the logical structure of the study, unlike that used in macro material, what is known as 'empirical history' (or 'scientific history'). The approach often used in microhistory is called 'the evidential paradigm' (Ginzburg 1989a: 96–125). The premise here is that research into small units calls for minute analysis of clues and signs in the sources; that in gathering evidence and proofs this principle is applied by detecting hidden clues in the text, and deconstructing the position of the individuals involved. In such a case, proofs as such can hardly exist in the same way as they may in the case of a statistical analysis for instance; but this approach can provide an indication of the way towards certain proofs and the path the case has taken. Thus the microhistorian discerns the *direction* of the case, and seeks to follow it up by analysis of clues and signs in the sources. The method is complex, and demands great attention to detail; in applying this approach it is necessary to bring out all the unique features found in the text – however trivial they may appear at first sight – and make them the subject of the study.

The microhistorian's research method has often been likened to the task of a doctor, who diagnoses a patient's symptoms which are not visible to the naked eye; or, even more aptly, the work of a detective who seeks to solve a crime. He/she searches out clues, but does not give too much weight to general data on norms of human behaviour. Such generalized knowledge is rarely useful is resolving the puzzle; hence 'Mr and Mrs Average' can be left in peace on the desk of the social historian (where they belong) while the detective work goes on.

It should be borne in mind that the traditional social or cultural historian generally seeks statistical data which can indicate how the mass of the population acted and thought in the context of the formal structure of society. For the microhistorian, as for the detective, such information is of limited value; the microhistorian is not interested in how the majority acted, only in what the individual under consideration did. For the microhistorian knows that each of us takes his/her own path in dealing with our daily lives, and that is the path the microhistorian seeks to trace. Due to this focus on the singular, many historians find it hard to accept that the subject of study cannot be placed within the framework of empirical history. And thus the questions are often asked: How typical is this subject? What does he/she tell us about society in general? Microhistorians have many ripostes to such questions.

When Natalie Zemon Davis's book was published in 1983, she attained almost instantaneous world renown. But not everyone was impressed. American historian Robert Finlay, for instance, made himself heard in the respected *American Historical Review* a few years after the publication of the book, with outspoken criticism of Davis's work (Finlay 1988: 553–71). To anyone who read Finlay's critique, it was obvious that the dispute was a matter of fundamentally differing views of history: on one hand the classic historical approach to history, based on the principle of sticking closely to the sources and restraining all flights of imagination which might tempt the scholar – embroidering as little as possible – and on the other hand the method of using limited sources to build up a narrative, utilising a broader range of evidence not necessarily directly relating to the subject.

Davis takes the innovative approach – in the microhistorical spirit of addressing a subject that is not central in the narrative, but appears to be peripheral to the tale – of focusing primarily on the position of the wife, Bertrande de Rols, and how she made the considered decision to play along when her 'new husband' turned up. In this way, Davis creates an opportunity to approach this often-told tale from an entirely new perspective; and she does so through a minute reading of clues and signs in the sources. She sets out to recreate Bertrande's world with reference to her environment in the past and in her own time. This is thus a good example of the microhistorical approach.

Davis maintains that Bertrande had in fact no option but to play along with the outsider as her position in society, as the wife of a man who had disappeared, was dismal: she was an outcast in her own community. The unexpected appearance of the imposter in her life offered her an opportunity she could not resist, the chance to wrest back her independence from her mother and the uncle (foster-father), and begin a new life. Although she formerly testified against her putative husband during the trials, she never abandoned him, but instead played a double role perfectly, Davis argues. And when the truth came out, she had an easy way out, without risk of official retribution. Thus, says Davis, Bertrande was able to manipulate her difficult position with admirable skill, just as a fully developed and independent individual might be expected to do.

Davis contrives to interpret the story in this way: by examining the sources in detail in the microhistorical manner while also taking account of the changes which took place in French society following the religious conflicts which had raged in Europe during previous decades. Reformist ideas spread throughout Europe, and that gives Davis an opportunity to speculate that the new ideas may explain Bertrande's decision. It could be argued that the couple did not view their marriage as a Catholic sacrament that required the approval of the Church, but instead as a relationship between the two of them and a higher power. At least it is easy to show that they shared a profound intimacy that gave them an opportunity to support each other's testimony when the case was tried.

Davis's effort to throw light on a French village community in the sixteenth century is entirely successful, and the method she employs is clearly in the spirit of the new social and cultural history of which microhistory was a part.[1] The focus on the lower classes of agrarian society, and especially the women, makes Davis's work unusual, when account is taken of the fact that she permitted herself to read into the established sources clues and signs which were not necessarily obvious. For example, she examines Basque customs and traditions – the Guerre family was of Basque origin – and speculates whether the two Martins may have met before the confrontation during the trial in Toulouse, and why the true Martin decided to come forward at that fateful moment.

Much of her research focused on the question of how it may theoretically be possible to usurp the place of another man as Pansette did, especially with respect to the wife who had, after all, been sufficiently intimate with him to conceive two children. She would have been in a better position than anyone else to tell whether Pansette was the real Martin Guerre. Davis went on to consider Bertrande's performance during the trial, and how she contrived to avoid being convicted as an accessory to the crime. All this analysis informed Davis's approach; she succeeded in throwing an interesting light not only on the case itself but on the mindset of these sixteenth-century French villagers. That includes a perspective on the village community and how it functioned: family life, marriage, gender roles, justice and religion, as well as the widely divergent social status of the learned and the common man.

Yet it was precisely this approach in Davis's work, *inter alia* the concept of 'self-fashioning' which she employed to demonstrate 'the molding of speech, manners, gesture, and conversation' of key actors in the drama, which so irritated Robert Finlay (Davis 1988: 603). He utterly rejects the idea that the sources provide a basis for any other reading than the traditional one, with Pansette at centre stage. Clearly, the entire community was hoodwinked by the imposter, including the woman he claimed as his wife. According to Finlay, Davis's handling of the story does not have a leg to stand on – she forces her modern ideology of the strong woman onto a person who was demonstrably the product of a society where women's rights were almost non-existent. 'But speculation,' Finlay continues, 'whether founded on intuition or on concepts drawn from anthropology and literary criticism, is supposed to give way before the sovereignty of the sources, the tribunal of the documents. The historian should not make the people of the past say or do things that run counter to the most scrupulous respect for the sources.' (Finlay 1988: 571). Finlay speaks of Davis's 'unfounded hypotheses', based on misconstrued evidence from the trial. Thus, he says, Davis subverts the true story, removing it from its true context in order to put forward contemporary ideas which have nothing to do with Bertrande's position in the sixteenth century. His criticism targeted cultural historians in general, and how they went about doing their business, and especially what he terms the 'psychological reconstruction' of the historical motivation of the main persons in the story – a refashioning of a human being. He also maintains that Davis's scholarly method obliterates the difference between history and fiction. And he asks the classic question: 'In historical writing, where does reconstruction stop and invention begin?' (Finlay 1988: 569).

The response this elicited from Davis was no less interesting. In an article in the same journal, 'On the Lame', Davis fiercely rebutted Finlay's criticism (Davis 1988: 572–603). She maintained that Finlay himself had used similar methods to hers in his previous work, i.e. considering his subject from the perspective of psychological exploration and literary interpretation. But her main criticism is that she feels that Finlay is guilty of ignoring many different possible facets of the case which can throw light on what happened. She ascribes this to pre-conceptions about how historical research should be carried out. Davis's objective is, as she puts it, the 're-creation of complexity in historical experience'. Here she is influenced by postmodernism and poststructuralism, where any event is seen as multilayered, having many different facets, which scholars should strive to bring to light (Megill 2007: 1–2, 4). A corollary of this is the loss of the synthesis, the continuous, clear narrative which states the 'facts' and elucidates them.

Davis certainly marks a new departure here. She adopts new methods, different from those used by traditional historians, and she goes further in recreating the past, employing methods that historians have never thought of using before. Hence Finlay's response is quite understandable. He was simply seeking to champion the methods and approaches which historians had learned, from generation to generation, throughout the twentieth century – but refused to recognize the developments which had taken place in the humanities regarding the relationship between the text or source and the scholar working with them. While that trend was no longer new at that time (in the late 1980s), the historians who should have been best equipped for the debate on postmodernism and poststructuralism were firmly entrenched in the old historical methods. It almost seemed that they lacked the confidence to address these new ideas on the basis of any other premises than those they knew and had always used. This may be seen in various ways in their discussion of the issue during the last decade of the twentieth century.

New methods, new approaches

I feel that social and cultural historians can learn a great deal from their own history, particularly with respect to the methodological structure of the discipline.[2] I believe it is possible to look *inwards* at the way in which social and cultural historians go about doing their business, to see how a substantial section of the discipline – the section that should have been best placed to take on the new ideas associated with postmodernism and poststructuralism – avoided the task or simply lacked the confidence to take it on. Here I am referring to the historians who were most closely involved with the concept of *mentalités* or 'mentalities' (the history of mentalities) in the late 1980s. Instead of working systematically on the basis of the ideology at the centre of this approach, scholars applying the history of mentalities looked in a quite different direction for methodological guidance, namely to quantitative analysis. It is hardly surprising that many historians who worked with *mentalités* at the time employed quantitative methods in their research, since the *Annales* scholars, who were beyond question the leading force within social history in the second half of the twentieth century, accorded cultural discussion, for instance on the mentalities, a lower status in the intellectual pecking order. This is noted by Christopher E. Forth in an article on the old and the new cultural history in a collection of essays called *Encyclopedia of European Social History*:

The *Annalistes* nevertheless failed to provide a rigorous theorization of the relationship between *mentalités* and other environmental factors, and some like Pierre Chaunu concluded that it represented a 'third level' of historical inquiry more or less determined by developments taking place on the putatively more primary level of social and economic life. Hence, the *Annalistes* contended that culture was at heart an expression of underlying structures, and shared the Marxist reluctance to accord it an autonomous status.

(Forth 2001: 87)

So we are forced to concede, whether we like it or not, that the leading ideology of the *Annalistes* never found a solution to the methodological problem facing their studies. It was enough for the scholars who worked with *mentalités* to follow methods and paths that had been developed by people in other areas in which the subject material was in any case bound up with the course of social and economic developments (Jarrick 1999: 124–25). In other words, according to the ideology of the *Annalistes*, the basis for historical analysis was not to be found in *mentalités* but in other areas of social studies.[3]

The reason for bringing up these patterns is that I believe strongly that social and cultural historians can learn from the sad case of 'the history of mentalities' and that it helps to explain the weak ideological basis of socio/cultural historical studies at the present time. As I have described above when discussing the case of Robert Finlay, many scholars have chosen to ignore new currents and movements within the humanities because those who were involved in 'the history of mentalities' and similar academic approaches were never really put in a position of having to test out whether it was possible to identify a particular ideological grounding for their work. As time went on, this intellectual focus began to lose its footing and eventually became just part of history, though without any formal notification of its demise. As I see things, social and cultural historians are facing a peril of a similar nature at the present moment, i.e. if they succumb to the temptation to carry on looking at their material with the same eyes as scholars have done in recent decades, there is a serious danger that much of the discipline's force and vigour will be dissipated.

American historian Nina Rattner Gelbart made the following observation in her book published in the end of the last century, *The King's Midwife: A History and Mystery of Madame du Coudray*:

For centuries history was written in an authoritative, detached voice, communicating an illusion of logical progression, objectivity, completeness. It claimed to have discovered 'how things really were', to be scientific and factual, and to present a linear, seamless tale. Recently such empiricist presumptions of certainty in the discipline have been attacked; recovery of the past once and for all, the 'whole story,' now seems a naive and strange conceit.

(Gelbart 1998: 9)

Gelbart notes that it has largely been feminists and postmodernists who have turned against these particular modes of thinking with a view to exposing the faults in the reasoning of those who advocate them. In conventional social and cultural history, the views of the 'others' were entirely discounted and there was a pretence that the vast majority of mankind did not exist or affect things in any way. 'Such energetic challenges,' Gelbart goes on to say, 'bring to the field tremendous new vitality and interest, but also considerable discomfort.' (Gelbart 1998: 9). With some justification one might say that what Gelbart is describing here lies at the heart of the conflicts that have been going on within history for the past few decades, conflicts that clearly materialized in the debate between Finlay and Davis. I have described how the scholarly world set about tackling the problem Gelbart alludes to, and come to the conclusion that, after a certain amount of dither and fluster during the 1990s, all too many social and cultural historians have elected to stick to the solutions and tactics of the old 'new history',[4] while accepting that 'the history of mentalities' is now entirely defunct (Magnússon 2001: 83–107).

There are, as I see it, two main reasons for this development. First, I believe that the scholars who were most closely associated with the area that was under attack, i.e. social and cultural historians working within the precepts of the history of mentalities, were ill-prepared for the criticisms of postmodernists and poststructuralists. As mentioned above, the weak ideological and methodological underpinnings of the history of mentalities meant that scholars lacked confidence to face up to the new challenges of contemporary scholarship (Jarrick 1999: 120–32). The discourse was unfamiliar to many of them, and scholars who had thrown in their lot with historical demography and quantitative analysis had no problem disregarding this criticism. This was also the recourse of social and cultural historians who had espoused the history of mentalities when the ground started slipping from under their feet late in the 1980s. For example, historians who had massed under the banner of quantitative analysis simply considered their theoretical position to be so strong that there was no need to waste their time on the kind of academic wrangling that postmodernist criticism was adjudged to be: the quantitative approach was tried and tested and, in the view of those who used it, had proved itself by its results.[5] Postmodernist currents could thus be left to their own devices.

Second, it was clear that the failure of the 'grand narratives' – so named by scholars working in fields such as literary analysis, philosophy, ethnology and anthropology – would mean a realignment of historical ideology, and entail that the work of historians who were then at the height of their reputation would need to be reassessed on new premises. So it is hardly surprising that many historians chose to shut their eyes to what was happening: the potential danger from the breakdown of the grand narratives was simply too great.

Reality check

What is so interesting about the development recounted above is that a large number of influential microhistorians who started out in the vanguard of the movement made the same mistake as many of the social and cultural historians I mentioned above. In spite of the fact that microhistory springs in many ways from postmodernism – and is in the mind of many historians one manifestation of postmodernism – Carlo Ginzburg and others fulminated against the new ideas. They refused to recognize their importance, continuing to focus, for instance, on contextualization in their research, i.e. placing the smaller research unit in a broader context.[6]

Norwegian critic Trygve Riiser Gundersen interviewed Carlo Ginzburg about his research in 2003 (Gundersen 2003). He asked whether there was not a certain contradiction 'between comparison and chronology', and explained further: Gundersen pointed out that Ginzburg's book *Ecstasies* 'starts with an account of the events of spring 1321,' and then he adds: 'You go from describing, by way of introduction, a couple of months in a specific year to wanting to say in conclusion something fundamental about the whole of mankind's existence on earth. How do you reconcile these two concepts?' Ginzburg replies:

> I regard *Ecstasies* primarily as a kind of experiment in size. The idea of combining the very smallest and the very largest in one book – micro- and macrohistory at one and the same time, you might say – attracted me. There is, moreover, a polemical intention underlying the way the book is structured: it may be read as a criticism of what one might term 'middle history'; the kind of history that uncritically accepts the explanatory levels we deem 'natural' in a given context – a nation, an epoch, a period of time, and the like. I wanted to show, if I could, that the scope of study never can be taken for granted. The scale we employ always determines what answer it is possible to arrive at in each case, be it at the micro- or the macro-level. So, the two levels you mentioned must be viewed together.

Ginzburg's answer undeniably expresses an interesting perspective: an unexpected, and really rather appealing, argument for how history can be done. It must be borne in mind that there is much that is unusual about Ginzburg and his distinguished career as a historian. He blazed the trail for analysis of material that has often been marginalized and dismissed as trivial by conventional historians. He has seized on the power of the narrative, and placed emphasis on telling an interesting and enchanting story, thus grabbing the reader's attention and drawing him/her with him into the events, making the reader a direct participant in analysis of the subject. Just as Davis did, he has applied approaches which are deemed unconventional, and read into the narrative clues and signs based upon the methods of literary criticism. For this reason Ginzburg has often been identified with postmodernism, as pointed out by Trygve Riiser Gundersen, who goes on to comment: 'something against which he has strongly protested'.[7] Gundersen continues: 'In a series of articles he has emerged as an ardent defender of the concept of historical truth and as a surprisingly fierce critic of the postmodern theory of history'. In truth, however, Ginzburg's opposition is less clear-cut than his declarations would indicate. He points out, for instance, that he can agree with much of what postmodernism stands for, such as that knowledge is never final, and that the historical text is a construct which has nothing to do with the past as such.[8] But that does not change the fact that he has taken a stance in absolute opposition to the relativism which is widespread in the works of those who tend toward postmodernism. Instead he focuses on the search for truth.

Obviously, there is a great difference between Ginzburg and Finlay: Ginzburg is one of the most vocal critics of the traditional history which Finlay champions. And that difference is revealed in Carlo Ginzburg's own words in the interview cited above:

> Nor is the act of remembrance without its problems. Consider everything 'that has taken place', as Benjamin writes, and how little we have preserved of it. Hardly anything! What is more, we have no guarantee that what we do know is what was important. Take ourselves, for example: we don't even know whether we remember what is worth remembering in our own lives. And whether what we do remember about ourselves is correct. Consider all the things of importance to us that we never think about, that we are never really fully aware of. The bulk of what is really important in the world will probably never be passed on, never be remembered.
>
> (Gundersen 2003)

This is the expression of the view of someone who has travelled a long way from the conventional historical approach, whereby it was deemed highly probable that the objective approach to history would lead to an understanding of what the past had actually been.[9]

I am of the view, however, that Ginzberg's intransigent opposition to postmodernism militated, in the end, against the influence of microhistory worldwide. Historian Tony Molho appears to take a similar view in a paper written in 2004, in which he states that Ginzburg has always taken the view that his scholarly methods should be 'incorporated in our discipline's dominant discourse'. He adds: 'But his rather lonely confrontations with the gurus of the linguistic turn and with the armies of their well disciplined followers raises questions about Ginzburg's ultimate influence on how we, historians, do (and will continue to do) our work'. (Molho 2004: 123). His opinion is interesting, in view of the fact that microhistory demonstrably has all the attributes of scholarly experiments in the postmodern vein – especially those which sought to emphasize the fragmentariness of the past, described so ably by Ginzburg (above). Such approaches to the past place a great strain on a discipline such as history and the parameters within which it has worked.

However, it should be pointed out that Natalie Zemon Davis does not accept that her book, nor those of Ginzburg or of Le Roy Ladurie (*Montaillou* (1975)), for that matter, should be classified as postmodern.

> When I think of the postmodern, I think of the focus on the importance of culture and language as conditioning everything, from the way we speak to

the way we think; and also of the postmodern approach's undermining of generalizations and preference for speaking about fragments, rather than about coherent wholes. All three books take local culture very seriously but they are also concerned with experience and with long-term traditions and structures of thought. I don't think that the postmodern label adds very much here. And as to the claim that these books are postmodern because they refuse to generalize, I would reply that, although different, all these three works were hoping to generate insights into processes that went beyond the individual case they were studying. All were generating suggestions about other cases, not only through the possibility of analogy, but also through communication networks and systems of power.

(Pallares-Burke 2002: 67)

Personally, I am of the view that Davis, like Ginzburg, comes very close to the ideas which are deemed important by many postmodernists. But I must admit nonetheless, as Ginzburg emphatically states, that they each go their own way in scholarship – ways which are both productive and interesting.

A group of historians have been willing to take on these challenges which postmodernism has had on its agenda in a systematic fashion, and attempt to consider the implications of these new ideas for the discipline as a whole and how it might be possible to work with them constructively within the field of history.[10] These historians have had the benefit of guidance from scholars in other fields, such as literary criticism, anthropology and philosophy (to name but a few), where similar criticism has been exerting an influence for much longer than in history. In fact, my own attempt at approaching the past in the light of the new poststructuralist perspectives has been through what I call 'the singularization of history', as described in my article in the *Journal of Social History* in 2003 (Magnússon 2003: 701–35). This approach, which draws on the experience and methods of many microhistorians, tries to address various significant criticisms aimed at contemporary history. The guiding principle is, to quote Gelbart, a frank acknowledgement and acceptance of the fact that 'historians always have to work with fragments and lacunae, with revelations and secrets. We may crave coherence and synthesis, but because much remains indecipherable we do not get it' (Gelbart 1998: 11).

The ideology of 'the singularization of history' is grounded in the fact that it is impossible to know more than a tiny fragment of the story, that the sources preserve only a minute selection of the moments, and that if the compass of the subject is increased, our chances of attaining an understanding of what has happened decrease still further. I see it as a major mistake on the part of the majority of microhistorians, and in fact of most social and cultural historians, to put the main emphasis on seeking ways to incorporate their own research units within greater wholes (contextualization). The grand narrative monopolizes attention, since academic tradition lays down as a condition that without such greater historical connections the research becomes incomprehensible (a condition that goes under the name of scientific working practice); odd disjunctive bits and pieces left behind from the past are not seen as valid unless placed in an analysable context. The grand narrative, whether masquerading under the name of modernization, the Enlightenment, Christianity, socialism or whatever, determines the questions that research is expected to ask, the form of the main argumentation and the positioning of the research within the world of academic study.

This rejection of the grand narrative is also advocated by some other historians, for example American historian Barbara H. Rosenwein in an article published in *American Historical Review* 2002. She discusses what has been called 'the history of emotions' and its status within the discipline as a whole, noting that scholars have tended to draw a supposed distinction, in accordance with modernization theory, between traditional farming communities in the early part of the modern age and the kinds of communities that began to coalesce towards the end of the eighteenth century. This has been especially marked in discussions of the emotional lives of ordinary people. Rosenwein rejects the grand narrative that has shaped the whole course of research in this area in recent decades, preferring to see people as having lived at all times in what she calls 'emotional communities', i.e. independent, fluid and unpredictable groupings. Each of these is subject to its own laws and customs and so needs to be studied on its own terms. 'There are two points here', says Rosenwein, 'not only does every society call forth, shape, constrain, and express emotions differently, but even within the same society contradictory values and models, not to mention deviant individuals, find their place.' (Rosenwein 2002: 842–43). What Rosenwein is saying here is that historians and others dealing with the history of emotions need to attempt to approach sensitive research material in ways other than those imposed by the grand narrative. The area for research needs to be broken down into small units. She concludes her case with this simple declaration: 'The grand narrative that has dominated emotions scholarship cannot stand. It is based on a debunked theory of the emotions and its concomitant, but flawed, notion of progressive self-restraint' (Rosenwein 2002: 845). This conclusion of Rosenwein's, in fact, highlights the greatest strength of the microhistorical method, i.e. the opportunity it gives us to break away from the shackles of the grand narrative and approach the research material free from the constraints of any pre-determined scholarly conception of what is significant and what is not, and where the difference lies.

Rosenwein noted that in the course of the twentieth century the scholarly treatment of emotions as a special phenomenon (or concept) underwent a series of changes. Early work was deeply coloured by what she termed 'the hydraulic model': the emotions were 'like great liquids within each person, heaving and frothing, eager to be let out'; 'unless given outlet, [they] would never cease to press forward', as Rosenwein described it (Rosenwein 2002: 836). Under this interpretation people are charged with emotions which are either displayed or contained, according to social conditions or personal wish. Later in the twentieth century this model was largely replaced by the 'cognitive view', in which 'emotions are part of a process of perception and appraisal, not forces striving for release'. Emotions are the result of judgements 'about whether something is likely to be good or harmful, pleasurable or painful, as perceived by each individual'. Certain 'basic emotions' are assumed to be 'true of all human beings' but, cognitive psychologists stress, different individuals will experience their emotions in different ways. Parallel to this model there developed another approach to emotions under the influence of 'social constructionism', in which emotions and their display are seen as being 'constructed, that is, formed and shaped, by the society in which they operate' (Rosenwein 2002: 837). Again, every society, Rosenwein concluded, has its own special peculiarities that are fluid and 'alive', constantly changing according to the individuals and circumstances in question. These changes of emphasis revolutionized the whole concept of 'emotional communities' and with it the ways in which scholars viewed the historical development of the 'culture of emotions'.[11]

I believe that the kind of history that seeks to reinforce the overall picture, to forge links with certain hypothetical threads that supposedly hold life together, is on the wrong track. This sets me at variance with distinguished scholars such as Peter N. Stearns, when he urges historians to stand guard over social history, saying that the best way to do this is by constructing powerful syntheses of the material the discipline deals with. 'We need renewed attention', says Stearns, 'to broader synthesis not only to address an endemic problem, but to respond to the additional, almost inherent particularism of the cultural turn.' (Stearns 2003: 13). As I hope I have made clear in this book, I find it preferable to place 'inherent particularism' at the very centre of what social and cultural historians – such as microhistorians – ought to be doing in the future.[12]

Notes

1 The position of microhistory within history is interestingly addressed in two readable books of interviews with well-known living historians (Pallares-Burke 2002; Domanska 1998). Both authors repeatedly ask the interviewees about the place of microhistory within the discipline, and what it means for scholarship. I shall return to these debates later in this book.

2 Part of this chapter is based on the text of my article in *Journal of Social History* 2006 (Magnússon 2006: 905–8).

3 A clear exposition of this can be found in Carrard's book, *Poetics of the New History* (Carrard 1992).

4 See for example this approach in a well known book of Appleby, Hunt and Jacob called: *Telling the Truth about History* (Appleby, Hunt and Jacob 1995). For a lively discussion of this book and the approaches of its authors, viewed from a variety of perspectives, see 'Forum: Raymond Martin, Joan W. Scott, and Cushing Strout on *Telling the Truth About History*,' (1995) *History and Theory*, 34: 320–39.

5 See for example a well known book by Iggers (Iggers 1997: 59–60).

6 See István Szijártó, pp. 74–6 in this volume.

7 See also discussion of the same issue in: (Ginzburg 1999).

8 See discussion of Ginzburg and Davis in the context of postmodernism: (Zammito 1998: 330–46).

9 Ginzburg maintains a similar perspective in an interview with Maria Lúcia G. Pallares-Burke in *The New History. Confessions and Conversations* (Pallares-Burke 2002:

205–6), in which he cites an interesting example to illustrate his stance, outside and above both the perspective of postmodernism and those who go along with positivism.

10 I take the liberty of making reference to a work of my own in this context, *Wasteland with Words. A Social History of Iceland* (Magnússon 2010), in which I seek to apply the methods of microhistory to subject matter which has predominantly been guided by the grand narrative – a general history of a country over a long period of time.

11 (Rosenwein 2006). See also: (Plamper 2010: 237–65; Reddy 2008: 81–100; Stearns and Stearns 1985: 813–36).

12 See important arguments in Cabrera, *Postsocial History* (Cabrera 2004), and Wilson, *History in Crisis?* (Wilson 1999).

7 New and old theoretical issues
Criticisms of microhistory

The revelation

> There are moments so beautiful, so rich in delight, that the tongue has no words, and the heart as it were shuts itself off against the articulation of emotion, and one of these has always come over me when I have been with you. I know well that you have gone through a baptism of fire of your innermost desires, and now look forward full of hope towards the future of our youths, now that we love each other through real experience and times of danger. But childhood love and the ardour of youth is the hottest of loves, the saying goes. So you will be my strongest spur, and a good woman makes the man steadfast, and the best wages I can have for my labour are if what I do may meet your approval. I would pray to God fervently and from the depths of my soul that he turn our plans to happiness, and strengthen us both on our way along the treacherous path of life.

This is the end of a love letter that Níels Jónsson, one of the brothers from the Strandir commune, wrote to his betrothed, Guðrún Bjarnadóttir, during their courtship in the final decade of the nineteenth century. Twenty-two letters of this kind from this young peasant son have been preserved, all of them long and elaborate, and almost without parallel. In 1997 I published a book based on my research on the brothers Níels and Halldór Jónsson and the people that came into their lives. The book was published, in Icelandic, by the University of Iceland Press, under a title that translates as *Education, Love and Grief: A Microhistorical Study of Icelandic Rural Society in the 19th and 20th Centuries* (Magnússon 1997).

A year after the book was published I received a letter from a farmer in Strandir, the same county where Níels and Halldór had lived their entire lives.[1] The writer talked about various aspects of my book and appeared largely in favour of most of what it said. But on one point he was in strong disagreement, and that was my portrayal of the emotional lives of Níels Jónsson and Guðrún Bjarnadóttir. His comments suggested that events had occurred that had cast a shadow over their life together, a shadow so long that he could not imagine that relations between these people had been as profoundly loving as the letters led one to believe. This was all he said, and with that concluded his letter of over twenty handwritten sheets.

I was naturally very curious to know more. When one has spent years of one's life working on a particular collection of diaries, letters and notebooks, one is liable to form a kind of emotional attachment to the subject. At least, that was how it was with me. After all this time I felt I knew these people almost as well as I knew my own family. My correspondent was suggesting, however, that I had missed something important. I wrote back to him asking him to give me the whole story, tell me everything he knew about what had come up in the couple's relations. Some time later, in the summer of 1998, an answer arrived. The writer took a long time to bring himself round to the main issue; it was plainly something he found difficult to talk about. Finally, however, the story emerged:

> I now come to the matter you ask me for clearer information about and that I touched on in my previous letter to you. I was clumsy enough to allude to what I believe turned into a long-standing anguish in the lives of the pair of them. It seems that Níels and Guðrún had not been married and living together long when signs of discord began to appear. Perhaps Níels failed to find in Guðrún the woman he had built up in his imagination while they were courting. There are no reports that one can take as being entirely reliable but I heard two stories on the subject. It was not long before jealousy raised its head and began to come between them. – Níels accused his wife of being unfaithful to him and she the same of him. So far as Guðrún was concerned, I do not think there was anything in this.

His source maintained that Níels had formed an attraction for a young girl at Gjögur:

> As a result, Guðrún accused Níels of cheating on her. Níels accused Guðrún of the same, without any real grounds. Níels became vehement and heated. To cut a long story short, at this point all hell broke loose.
>
> During these years their daughter Elísabet had been born and she was probably then 2–3 years old. Somehow the child became mixed up in this quarrel of theirs. In one of their bouts of recrimination things got so heated that Níels stormed out with threats aimed at Guðrún, including that she would not need to have any more children bearing his name, nor would they need to argue about other children. He rushed off in a furious temper. A long time passed and Níels did not return. People went out to look for him. He was found somewhere a fair way off, racked by torment and helpless with pain, so that they feared for his life.
>
> In his rage he had drawn a cord tight around his testicles and torn them off.

I was dumbstruck and had no idea how to react. The farmer's account of how Níels had castrated himself affected me so deeply that I could never bring myself to answer his letter and thank him. Shortly afterwards my correspondent died at a ripe old age, in his late nineties, without my ever having found myself able to write back to him. And for more than ten years I could not bring myself to deal with the letter. It just sat in my drawer all this time.

But Níels survived the incident and lived into old age.

My acquaintance with Níels and his people was such that the whole thing seemed inconceivable. I immediately started asking myself whether the sources I had been working with were, by their very nature, simply not to be trusted. I told myself that these events fell outside the scope of my research, since the subject I had actually been interested in was courtship and I had only followed the lives of Níels and Guðrún through that period of their relationship. I tried to take the attitude that what became of them after they were married simply did not matter: I was not writing their biography; my book was about the interplay between education and emotional life (love and grief), and to this extent the emphasis was not directly on these two people and their lives. Even so, I was filled with an uncomfortable sense that I had failed to recognize these extreme and violent tendencies in Níels's character, and what they meant. Could his desperate action be seen as a question of honour, a statement about his integrity, which uncovered his true character? Could he have been unjustly accused, and responded in this way to remove all possible doubts of his honour? It is, of course, impossible to tell.

The only account of a similar event, that I know of, was in a book by British-born historian Jonathan D. Spence, *The Death of Woman Wang*: 'But in 1651, before the official marriage had taken place, Liu was slandered for having illicit relations with his widowed sister-in-law; with some impetuous notion of clearing her good name and proving his own integrity, he castrated himself' (Spence 1978: 101). It must be reiterated that it is hard to understand the truth of what happened in Níels Jónsson's case: was he making a symbolic point to his wife and others, or did he act in a moment of madness? One thing is for sure: for many years I had pored over the writings of this man and his brothers, wondered at their fortitude and perseverance, tried to put myself in their shoes and understand all the intricacies of their thoughts and deeds. And yet, despite this, I had managed to miss such a profound defect of character as the one that had manifested itself here in so macabre a fashion. So I kept asking myself one simple question: How could such a thing happen?

The bull's eye

Metanarratives ('grand narratives'),[2] whether guided by modernization theory[3] or anything else, are 'constructs' which have reference only to traditions of research that are integrally bound up with the academic network, 'constructs' which have taken on the form of phenomena with independent lives unconnected to the past and the events related to it.[4] I have regarded microhistory as the scholarly experiment which had the most potential to counteract the influence of metanarratives, for the following reasons (Magnússon 2003: 701–35):

Admittedly, a certain problem exists in the approach of the vast majority of microhistorians; they never lost sight of broader historical and political contexts. Their method was supposed to test grand generalizations, and this has characterized the arguments of some key players of microhistory, like both Giovanni Levi and Carlo Ginzburg, and in fact, most other microhistorians around the world (Ginzburg 1993: 10–35). In short, for the majority of micro-historians, it has been their explicit intention. Levi, for instance, maintained in a well-known paper: 'The unifying principle of all microhistorical research is the belief that microscopic observation will reveal factors previously unobserved' (Levi 1992: 97). He adds the following about the nature of microhistory:

> Phenomena previously considered to be sufficiently described and understood assume completely new meanings by altering the scale of observation. It is then possible to use these results to draw far wider generalizations although the initial observations were made within relatively narrow dimensions and as experiments rather than examples.
>
> (Levi 1992: 97)

But microhistorians have always 'failed to escape from a notion of modernization, now seen mostly as a destructive force that impinges on the microscale of local history', as Georg G. Iggers argues (Iggers 1997: 139). American historian John Brewer picks up a similar point when he states that the microhistorical focus certainly offers complexity, but also greater completeness: 'For certain sorts of microhistorians may confess themselves dissatisfied with grand narratives but still aspire to a notion of total history' (Brewer 2010: 8). He maintains that this point of view is more likely to be found among French and Italian micro-historians 'who both react against but want to remain within the great *Annales* tradition of *histoire totale*, writing what Revel has described as "a total history, but this time built from the ground up".' Brewer points out that completeness in history writing is 'the most exclusionary version of historical narrative', adding that: 'It supposes one true history rather than competing histories' (Brewer 2010: 8).

For the above reasons, I set out to clarify the concept of microhistorical methods through the idea of the 'singularization of history,' as mentioned in the last chapter (see p. 115). The model is based upon utter rejection of the impor-tance of the grand narrative. The general idea was based on the following: the model looks inward, and studies all aspects in close detail, bringing out the nuances of the events and phenomena we choose to investigate. The idea is that the focus will always be fixed on the matter in hand and on that alone. The ideology consists in investigating with great precision each and every fragment connected with the matter in hand for which there are sources, and in bringing up for consideration all possible means of interpretation that bear directly upon the material. Even if the scale is reduced in the way envisioned here, one must still expect some structural orientation within the frame of reference. But this structure must always be subject to laws other than those imposed by the traditional metanarratives and, because of their scope, must be more malleable, i.e. the frames must be more limited and more easily controlled. In this way there is the opportunity to give the full range of voices within society easy access to historical research. The singularization of history in this sense provides the researcher with a means of bringing out the contradictions that exist between the different 'discourses' of individual groups, and this is a precondition for our being able to approach ideas and points of view that in the general run of events do not come to the fore.[5] It needs to be stated that this model does not offer *completeness* in any shape or form.

Therefore this ideology brings into prominence the contradictions and inconsistencies in the mind of each and every individual, and heightens the paradoxes that exist within each living person. To allow the contradictions and paradoxes freedom of expression, the emphasis must always be kept squarely on the subject matter itself, and on nothing else. The key word here is singularization; the singularization of history is first and foremost a search for a way in which history can research its proper subjects in their proper logical and cultural context and thus dissociate itself from the 'manmade' ideological package of the metanarratives.[6]

It was precisely within the parameters of the above ideology that I believed I was working in my study of the brothers from the Strandir commune. Hence I was taken aback to receive information about the life of Níels Jónsson which was so utterly at odds with what I believed I had learned, guided by the ideology of the singularization of history. I asked myself whether I had utterly failed to draw up a significant picture of the life of these individuals, since such a dramatic event had taken place without my noticing it in the sources, in one way or another.

In spite of these provisos regarding my research on the material, and additional material I received later, the fact remains that the 'method' or 'model,' as applied in my study, did not work. I felt that I must face this fact, and work systematically through the difficulties in which I found myself. I asked myself: Was the criticism of microhistorical methods levelled at microhistorians by respected historians justified, after all?

Upstream

Ego-documents of various sorts can certainly open up new and exciting opportunities once the past is analysed. The problem has been, however, that it has been hard to find these 'hidden treasures', mainly because many archives have been poorly indexed and catalogued, so the material stored there has not been accessible. There are also well-known cases of women's writings not being catalogued at all, to all intents and purposes 'hidden' by their anonymity in archives around the world.[7] Gaining access to such material can make a crucial contribution to research, changing the scholar's frame of reference, and the opportunities for examining large groups of people. For example, what made my research on the two brothers special was the excellence of the material I had to work with, i.e. the diaries and many other personal writings of the brothers. In retrospect I realize that I failed to utilize it fully when forming my argument because, in spite of everything, I was so taken up with writing the argument into the metanarrative, to serve the insistence of the community of scholars that I connect my arguments to a bigger picture. Instead of fixing my gaze on the subject matter itself and the sources at my disposal I concentrated on placing them within wider contexts – the contexts of laws and regulations on the education of children in Iceland, and of general discourse about such matters in newspapers and journals in the country – and ended by linking this debate with scholarly discussion of education and the emotions on a worldwide level.

It could be said, perhaps, that I was not conscious of an important mode of thinking which is entailed by the use of the methods of microhistory, i.e. asking the question: What kind of documentation is needed to present a convincing argument? Tony Molho considers this precise point in a paper (2004) in which he examines the links between the writings of the inquisitors and the beliefs of peasants as they appear in Carlo Ginzburg's research. He concludes: 'It is the "discrepancy" or "gap" between the questions asked by the Inquisitors and the peasants' initial responses to these questions that enable the historian "to reach a level of genuinely popular beliefs".' (Molho 2004: 129). And it was probably here that I myself went astray, by not considering a certain problem that could be seen in the sources themselves, on close scrutiny, which could have pointed me in the right direction, towards the puzzle revealed in the old farmer's letter. In other words, despite all good intentions, I ended up carrying out this research mostly in the way I had been taught, and nowhere deviated from the conventional frames of reference in social and cultural history, i.e. to connect the material with a greater whole and allow the metanarrative in large part to dictate the outcome. At the same time I missed the opportunity to use the material in the way I had intended, guided by the methodology of the singularization of history; the extraordinary sources I had at my disposal were straitjacketed and distorted by the frames of reference I had shaped for myself, or learned long before, under quite different circumstances.

My approach to historical subjects sprang from a deeply felt discontent with the development of social and cultural history.[8] I felt that I had failed in my ambition to bring out the role of ordinary people in developments over recent centuries. The broad-brush approach of historians, dealing with society as a whole, meant that actual people disappeared from the picture. By suggesting a narrower approach, I sought to achieve a better understanding of the mindset of ordinary people than had been achieved before. I was not alone in this; such dissenting voices spoke ever more loudly in the closing years of the twentieth century. Yet, even though scholars were ready to admit that social and cultural history was in difficulties, few of them favoured a narrower approach. The majority advocated a move in the opposite direction, i.e. widening the field of research towards a global perspective. And again, Peter N. Stearns is a case in point when he says of this movement within the discipline: 'History as discipline is departing from the national unit, however haltingly and with real political risks, but it (like the world around us) is looking for bigger, not smaller, units of analysis; and social history is participating, and should participate, very strongly in these explorations' (Stearns 2007: 21).

Despite the indisputable change of direction inherent in the ideology of microhistory – as I see it, a change for the better – the problem with this new mode of thinking has lain particularly in the inability of scholars to break loose from the older methods of social and cultural history, viewing microhistory rather as an adjunct to them. One might say that this feature of the status of microhistory within social and cultural history is absolutely in line with that of other movements within the discipline, such as the cultural and the linguistic turns, movements which perhaps seemed more likely to change the status of social history. These movements have been accorded unequal welcomes, but the outcome has, it seems to me, been the same in all cases, that sooner or later the sting has been taken out of them, and they have been smothered within the embrace of the discipline, as was discussed in the last chapter.

To be sure, the discovery of culture and the individual as historical phenomena had a huge influence on the ideology of the microhistorians, but they seemed to lack the self-confidence to take the final step and declare that their research could stand on its own two feet, free from connections to the greater whole. There are always, according to the great majority of microhistorians, distinct limits as to how far it is possible to use such research in explanations of the development of a community, as Ginzburg argued in the interview with Norwegian critic Trygve Riiser Gundersen. On the basis of current practice, Iggers puts it this way: 'The charge that microhistorians examine small communities with little or no reference to a broader context is not justified' (Iggers 1997: 112). Towards the end of his book, he goes further, concluding:

> We have seen how the microhistorians in Italy and Germany, despite their concentration on the local, never lost sight of broader historical and political contexts. In fact they believed that the concentration on the local, which always differed from the 'normal', made it possible to test generalizations.
>
> (Iggers 1997: 139)

All things considered, the influence of the microhistorians and those associated with the cultural turn on the traditional research methods used by historians has been conspicuously small. This comes out quite clearly from a cursory glance at the subjects represented in scholarly journals, where the same themes recur year after year, or even decade after decade: class, race, ethnicity and gender, in macrohistorical contexts.[9] Beyond this, the use of statistical records continues to develop as if nothing had happened, and such research bears witness to the conviction of its practitioners that it is feasible to produce coherent social explanations in which discrete and limited research projects act merely as pieces in the overall jigsaw puzzle.[10]

My personal disappointment is not directed solely at this general line of development within social and cultural history, including the experiments conducted in the spirit of the cultural turn, but also at the fact that microhistory has as yet failed to make any significant impression on contemporary historiography, owing perhaps to a lack of conviction or initiative among microhistorians themselves.

.his is highly regrettable, since I believe that the ideology of microhistory has much to offer if taken at face value.[11]

The problem of microhistory relates to some extent to the development of social and the cultural history in the latter part of the twentieth century, as discussed in the last chapter. The emphasis which has been placed on the empirical approach of the discipline – making social history especially a 'real science' – has prevented phenomena such as microhistory from escaping the discipline's requirement for conventional empirical methods. In the end, the argument has prevailed that scholarly experiments such as those known as microhistorical must comply with the same rules of proof, contextualization and other similar quests for historical truth. This trend can be shown clearly and simply in a schematic diagram:

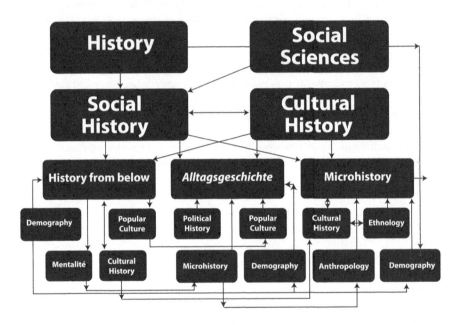

Clearly, the microhistorical approach set out to enrich social and cultural analysis by introducing new, more complex, and more flexible variables. There are, however, limits to such methodological individualism, since we are supposed – according to the 'rules of the discipline' – to seek to discover the patterns governing the formation and functioning of a social entity or, rather, a collective experience (Revel 1995b: 498). This is in full accord with many microhistorians, when they point out that these links are inevitable and unavoidable, that it is impossible to conceive of a historiography without these connections to meta-narratives. There would in fact be no point in all the effort if historiography was not to be connected with greater wholes (Pomata 1998: 99–124).

The flow chart shows why microhistorians never fully succeeded in breaking away from conventional historical methods: their subjects fell within the frames of reference that historians were accustomed to working within, and accepted. But this debate relates mostly to historiographical development in the last decade of the twentieth century. Perhaps there is reason to believe that micro-history has changed since the turn of the century, when most had moved on from postmodernism and taken their approach into new fields of history.[12] There is, at least, every reason to believe that the methods (or ideology) of microhistory have changed in keeping with new trends and directions.

Microhistory in the new century

American scholar Richard D. Brown has written a paper on 'Microhistory and the post-modern challenge', in which he addresses aspects of historical research similar to those I have written about.[13] Brown maintains that microhistory means a focus on small incidents, insignificant in themselves, which reveal larger structures. He underlines particularly that many microhistorians focus on the broader context and believe that they are recounting a story which extends far beyond their actual subject. It may be so in the case of apprentices and journeymen in a French printing shop killing their master's cats, as revealed by Robert Darnton in his famous book; the man who returns from the war claiming to be Martin Guerre, as Natalie Z. Davis shows her readers and that we have already discussed; the inquisition's interrogation of a miller by the name Menocchio in an Italian town because he believes that the world was originally created as a giant cheese, as explored by Carlo Ginzburg in his well-known book: all these writers, and others like them, strive to hitch the subject of their study to far more extensive themes than the study in itself would justify.[14] And, in addition, such academic arguments are based on an excellent theoretical foundation.[15]

In Hayden White's terminology, studies like these rely on the literary trope of synecdoche: a small part represents a larger whole:

> By the trope of Synecdoche [...] it is possible to construe the two parts in the manner of an *integration* within a whole that is *qualitatively* different from the sum of the parts and of which the parts are but *microcosmic* replications.
> (White 1973: 35)

The example given by White to illustrate this point is the expression 'he is all heart'; a part, or phenomenon, stands for the whole. Finnish microhistorian Matti Peltonen observes that his colleagues 'are actually trying to discover very big things with their microscopes' (Peltonen 2001: 350). Richard Brown explains further the provenance of this ideology: 'Like ethnographers, they use the micro study to discover variations in general patterns of behavior, or to reveal larger patterns that have otherwise been hidden' (Brown, R. D. 2003: 15). In other words, this approach derives from cultural anthropology, with its focus on symbols and rituals that represent a common shared culture, under the influence of Clifford Geertz. As is well known, anthropologists generally do field work in only one village, but from their micro-study they claim to derive conclusions about the wider field in which their place is located. Geertz clearly does not see the Balinese cockfight just as an intriguing game, but as an event that reveals basic understandings of the Balinese about what their lives mean. Here we see that Geertz's ideology has obviously blazed a trail for works such as Darnton's *Great Cat Massacre*, mentioned above.[16]

American scholar John Brewer points out that the difference between these two approaches – micro and macro – can be complex, but that it is first and foremost a 'contrast between two very different styles of historical writing,' as he puts it in a very interesting paper on microhistory and everyday life: 'These differences can be expressed in many different ways: as a contrast between structure and narrative, determinism and agency, science and humanism, grand narrative and micro-histories, or as a difference in the poetics of history' (Brewer 2010: 3). In his view there is not much real difference between these two forms, because 'as any theorist of narrative will tell you, there is no *formal* difference between grand narratives and micronarratives' (Brewer 2010: 8). And the reason is precisely that 'they necessarily involve choice, inclusion and exclusion'. His reference here is primarily to the narrative mode, while the idea 'that closeness will lead to different sorts of explanations – is entirely plausible as a methodological or epistemological claim' (Brewer 2010: 9).

Brown states that the conclusions reached by microhistorians can be both incautious and tenuous – whether the work of Ginzburg, Davis and Darnton, for instance, or other lesser known scholars; the truth is that microhistorians have a tendency to expand their generalizations far beyond the material with which they are working. I would wish to add to Brown's comment that, as a consequence of this, they often lose precisely the virtues of the microhistorical focus. Their gaze becomes diffused, from the actual subject of research to the perceived context.

Richard Brown also takes an example of a microhistorian whose focus is entirely on the subject, and hence succeeds in revealing factors which a macro-historical approach would never have brought to light. This is Patricia Cline Cohen and her book *The Murder of Helen Jewett*, in which she explores sexual behaviours in nineteenth-century New York which were probably, strictly speaking, illegal, and which were certainly not 'moral' by the standards of the time.[17] By focusing on one murder case, Cohen succeeded in documenting 'a flourishing, customary sexual counter-culture of astonishing richness and vitality', in which thousands of men and women were involved in New York alone (Brown, R. D. 2003: 16). Brown adds an important point: 'If by reading *The Murder of Helen Jewett* we are holding our eye up to a peephole, that peephole reveals a wide expanse of culture and society, not a tiny chamber' (Brown, R. D. 2003: 16). In other words, Brown demonstrates that those who focus on the subject – and do not seek to generalize beyond what is justified – are more likely to uncover important knowledge about a field which the academic world has believed it understood but, in the end, did not.

Let us recall that American microhistorian Guido Ruggiero has maintained that the works of those who deal with the methods of microhistory are more complex than is generally believed. Those who have criticized microhistory have, he says, 'also tended to call into question the validity of arguments based on single cases. This last critique is easily dealt with, for while many micro-historical narratives focus on one case, they are usually based on much broader research' (Ruggiero 2001: 1146). This is exemplified in his own research, and that of almost all microhistorians I know of. Ruggiero refers here to the way in which many critics of microhistory have remained stuck in the quantitative mode of scholarly research when addressing microhistory; the question of how 'representative' the subject of microhistorical study is becomes an almost over-whelming focus of the critic's interpretation. Here the question turns, of course, on the relationship between the fragment and the whole – micro/macro approach. Hans Renders and Binne De Haan from the Netherlands take a rather favourable view of the debate on the 'representativeness' of each subject, by pointing out that:

> the supposed representativeness of an individual, a human being from the past, contributes in the first place to a better understanding and confirmation of exactly those historical structures and categories for which he or she is considered representative.
>
> (Renders and De Haan 2011: 41–42)

The authors also make a very interesting point about the academic relationship between the fragment and the whole:

> Too often it has been assumed that research on small social communities would teach us something about regional or national history. That is only partly the case, certainly from the perspective of representativeness, and more likely the concept of 'normal exception' fits better in these cases. It teaches us rather more about other social relationships which exercised unexpected impact on general history.
>
> (Renders and De Haan 2011: 39–40)

All four of these – Brown, Ruggiero, Renders and De Haan – underline important factors relating to the practice of history in general. While I do not, for example, share Brown's upbeat view that the microhistorians' approach to their subjects is generally justified, I am convinced that the methods of microhistory have much to offer the discipline, but only if handled correctly. Brown writes:

> Avoiding the broad claims and overarching titles that are the inevitable companions of grand narrative synthesis, they would prefer to lower read-ers' expectations so as to make sure that as authors they can, at the very least, live up to their titles. Though microhistorians may in fact be just as ambitious as synthesizers, their approach is based on a different strategy of persuasion.
>
> (Brown, R. D. 2003: 16)

This is undoubtedly correct. But unfortunately it seems to me that the demand for contextualization overwhelms the emphasis on the importance of the unit of study. 'Yes, the author will admit, my case is exceptional and unrepresentative in some respects, but surely not in every respect', as Brown argues in his article (Brown, R. D. 2003: 16). Brown maintains precisely that microhistorians are motivated by a scepticism about their 'minimalist' approach, which often leads them to contextualize far beyond their actual subject; that they justify this by claiming that they base their studies on real sources, unlike those who work within a broader chronological and geographical framework. 'Though some of historians' large generalizations are fictions, microhistorians believe that is due to the method of generalizing from scattered, inadequate evidence' (Brown, R. D. 2003: 18). The methods or the ideologies of microhistory are thus superior when it comes to the reliability of research findings.

There are of course others, both in the scholarly world and among readers, who have taken an entirely different view of the position of microhistory. German historian Jörn Rüsen explains the unusual attraction of this discipline for many, in an interview with Polish historian Ewa Domanska in the volume *Encounters: Philosophy of History after Postmodernism*:

> If you look at this sympathetic miller's qualities [Menocchio], you find that he accumulates many qualities that the intellectuals of '68 wanted to become cultural values in their society by revolution. For me this is, at least, one of the reasons for the success of this book. It presents a historical image, the realization of the ideal of the '68 generation. They have lost their future in the past. This is compensation: loading the past with disappointed hopes for the future.
>
> (Domanska 1998: 146)

Rüsen stresses here that authors like Ginzburg primarily present material which appeals to people – that their attraction 'lies in the fact that they present counterimages to our present-day life experience', as he puts it. On the other hand, he does not address the route taken by the microhistorian to his/her subject.

Brown, in contrast, is of the view that:

> the glory of microhistory [...] lies in its power to recover and reconstruct past events by exploring and connecting a wide range of data sources so as to produce a contextual, three-dimensional, analytic narrative in which actual people as well as abstract forces shape events.
>
> (Brown, R. D. 2003: 19)

One can certainly agree with these words, and with Brown's view that the microhistorical approach opens up the possibility of emotional connections with our subjects – as I have sought to describe in these chapters, based on my own experience.

Yet others view the position of microhistorians, and the opportunities offered by the microhistorical way of doing history, within the contours of traditional history writing. That appears, at any rate, to be the perspective of Lynn Hunt in her postscript chapter to the book mentioned above, *Encounters*. Examining the position of well-known works by Ginzburg, Davis and Le Roy Ladurie, her conclusion is that they are not consistent with the postmodern agenda:

> These works may exemplify a loss of belief in metanarrative and reflect the fragmentation of knowledge, since they are so insistently local in focus. Yet they brim with confidence in the historian's power to evoke, recapture, and yes, tell the truth about the past, even while raising questions about the way the sources work to distort and distract our vision of what happened. They reflect the best of the current interest in the seemingly insignificant and peripheral things of life, because they insistently use those tiny things to illuminate much broader questions about religion, scientific knowledge, family life, sexual relations, and lower-class aspirations in the past. They certainly do not represent a giving up on history or a loss of conviction about reason; in many respects, Le Roy Ladurie, Davis, and Ginzburg are among the most resolutely 'modernist' of historians, because they push on the constraints of conventional forms, even while writing out of a deep sense of affirmation of the future.
>
> (Domanska 1998: 273)

Hunt's inference appears to be that the days of microhistory, and even of cultural history in general, are numbered; she cites an interview with Peter Burke, to whom this view is attributed, pointing out that 'without careful attention to larger structures of explanation, the local focus loses its edge' (Domanska 1998: 274). The conclusion is thus clear in Hunt's mind: 'The tried and trusted techniques of historians do not seem so out-of-date after all'. While I cannot agree with those words, and am in truth far from sharing that view, I will admit that the big question remains: How can we rely on microhistory continuing to function as an important force within the discipline, and one that is listened to?[18]

Notes

1 Part of the story told in this chapter is taken from my book *Wasteland with Words. A Social History of Iceland* (Magnússon 2010). Acknowledgments to the publisher Reaktion Books in London.
2 For a collection of essays dealing with the concept of metanarrative, see: (Fox and Stromquist (eds) 1998). Allan Megill makes a distinction between 'master narrative' and 'grand narrative'. A master narrative he sees as a 'big story' overshadowing all the small stories; it is often hidden and waiting for the historian to discover it. In other words, his 'master narrative' is what I call macrohistory, i.e. historical studies which extend over large geographical areas and time frames. Thus, to Megill (and me), 'master narrative' is more limited than 'grand narrative' (also named metanarrative), and it is the latter which is likely to give the reader 'the big picture' (Megill 1995: 151–73). Other scholars use these words and concepts in different ways: see for example (Ross 1995: 651–77; Klein 1995: 275–98).

3 See an interesting discussion of the modernisation theory in Brewer, J. (2010) 'Debate Forum: Microhistory and the Histories of Everyday Life', *Cultural and Social History* 7:1: 87–109. Also published in CAS-LMU e series 2010/5: 5–7 which is used in this chapter.

4 The following publications address, in their different ways, the power of the grand narrative: (Berkhofer 1995; Fuery and Mansfield 1997; Hoffer 2004; van der Linden 2003: 69–75; McDonald (ed.) 1996).

5 See interesting discussions, both regarding the importance of microhistory for bringing out different voices in history, and criticism of those methods, in the following articles: (Bruegel 2006: 523–53; Lamoreaux 2006: 555–61).

6 This is related to, though perhaps less radical than, the use of the term singularization by philosopher Gilles Deleuze and psychoanalyst Felix Guattari in their 'schizoanalysis'; the 'process of singularisation' questions the regular hierarchy – the order of values – and actually calls for the inversion of the system of values. See, for example: (Deleuze and Guattari 1983).

7 In this regard I would like to point to a research project under the name the Perdita Project: Early Modern Women's Manuscript Compilations, carried out by a team of scholars based at Nottingham Trent University and Warwick University in England with the aim of creating a database of women's manuscripts from various parts of the world. Publications arising from this project include (Justice and Tinker 2002; Burke and Gibson 2004; Millman and Wright 2005). For further information on the Perdita Project, see www.warwick.ac.uk/english/perdita/html/.

8 A very similar view on the status of social and cultural history may be found in Martin Bruegel's article (Bruegel 2006: 523–61).

9 See also (Stearns (ed.) 1994) which contains a good summary of the kinds of subject worked on within the realms of social history.

10 Such views are widely expressed, i.e. regarding the importance of quantitative methods and their superiority to 'impressionistic sources.' See, for example: (Lamoreaux 2006: 555–61).

11 I wish to draw attention to the fact that I refer to microhistory, from time to time, as an ideology rather than a method. I take the view that microhistory is first and foremost an ideology combining both a methodological and a conceptual framework, even though I refer to it most often as 'the methods of microhistory'. At some level, the word 'method' fails to cover the mode of thinking behind microhistory since it suggests that the phenomenon is of a purely technical nature. See a discussion of these terms and their use in Fairburn's book, *Social History: Problems, Strategies and Methods* (Fairburn 1999: 4–5).

12 See a recent discussion of the status of history after the cultural and the linguistic turns in *AHR* Forum: Historiographic 'Turns' in Critical Perspective. *American Historical Review* 117: 3 (2012). See the following articles: (Surkis 2012: 700–722; Wilder 2012: 723–45; Cook, J.W. 2012: 746–71; Ghosh 2012: 772–93; Thomas 2012: 794–803; Perl-Rosenthal 2012: 804–13).

13 (Brown, R. D. 2003: 1–20). Recently several papers have been published which address microhistory from different aspects. See, for example: (Mosley 2006: 915–33; Brewer 2010: 1–16; de Vivo 2010: 387–97; Sandwell 2008: 124–38; Aljunied 2011: 22–35; Barth, V. 2008: 22–37; Szijártó 2008, 2002: 209–15). See also: (Sogner 1995: 347–59).

14 At this point it may be helpful to specify various writings that fall under the heading of microhistory, though clearly one might argue endlessly about what qualifies or does not qualify to be on such a list. Not all the works listed here can necessarily be classified directly as microhistory, but all employ its methods in one way or another with the broad picture in mind: (Berenson 1992; Berenson 1988: 31–55; Brown, J. C. 1986). Brown's book spawned an interesting discussion within the academic world: (Bell, M., and Brown, J. C., 1987: 485–511). See also: (Brucker 1986;

Kuehn 1989: 512–34; Molho 1987: 96–100). Also: (Clark 1990: 47–68; Corbin 1992; Cook, H. J. 1994; Duggan 1993: 791–814; Egmond and Mason 1997; Muir and Ruggiero (eds) 1994; King 1994; Kingdon 1995; Martin 1992: 613–26; McLaren 1993; Muir 1991a: vii–xxviii, 1991b: 123–25; Ozment 1986, 1996; Pucci 1997; Muir and Ruggiero (eds) 1990; Sherr 1991: 1–22; Srebnick 1995; Wolff 1988). Two other well-known and outstanding works of scholarship should also be mentioned, which display affinities of one sort or another to the methods of microhistory: (Cipolla 1979; Le Roy Ladurie 1978).

15 See (Davis 1983; Darnton 1984; Ginzburg 1980).

16 See discussion of this issue in: (Magnússon and Ólafsson 2012: 495–524).

17 See some of her other works on similar issues: (Cohen 1993: 133–45, 1990: 374–89, 1992: 33–52, 1995: 34–57).

18 For further discussions on the development of the methods of microhistory see the following monographs and collections of essays: (Castrén, Lonkila and Peltonen (eds) 2004). See for example essays in these books by: (Cerutti 2004: 17–40; Ago 2004: 41–50; Levi 2004: 71–86; Peltonen 2004: 87–101; Gribaudi 2004: 102–29). See also: (Brooks, DeCorse and Walton (eds) 2008; Ulbricht 2009; Budde, Conrad and Janz (eds) 2006; Lima 2006; Amato 2008; Ouwenell 2005; Chin 2011: 341–57).

8 A West Side story, and the one who gets to write it

Beat! Beat! Drums![1]

In recent years there has been a revolution in scholarly circles in the ways in which historical sources such as manuscripts and private documents are used and thought about. The 'cultural turn' and the new perspectives it has opened up have attributed great importance to the direct, first-hand testimony (ego-documents) of people from all levels of society, and sought expressly to direct a spotlight on those who have experienced or taken part in historical events. A high value was placed on people's actual personal experience of events and phenomena. This has provided opportunities to analyse people's understanding and perceptions of life, the workings of the institutions that form part of their daily condition, and their links with other individuals in their immediate environment. Ego-documents of various types have taken on greater significance within the world of scholarship.[2]

In a methodology which I have been developing in recent years called the 'textual environment', I set out to address certain central issues regarding ego-documents and their use and meaning. Subjects for investigation include how the individual is shaped by text, how scribal culture, for example, has had a formative influence on people in past times, and the nature of the interplay between texts (narratives) and life (reality). The basis of the scribal culture and the way it has developed have been considered in an international context, with regard to the semiotic status of manuscripts.

In parallel with the changes in outlook associated with the cultural turn, the linguistic turn has led to a major rethinking of the concept of the individual as an independent entity of expression. How was it possible for the testimony of an individual to be of any value, when that person's mode of expression was so inextricably bound up in linguistic systems that there was no way of communicating experience from the past on the basis of the thoughts and feelings of the person involved? Poststructuralists have attempted to address this question in a variety of ways, but to some extent it seems fair to say that the approach offered by discourse analysis – in which significance is read into discrete narratives of events, phenomena and people that would otherwise be difficult to approach – has taken on increasing importance. By investigating all the strands of such a discourse as minutely as possible, the scholar provides himself with a means of deconstructing courses of events and ideas that would otherwise be concealed within the complex web of the 'official' discourse of the grand narratives that stand in an imagined relationship to 'the past,' conceived within the mind of the historian.[3] The new intellectual insights require historians to seek ways of approaching their research material from different perspectives than the ones offered by official or public discourse – to open our ears to the multiplicity of voices that are invariably raised on any subject and be prepared to come to grips with the contradictions and inconsistencies that resonate in the text. The 'singularization of history', which I have already discussed at some length in this book, is aimed precisely at defining the opportunities that sources give scholars to talk about the past in as varied a way as possible, without becoming trapped within the received channels of the grand narratives.

The central element of the analysis has been the manuscripts themselves, their creation, their context within the events they describe, the opportunities they present for analysis, and how they tie in with events that take place when they are used. What kind of meaning can be attributed to manuscripts or texts of any sort that express people's personal opinions? And how can we justify their use in academic research? This approach is, no doubt, essentially a historical one, but at the same time it has taken cognisance of the philosophy of the text – its metaphysics – in the sense that I have addressed the underlying premises behind text creation, how this creation finds correspondence in life as people perceive it. As a fundamental working principle, I have made an attempt to consider the interplay of *events*, *narrative* (*conscious and unconscious*), *analysis* (*conscious and unconscious*), and *new events* that arise as life moves forward. This 'living' research model I call 'the textual environment,' extending to all the aspects noted above. I say 'living', since I take into consideration events that impact on the form of the narrative and the analytical process during the creation of each.

The thinking behind the 'textual environment' is to draw scholars' attention to both the content of the source – the textual space – and to its embracing environment – meanings and connections that constitute the textual whole. The approach extends to aspects such as vocabulary and general diction, spelling, foregrounded textual elements of various types, abridgements and the presentation of the manuscript, in addition to other factors related to both the manuscript and its creation (type of paper, writing implements, working procedures, etc.), as well as the use to which the manuscript or text can be put under various circumstances.[4] The 'textual environment' is the totality of the space that makes the text (narrative, things, illustrations) the medium that its contents and outer form have to offer. This research model is certainly under the influence of Ginzburg's 'evidential paradigm', where the principle is to study the most trivial details of each subject matter at hand, as the famous Giovanni Morelli used to do when studying the details of a work of art, in order to identify its deeper meaning (Ginzburg 1992).

Language is of course crucial here: how the person expresses him/herself about him/herself, the community around him/her – daily life – and the mindset of contemporaries. Accounts of events and circumstances, conversations, wordplay, self-image and other factors regarding the individual concerned provide a basis for bringing out the *polyphony* of the text – the paradoxes and the multiple viewpoints which are likely to reveal the evolution of society in a more diverse way than has been done before. We are all familiar with such contradictions in our own lives: at times they may become overwhelming, as one 'misguided' decision follows another, propelled by chance, or by primal urges. The continuous narrative of conventional history seeks to eliminate such contradictions, because they muddle the storyline and the 'progressive' vision which is an inevitable adjunct of such history-writing. The discourse analyses recommended here thus focuses on the language and its position in the past, as this is where we are most likely to find an autonomous manifestation of the past.

Scholars within the field of book history have worked with similar ideas under the English term 'paratext,' denoting the various forms of books and additional material to be found in them that give a particular indication of the true meaning of their contents.[5] This concept draws on the ideas of the French literary theorist Gérard Genette, who terms this part of the 'intertextuality' of a work, i.e. everything that, explicitly or implicitly, forms connections between one text and others (Genette 1997; Helgason 2007). With the 'textual environment,' however, the intention was to go further, to immerse oneself in the wider context of the work and investigate how it becomes a part of the scribal culture of any area and at different times. The approach is in fact what might be termed a 'sociology of texts': everything that touches the scope of any manuscript, wherever and however it enters the frame (Spiegel 2005: 1–31). This interplay between sources and the past, particularly the sources' muted echo of historical time, means that it is important to work with the 'textual environment' in a unified and holistic way and avoid rupturing the inherent context of the text.

American anthropologist Joanne Rappaport presented a most interesting approach to the use of sources in her book *Cumbe Reborn*, on the society and history of indigenous peoples in South America (Rappaport 1994: 20–23, 65–70). She places emphasis on the concept of 'living archives', to direct attention to the fact that the sources that exist in various manifestations are often a part of the daily life of ordinary people in the present, as well as being part of the conceptual world of the scholar once he/she starts to work on them. Viewed in this way, sources are seen as ever-changing and 'living' phenomena. A similar approach is found in the work of American historian Luise White in her book *Speaking with Vampires*, in which she tackles the history of peoples in Africa who in the vast majority of cases had no written sources from earlier times (White 2000: 3–86). Here 'texts' of other kinds became a motive force in people's lives: material that directed how they thought about and interpreted the past and their history. In these works, the distinction between public sources and oral sources, between sources that are part of the man-made landscape of societies and written sources in whatever form, breaks down; the only thing that matters is how the sources are used in the context of time and space. The rationale for this approach lies in the perception that the sources are not solely pieces of information, but phenomena that are 'alive'. They are used to explain the background to specific conditions that are always contingent on the thinking and ideas of those who speak about them. They can be used if the 'textual environment' is clear.[6]

The individual in history and the biographical method

But what kind of history am I proposing in this book? I am, certainly, urging scholars to give plenty of thought to the sources they work with – to seek to approach them on their own terms; to consider their context, the environment from which they emerged, how they have been preserved and how used, and to examine their status in the present day. All these factors yield information about those who are in some way connected with the sources: those who create them, shape the ideology that lies behind them, preserve them from one period to another, and work with them, in real time.

I have also called upon historians to approach the perspective of the individual as closely as possible. It makes no difference here what the subject is. As soon as one seeks to examine it from the viewpoint of those who are connected with the subject, directly or indirectly, the potential of analysis is transformed, and new dimensions are thrown open. I am of the view that microhistory which places an emphasis on sticking to the subject, and striving to analyse it as minutely as possible – and from the perspective of the individual – constitutes an important experiment in approaching the past in a different way from what has been done before.

The question may be asked: Am I proposing that microhistorians should confine themselves to writing biographies? What is the relationship between microhistory and biography?[7] It must be borne in mind that historians in the western world have been abandoning biography in droves, as a tool for historical analysis, although scholars from other disciplines have enthusiastically seized upon it (Renders and De Haan 2011: 40). It has been pointed out that history students have rarely been permitted to write doctoral theses which might be classified as biographies; cutting-edge academic journals will not accept papers based upon biographies of individuals, and are reluctant to review published biographies; in university promotion systems, academics receive no points for published biographies; and academic historians who use the biographical form refuse to be labelled biographers (Nasaw 2009: 573–78). If they have been tempted – as they often are – into biographical writing, they are reluctant to admit any familiarity with that tradition, or recognize that they belong to it in any way, shape or form.

But, in the end, the *biographical method* (note how I use the concept) is an important analytical tool for historians, regardless of how it is applied.[8] Thus the biographical method in various guises has established itself in the field, and has often given rise to productive and interesting analysis, *inter alia* by well-known microhistorians, of phenomena of which little was known before. At the same time, the conventional biography has retained its place, primarily due to its popularity with the public. Writers know that biography is the way to the heart of many readers. Its appeal is indisputable.

In the last decades of the twentieth century biography as a historical method was reborn in many western countries, especially in the approach of specialized cultural and social historians.[9] The most striking quality of such works is that they address new social groups, studying people of the working and peasant class, often in a highly original and interesting way (Renders and De Haan 2011: 41). The writers and politicians – or simply the great and the good of the relevant country – who had been the most popular subjects for biography, were no longer in the limelight, although stories of such individuals retained their appeal for many readers. Common people who had never been famous had, nonetheless, left some traces which had survived, and with which historians could work. In many cases this was because the individuals had been in trouble with the law, while some had written down their own ideas and thoughts about their lives. Material of this kind was often useful in historical research which applied the *biographical method*, whose strengths lay in the methods of microhistory, as witness many examples discussed above. In such works the biography of the individual did not comprise the bulk of the study: in general some fragmentary knowledge of such a life, or some specific aspect of it, was the focus. This kind of history had moved a long way from the conventional biography, which generally traces the course of a life from the cradle to the grave.

Experiments of this kind went so far that scholars started to work on the lives of people about whom few, if any, sources survived.[10] Such ventures coincided with the fundamental ideas of many microhistorians, who sought all possible ways of showing ordinary people in an illuminating way, as agents in their own life.

The biographical method thus evolved towards scholarly experiments which have focused on research on 'the self': how the self has evolved and been influenced by diverse factors which are part of a person's life and work – gender, nationality, class, educational background and so on – including even minor aspects of daily life. Research on 'the self' aimed to achieve an understanding of how people dealt with fashioning themselves in the context of their own time, and how people were equipped to be agents in the sequence of their own affairs. At that same time, the 'objective' scholarly focus which had been predominant through most of the twentieth century – the nuts and bolts of the historian's craft – was increasingly being called into question, as a desirable objective, or even a possible perspective (Novick 1988). The 'subjective' approach was, at that same time, gaining a following. Scholars were seeking to bring out in their work the individual's experience of life and existence, and of the phenomena they were researching. Historians too stepped boldly into their own texts, and took their place beside their subjects.[11] Research on 'the self' thus became one aspect of interesting scholarly experiments which aimed to juxtapose the individual and known resources on his/her life, with analysis of the self-fashioning both of the subject and of the historian him/herself. The 'biographical approach' hence became part of the apparatus used by microhistorians in their research, and the emphasis on the 'self' of the individuals involved became one of the characteristic features of such studies (Jarrick 1999: 181–87).

The 'self' in public sources

A personal perspective on the past is undeniably to be found in many sources. We tend to think primarily of first-person sources (ego-documents) in that context, but such perspectives may nonetheless be found in other sources, for instance *public sources*. Study of these can, if correctly handled, yield impressive insights into the lives of the individuals who are the subjects of the sources. The reason for this is first and foremost that the sources tend to have been prepared with some specific public objective in mind, which bears only indirectly on the historian's subject. So scholars or others who gain access to such sources have an unusually good opportunity to study the personality, as the subject is approached from an unexpected direction. 'One night in 1980, when I was living as a student in East Berlin, I came back with a girlfriend to my room in a crumbling Wilhelmine tenement house in the borough of Prenzlauer Berg,' writes Timothy Garton Ash, a journalist and professor at Oxford University, in his book *The File*:

> This was a room with a view: a view into it. Large French windows gave directly onto a balcony, and, were it not for the net curtains, people living across the street could look straight in. As we embraced on the narrow bed, Andrea suddenly pulled away, finished undressing, went over to the window and threw open the net curtains. She turned on the glaring main light and then came back to me. Had this been, say, Oxford, I might have been a little surprised about the bright light and the open curtains. But this was Berlin, so I thought no more about it.
>
> (Garton Ash 1997: 5)

The author recalls this event as he sits holding his 'file' for the first time – a collection of secret information about himself! The file contains detailed reports on his conduct and actions during his student years in East Germany in the late 1970s; the secret police (Stasi) had observed his every move. After the fall of the Berlin Wall and the collapse of the regimes to the east of the notional Iron Curtain, Garton Ash – known to the Stasi as 'Romeo' – had the opportunity, like tens of thousands more who had been under Stasi surveillance, to read what had been written about him. He returned to Germany in the early 1990s, to be met with a horrible sight. In a file which contained 325 pages of information about him, he was able to read reports by Stasi personnel and their informers about his own life (Garton Ash 1997: 22). The Garton Ash file was not particularly large; he mentions the world-famous musician Wolf Biermann as an example of a person under far more detailed surveillance, as witness a Stasi file of about 40,000 pages. Garton Ash discovered that some of his friends had reported to the Stasi on his actions and ideas. One in every fifty East German adults is believed to have been a Stasi informer at that time; this is an extraordinarily high proportion, practically unparalleled in history (Garton Ash 1997: 84). Friends informed on their friends, relatives informed on each other, and even husbands and wives! Garton Ash says:

> The effect of reading a file can be terrible. I think of the now famous case of Vera Wollenberger, a political activist from my friend Werner Krätschell's parish in Pankow, who discovered from reading her file that her husband, Knud, had been informing on her ever since they met. They would go for a walk with the children on Sunday, and on Monday Knud would pour it all out to his Stasi case officer.
>
> (Garton Ash 1997: 21)

Vera Wollenberger refers to her husband as 'Knud-Donald' in the memoirs she wrote later; 'Donald' was his Stasi code-name. It need hardly be added that the couple separated after the truth came out!

In his Stasi file Garton Ash was able to read about his own life as recorded by a public agency, cross-check it with his own diary of that time, and recall innumerable memories which had surfaced as he read the file – to study his own 'self'. So what did Garton Ash intend to do next?

> My plan of action, now, is to investigate their investigation of me. I shall pursue their inquiry through this file, try to track down both the informers and the officers on my case, consult other files, compare the Stasi record with my own memories, with the diary and notes I kept at the time, and with the political history I have since written about this period. And I shall see what I find.
>
> (Garton Ash 1997: 17–18)

And that is precisely what Garton Ash did, demonstrating how it is possible to make use of unusual public records to throw light on an individual's life, and on society in general. This spectacular work also leads one to think of the amount of data amassed in various ways about the citizens of democracies.

We do not necessarily need Stasi files in order to approach the individual and his/her actions in a new and unexpected manner. It is entirely possible to imagine carrying out an experiment by following a person through his/her life through public sources relating to him/her. These might include, for instance, various financial data kept by banks and other financial institutions (such as credit-card transactions), medical records, judicial documents (if the person has come up against the forces of law), educational records, and other sources for the person's dealings with public bodies. Such documents are all chock-full of personal data, which conform, however, with the laws of sources. They must, in other words, be deconstructed – to bring out, for instance, how the forms of the sources determine the place of the fragments of knowledge they contain. These sources could then be compared with the personal recollections of the subject, including extant ego-documents: letters, diaries, memoranda, photographs, school assignments, and so on. Thus the possibility would be created, as for Garton Ash, to approach an interesting picture of people in society – to bring out how the 'self' is brought into existence in a dialogue within the private and the public space. The problem entailed by analysis of this kind tends to be that it is hard to define the interaction of sources and the people involved. The classic question is, of course: How well does the source depict the life of the people involved? And that question entails another, no less important: How does a source come to be?

A twenty-first-century love story

After many years' experience of the use of life writing or ego-documents in academic research, covering all types of personal sources as well as other related manuscripts, as recounted in Chapters 5 and 7, I wanted to explore their actual significance and meaning for scholarship in greater depth. My discovery of the tragedy of Níels Jónsson, after I had completed my study, motivated me to consider the place of sources in historical research. In fact, I wanted to examine the interplay between the sources and the individuals to whom they relate, directly or indirectly. To be able to follow the previously-mentioned approach, I became fully aware of the fact that I had to step forward in person into the research arena as an active participant, the person who records the narrative, analyses it and lives and moves within the events associated with it. In fact, I wished to make an attempt to adopt positions both in 'the past' and in 'the history,' so to speak – to assess my own actions in a historical text and investigate how 'the narrative' has influenced my experience of 'what happened'. In this way I wanted to create an opportunity to compare and analyse problems that one generally faces with sources from past times, and address the question of how best to work with such material in academic research. I was aware, however, that it could prove very difficult to gain such an opportunity – that such circumstances would not often arise in the life of one person.

And yet, out of the blue I found myself in the situation of sitting at every place at the table: being part of the past, and the one who studied it, wrote about its context, and experienced in real time all that the process offered. In other words I was given the opportunity to test my own ideas, in my own personal life. This approach of mine requires some explanation, since it provided me with an unusual opportunity to analyse the interlinking of *events*, *narratives*, *analysis*, and *new events* – the research model I explained earlier in this chapter. What I intend to consider here are both some book projects that I produced a few years ago, that may be viewed as 'academic happenings', and the events on which they were based.

On Gay Pride Day (August 12) 2006 in Reykjavík, I met a woman with whom I developed a close relationship. This romance was from the very outset extremely intense, as manifested in a constant flow of letters and e-mails, text messages, long entries in my diary (I had been a passionate diary-writer since 1996) about the affair and the woman who occupied my thoughts, countless phone calls, and hours together every day. As things worked out, before long I set about writing a book that I published at Christmas 2006, a book project that was produced just like any other book, 166 pages, but printed in only two copies, under the title in Icelandic *Næturnar hafa augu eins og þú: Saga úr Vesturbæ* [The Nights Have Eyes Like You: A West Side Story].

The concept of the book was that I invented a narrator – a historian – who had acquired all the above-mentioned sources, and spun from them the tale from the beginning until December 2006, when the book was published. The fact was that the woman I had fallen for had wanted to break off our relationship soon after it began, when she realized that I was only slightly younger than her parents, and that I had a strong, though indirect, connection to her past. She was born when her mother was only 18 years old; she grew up on the same street as I in Reykjavík, and of course everyone in the street knew when the baby was born – and also knew when the young mother tragically died when her child was only six years old. I still remember the affectionate feelings I had for the little girl who had lost her young mother. But I did not keep tabs on her later life – the age difference between us being about 17 years. In 1996 we met again, and by chance I realized who she was. We met at the History Department of the University of Iceland, where she was a student and I a teacher. But at that time our acquaintanceship was brief and distant.

Ten years passed before I met her once more, on Gay Pride Day 2006. Our relationship progressed rapidly. But when she became aware of the old connection, she was distressed, and plainly told me she wished to end the relationship. I was desolate, as I had fallen for her in record time. I wrote to her a declaration of my love. And the letter had the desired effect; after some thought and consultation with her friends, she decided to go on. But I continued to write her letters, in which I described my feelings in some detail as I experienced them. She received such epistles every two or three days, and after the tenth she remarked, 'we really ought to keep all this writing organized'. At that point I was struck with the idea of documenting the entire relationship from start to finish, with the idea of publishing it in book form in due course. And it transpired that I had a remarkable amount of written material about our relationship – the main part consisting of diary entries, naturally. I often used my diary to record my emotional state, as I passed through one whirlwind after another. Our feelings went from one extreme to another: we spanned the whole emotional scale – wept and laughed alternately, and everything in between.

In the end, the written material was all available, and the course of events was rapid and gripping. Once the decision had been made that I would write a book about us, in some form, I pursued it with passion, and worked energetically to keep records of the whole storyline in our lives – to describe the emotional roller-coaster ride of the first four months of our relationship. I wanted to convey to her, as accurately as I could, how I was really feeling. It was of course a bold notion, but a tempting prospect for one who has focused on minute analysis of events from the past.

At a certain point, when it became clear that there was a real possibility of the book coming into existence, I started to consider the question of production. I realized that I would have to tell her that the publication was forthcoming, as she had not realized this before. I had to inform her that I must send the work to be printed, and that this meant that various strangers would see the text. As the descriptions of our love affair were very explicit and personal, I wanted her permission to continue. In brief, she approved. And, what was more, we agreed that she would compile material from e-mails between her and three close women friends about our relationship. For she had told me at the start that she would share 'everything' with them about our romantic rendezvous. I must admit that, at the time, I was far from happy with this arrangement, but had to accept it. But when I received the e-mail correspondence, (more-or-less) anonymized, the new text added a vast amount to the narrative of the book. The narrator had, in other words, plenty of material to work with; and the result was a 166-page book about the first four months of our life together!

Initially I was proud of myself for putting together this book which, if I may say so myself, was remarkably coherent, and captured the attention of both its readers (my girlfriend and me). She had been expecting a few A4 pages describing how we had come together, but when she received a proper book – a printed, bound hardback with a real cover design – she was both thrilled and speechless. And I went a step further: at the same time as the book was published I had an image of a seahorse and the lady's nickname tattooed on my right leg. Both – the book and the tattoo – were obviously over-the-top declarations of my love for her. My emotions were literally boundless. I had to express my love in as extreme a fashion as I could, and those were the ways I chose. Never before had I lost control of myself in this way. And at every moment I was possessed by the whole experience. I was, naturally, living in the now – feeling her love, and specific events relating to our life together – which passed, however, at breathtaking speed. But between our lovemaking, I worked through the relationship in text, in such diverse ways that the experience acquired manifold significance.

Though the work was intended first and foremost as an expression of my mind, an attempt to explain my deepest emotions to a woman who had come into my life, while also being a somewhat ingenuous declaration of love, I swiftly realized that what I had in my hands was something that was in many respects unusual, in that I had myself been part of a creation process in the events, narrative, analysis and then new events that occurred as our lives moved forward. It dawned on me that what had been created here was an opportunity for an innovative analysis of how a 'text' comes into being and what effect it has on the 'course of events' that the narrative is supposed to describe – and *vice versa*, how the events can come to influence the text. The following schematic diagram is drawn up based on what happened, and to illustrate the situation created in this case by the interplay of text and events/situation:

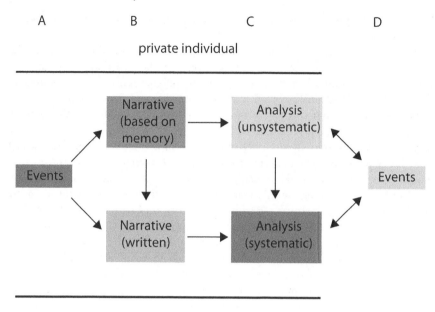

academic observer + private individual = *Næturnar hafa augu eins og þú*
– book + event
– A + B = traditional object of academic study
– C = usually carried out by an outside party (academic)
– A + B + C = processing calls for discontinuity; two-way link between A and B is broken
– A + B + C generate D, a new event commanding greater scholarly interest
– S. G. Magnússon as participant at all stages as both private individual and academic observer

Through writing books, a way opens up to study the process outlined above and orient oneself as to how important the *narrative* could be for the individual's (my own) perception and emotional involvement in what was happening – in fact, in the whole unfolding of the relationship. Though I may have started out from the events surrounding the way we were drawn together and what led up to it, it was in the narrative that they took on the significance that turned them into something that seemed of high importance. The experience was, that is to say, dressed up in specific clothing by the text, and this came to have by far the greatest significance within the narrative in which this significance arose. Thus, the narrative is in this sense the key to the past on its own terms. This at least is the hypothesis from which I start in my approach. It can hardly be otherwise, since the scholar's focus on and involvement in other people's texts can scarcely be other than a fragmentary and disjointed realization of what actually happened. For these reasons I believe that the scholar needs to look to ways of studying texts on their own terms, and one option here is to employ my concept of 'singularization', possibly with the aid of the research model which I have referred to as the 'textual environment'.

Immediately after the first book was published in 2006, I started work on a sequel – but now with my eyes open to the multifaceted relationship between events, narrative, analysis and new events. The writing was completed in December 2007 – a year after the first book was produced – and the book came out under the Icelandic title *Andardráttur þinn er tungumálið mitt: Ástarsaga úr Vesturbæ* [Your Breath is My Language: A Love Story from the West Side], 309 pages. The whole book project ultimately became a trilogy with the publication of *Spánar kóngurinn: Ástarsaga* [The King of Spain: A Love Story] (Reykjavík, 2009), a work of 149 pages which, unlike its predecessors, was issued for general readership in September 2009. Here I go the whole way and describe both how the relationship has reference to the pasts of the two lovers, and how it has been shaped in a 'text' that came into existence simultaneously with the events, and moved forward in the present.

It is against the background of these three works that I have had an opportunity to investigate more closely the interrelationship between the four factors outlined above: events, narrative, analysis, and new events. It is clear to me that the complexity level of each factor can increase sharply as new information enters the scheme (as, for example, with the publication of *Spánar kóngurinn*), since new events and new situations can have a major impact on the individual factors within the model. The processing itself ends in a new narrative, which again calls for a new analysis which affects events going forward into the future. This intricate and many-sided course of events has been one of the main subjects for the research I have presented here in this book. The process described above demonstrates that it is of great importance for historians to examine a source from as many different perspectives as possible, and seek to deconstruct its meaning and position within its proper context.

The woman who seized my heart and soul as described above in the autumn of 2006 is named Tinna Laufey Ásgeirsdóttir; she is now my wife.

We have moved a long way from conventional notions of the connections between events, narrative and the 'reality' that is supposed to lie within the narrative. Through the creation of the two book projects, and of the more traditional third book, ways open up to explore in depth the interplay of different aspects of manuscripts and how the 'textual environment' shapes its individual elements. Whether biographical method, or some other, is used in that analysis, I am of the view that accurate textual analysis in the spirit of the 'singularization of history' method will be a beneficial influence on the research of scholars in the future.

My conclusion, which I draw from the experience of the 'fate' of my research project on the two brothers from Strandir, discussed earlier in the book, is that one must not depart from the subject itself; that it is important to stick to the sources with which one is working, and that this is also likely to produce insights and revelations which will be important for people's understanding of the past. First and foremost, I urge scholars to look at the sources they have, and to do their utmost not to be drawn into the grand narrative, which will govern their interpretation of the subject. Every individual subject contains such a big story, such a complex of connections, that there is no need to look beyond the framework of the study.

Notes

1 Title taken from Walt Whitman's poem 'Beat! Beat! Drums!' which was a patriotic call to arms for the North, written as the American Civil War was beginning.
2 See an important article by Rudolf Dekker on the formation of the concept of ego-documents: (Dekker 2002: 13–37). See also the following articles: (Fulbrook and Rublack 2010: 263–71; Magnússon and Ólafsson 2002: 175–209).
3 These issues have been much discussed in recent years. I refer here to several publications which have had a positive influence upon my thinking: (Biernacki 2000: 289–310; Cabrera 2004; Munslow 1997; Wilson 1999).
4 There has been considerable discussion of this issue among publishers of documentary sources in the western world. Philologists such as Stephen Orgel, David Scott Kastan, W. Speed Hill and others have addressed, for instance, the role of the editor in the publication of texts in a special edition of *Shakespeare Studies*, led by Susan Zimmerman. See the following papers: (Orgel 1996: 23–29; Kastan 1996: 30–37; Hill 1996: 38–46).
5 Important contributions to research in this area include: (McKenzie 1986; Richardson 1994; Burke, P. 1996).
6 Philosophers such as Paul Ricoeur have also investigated the semantic and hermeneutic properties of texts, and by delving deep beneath the surface of the texts themselves drawn attention to the complex interplay of images and symbols in them and their connections with their environment. See (Ricoeur 1981, 1984).
7 I wish to refer once more to a most interesting paper by Hans Renders and Binne De Haan, which discusses among other things the relationship between biography and microhistory: (Renders and De Haan 2011: 32–42). See also a well-known paper by Lepore, 'Historians Who Love Too Much: Reflections on Microhistory and Biography' (Lepore 2001: 129–44).
8 See books such as: (Ginzburg 1980; Davis 1983; Le Roy Ladurie 1978; Kates 1995; Ozment 1986; Tillyard 1994; Reay 2002).
9 Much has been written in recent years about biography. Suffice it to mention here an enlightening recent roundtable which took place in 2009 in the *American Historical Review* on the academic status of biography. See *AHR* Roundtable: Historians and Biography, *American Historical Review* 114:3 (2009): (Nasaw 2009: 573–78; Banner 2009: 579–86; Brown, J.M. 2009: 587–95; Brown, K. 2009: 596–605; Fleming 2009: 606–14; Hellbeck 2009: 615–24; Kessler-Harris 2009: 625–30; Mann 2009: 631–39; Taylor, B. 2009: 640–51; Vardi 2009: 652–61).
10 See also an interesting paper by Robin Fleming, 'Writing Biography at the Edge of History', cited above, abut biographical writings in the near-absence of sources. The same applies to Kristján Mímisson's archaeological research, discussed in his paper: (Mímisson 2012: 455–71).
11 See, for example, the following books on the issue: (Stanley 1992; Eley 2005; Sewell 2005). Also Spiegel's study (Spiegel 2007: 1–19), which addresses the place of the individual in the postmodern and poststructural scholarly discourse. Finally I wish to mention a recent issue of *Rethinking History* (2009) which addresses similar issues to those discussed here. See, for example, a paper by (Hollow 2009: 43–52). I myself have stepped into the scholarly text in my works (Magnússon 2007), and also in the second part of this book.

Postscript

To step into the same stream twice

What is microhistory? As indicated in this book, the question can be answered in many different ways. But there are a number of factors that are central to a discussion of microhistory, which are generally recognized as being indispensible on the agenda of this type of history. The following matters have been touched on in this book in one form or another: (1) the role of narrative; (2) synthesis in history; (3) history and fiction; (4) historical subjectivity; (5) normal exceptions; (6) the reduction of the scale of observation; (7) the individual and the past; (8) ethnological and anthropological methodology; (9) microhistory and relativism; (10) contextualization. I shall briefly discuss some of them here in the final chapter, with the intention of summing up the principal features of microhistory as they have been addressed in the book as a whole.

The methods of microhistory

After microhistory gained prominence in the 1990s, having existed for over twenty years as a more-or-less peripheral phenomenon, a great deal of debate took place about the characteristics of microhistory, and its position within the humanities. The reason for this was, naturally, the advent of postmodernism and poststructuralism in international historical discourse in the late 1980s.[1] The urgent questions were: Where should microhistory be placed? Was it a part of this new wave of scholarly focus? Or was it simply a high-flown version of conventional personal history, or even vernacular lore, or part of the local tale tradition around the world, as was maintained by some?

It must be admitted that those who have addressed the idea of microhistory have been ambivalent in their attitude to it and to the new trends in scholarship. While keeping a half-open mind with regard to these scholarly experiments, they have also been highly critical. Comments have transmitted the message that microhistory is seen as a systematic ideology which conforms to certain laws. The focus has been particularly on the reduction of the scale of observation and the level of generalization offered by the subjects of microhistory: whether microhistorians can say something about the 'bigger picture' in history which relates only indirectly to the subject. Conventional history has, from its earliest days, primarily focused on the latter aspect: aiming to throw light on developments over long periods, on large geographical areas, and on dramatic events. So there was nothing surprising in the title of American social historian Charles Tilly's book *Big Structures, Large Processes, Huge Comparisons,* published in the 1980s (Tilly 1984). And it is on this same ideological basis that microhistory has often been judged, generally from the perspective of empiricism. In a review essay in the journal *History and Theory*, Brad S. Gregory makes the point that the difficulty of the microhistorian is great, because most people assume that the material they work with will have some application to a broader context. But in fact, he says, this is not so:

> To be consistent with their own empiricism, systematic microhistorians must recognize the restricted character of their work. One could simply eschew a wider context altogether, but this would contradict the desire to investigate broader processes 'on the ground'. If a particular village is to tell us about something more than itself – and systematic microhistorians certainly intend that it do so – then one must presuppose, know, or expect something about larger patterns.
>
> (Gregory 1999: 108)

In other words, the methods of microhistory cannot, on their own, serve the needs of ambitious research into the past. Gregory is of the view that if 'historical transformations are embedded in individual interactions', as many microhistorians maintain, it is almost impossible to infer anything about 'large-scale phenomena'. The discipline of history thus faces a paradox which has not been resolved.

This is a view often aired by critics of microhistory. The result has been that the subjects of microhistory are often regarded as interesting, but lacking in depth. Reactions to microhistory have, however, without exception been interesting, and have been conducive to ongoing debate on this matter.

I want to stress that microhistory is highly diverse, so it is misleading to refer to it as if it were a single, consistent ideology. The ideology of microhistory is sometimes more visible, sometimes less so, depending upon the nature of the research and the scholar's approach.[2] Scholars' methods also vary somewhat from one country to another, as has been mentioned in this book; the principal variants are to be found in Italy, Germany and the English-speaking countries.[3] Common to all microhistorians, however, is that they uphold the importance of contextualization – placing the small unit of study in a broader context – *inter alia* as a response to criticisms of the narrow perspective of their studies. Without this, microhistorical studies are deemed to have little meaning – they are dismissed as insignificant in comparison with 'real' (empirical) scholarship. I have opposed this view, and in the latter part of this book I reject it utterly. There are, however, other significant factors in what most microhistorians have in common, some of which will be discussed below.

Normal exceptions

Microhistory is grounded, essentially, in the same principles as the qualitative approach.[4] It pursues the idea that a small unit (an individual, event or small community) can reflect a larger whole, and how such an approach differs from the quantitative methods which are typical of phenomena such as historical demography within the discipline of social history. One of the cornerstones of microhistory is the concept of *normal exceptions*, highlighting the importance of focusing on individual units and demonstrating their significance in historical debate. An individual who is perceived to stand out in some manner from the crowd, through his/her conduct or thinking, will generally be judged on the premises of those who have power. Such an assessment may, however, be at odds with the person's social status or life history, as lived out in an ordinary way in the hidden crannies of society. Thus a man may be condemned for a 'crime' in a certain setting, but praised for the same action in another context, in his own environment. The situation of such a person is classified among *normal exceptions*, and the microhistorian strives to assess the circumstances and sources in that light – to recreate the relationship between the text and the people involved.

The concept of *normal exceptions* also refers to the problems entailed when a contemporary scholar 'discovers' material which is, by modern standards, exciting, even irresistible, and quite certainly marginal 'but that, when properly investigated, i.e. placed or coded in its proper context, reveals its own logic and order' (Brewer 2010: 9). This cannot be done, in the view of most micro-historians, unless the research topic is of manageable size. This principle has been much discussed in the works of microhistorians, directly or indirectly, as it is an issue many critics have raised. They tend to ask: How enlightening or typical for the whole is the 'case' selected by the microhistorian? Thus they approach the microhistorians' subjects on the premises of empirical analysis, like those who base their work on quantitative methods. But in the most successful instances the microhistorian's subject is deconstructed within its own framework; a large range of factors that relate to the subject are examined and analysed as precisely as possible, applying all the scholarly tools available.

It must be reiterated that many academic critics of microhistory have fixed their attention on the question of how 'representative' the individuals, events or other small units selected by microhistorians are for the larger whole. And here they fail utterly to understand the basis of microhistorical research. Micro-historians have, in fact, untiringly pointed out that it is necessary to approach the logical structure of a study of a small unit differently from macrohistorical analysis, i.e. material classified as 'empirical history'. The method applied in microhistory is termed the 'evidential paradigm'. The premise is that a study of a small unit requires a minute analysis of signs and clues in the sources, and that in gathering sources and evidence that objective must be taken into account, by 'reading into' the text and deconstructing the position of the people concerned.

Let us recall that the conventional social historian will generally look for statistical data which indicate how the mass of the population behaved and thought, in relation to the formal structure of society. The microhistorian, on the contrary, cannot make use of such data in researching his/her hypothesis, except in a very limited way. The microhistorian is not interested in how the mass of the population lived their lives, only in how the subject of study managed his/her own affairs. For the microhistorian knows that each of us walks his/her own path when we grapple with living our lives, and that is the path the microhistorian seeks to trace.[5]

The narrative

Historians often draw a sharp distinction between the scholar (the academic historian) and the disseminator of scholarship (e.g. the teacher) in their analysis of the role and meaning of the narrative in historical research. There is often an assumption that these are two different aspects – on one hand the narrative, and on the other analysis to scholarly material. Many see it as desirable that narrative and analysis should be brought closer – in such a way, for instance, that the researcher should master the presentational approach of the teacher; that he/she should be able to make his/her research findings accessible, and possibly even entertaining.

I take the view that it is important to take a bigger step, by rising up above the dichotomy on which this discourse is based. Thus the presentation of a scholarly text will no longer be seen as an ornamental flourish pinned to the phenomenon studied after the research is completed, but an integral part of the research method. Instead of differentiating between language and reality, as the conventional argument tends to do, the premise here is that reality is only accessible via language, as demonstrated in Chapter 8 (Munslow 1997: 25–26, 41–44, 62–66; Jenkins 1991: 47–53). This is an essential understanding of the ideology of microhistory, an important scholarly approach which has significance for the study and its findings. The premise here is that historical research is not a matter of recreating the reality of past times, but of examining the fragments of reality we have, with all their concomitant limitations. Hence it is necessary for the scholar to make the study itself part of the narrative and the process it follows. So the 'search for lost time' may be said to become part of the narrative; and in that way the point is made, first and foremost, that historians do not have all the answers – that the gaps in their knowledge are inevitable, and sometimes overwhelming.

What typifies the work of the microhistorian is the quest. We call that quest *research*. In order to connect it with the narrative we must offer the reader the opportunity to participate with us in the research process, by providing information on the researcher's material (sources) and the gaps that exist in knowledge of the subject. The reader thus becomes, on his/her own terms, a participant in the revelation of historical knowledge (or the lack thereof), and is hence able to enjoy it as far as imagination and the sources permit. So the microhistorian becomes the narrator in his/her own study – like the narrator I created in my own love story, as recounted in Chapter 8 – who focuses not only on telling the story of the historical events, but also on analysis of individual aspects of them, and exposition of the form and origins of the extant sources. This provides the opportunity to *slow down* the research process, to examine each fragment of knowledge, and place it in the context of other knowledge possessed by the researcher. In this way many of the best-known findings of microhistorians have come into being.

Worth a mention in this context is the 'slow' ideology which has appeared in recent years, and has a contribution to make to this aspect of microhistorical studies. 'Slowness' calls for creativity: sensitive, imaginative contemplation of phenomena concerned with people's everyday lives. *Slow* is the watchword of a range of movements in the arts, architecture, spatial consciousness and studies of time, reflecting individual and collective awareness of the quality of life: how to resist that perception of reality which demands quick responses – glib and shallow statements, generally based on some momentary instinct: a straight line from A to B, consumption that prioritizes speed ('fast food') and maximum calories in the minimum time, spaces providing low-maintenance comfort and convenience, looks that hide people's soft spots.[6]

The basis of the *Slow* ideology is precisely the opposite of this: not to seek to smooth out people's rough surfaces, but to find opportunities to demonstrate the positive side of the fact that not everything, and everyone, is the same. It is important to give oneself time to consider the qualities of people who have walked a rocky road in their lives, and not the smooth, straight path. Every person's manner and body language has its own qualities which give meaning to life; but these can only be discerned by scrutinizing all the details of each subject. This ideology opens up an opportunity for microhistorians to examine their subjects minutely, and to discuss them in an enlightened manner. This ideology often leads to such detailed examination of objects and materials on the scholar's desk that the result may be *neo-materialism* – an ideology which requires minute scrutiny of the material under consideration.[7]

The sources

The microhistorian's approach is grounded in the certainty that every source is ambiguous and requires exegesis (Munslow 1997). It is inconceivable that a source could shed light on some event or phenomenon without first passing through the hands of a researcher – whether a historian or some other scholar. So the source acquires value when it has been examined, and when some conclusion has been drawn about its genesis. Whether the source is a diary, a collection of letters, an autobiography, a parish register or statistical records is not important: all these documents are the work of people who had some specific idea in mind – some motivation for their task.

Let us start by considering purely statistical sources: clearly, the categories of the statistics, together with the questions asked to elicit the information, make for data collection that is slanted.[8] We tend to see historical statistics as standardized sources, untouched by human hand or mind, we may overlook the fact that it was some specific society that had the figures compiled, and that the data have been collected to serve some specific purpose. Sources gathered for no obvious reason – and for some reason left outside the framework of the data collection – may be viewed in a subjective light. For example, let us consider records and tables, which unavoidably include the heading *Other*. That is where all those who do not fit the system of classification are lumped together, without recording any more specifics about them.

Anyone who has had anything to do with statistical data or historical demography will recognize the *outlier*: the items that are at odds with the mass, and are discounted, so that they will not affect the medians, means and averages. This category may cover a multitude of variants, and it can provide an interesting subject of study regarding the ideology on which the data collection is based. One may imagine that someone who was placed in the *Other* category might, in some other time, and some other collection of data, be in one of the main categories – since such a classification is always grounded in certain given premises (Anderson 1991: 165–66). In other words, the creation of records and tables is always carried out with some objective in mind, and that determines where the subject is placed. The researcher must begin by uncovering this hidden agenda, regardless of the type of source, before the source can be used as a means of analysing phenomena in society.

Microhistorians approach this research material differently: they specifically search out the outliers, as these offer the opportunity to study the lives and behaviour of those who, for one reason or another, have not trodden the usual path of their time. At the same time, the researcher has the opportunity to explore how the institutions of society responded to such departures from the norm (Ginzburg 1979; Levi 1988). Those whose behaviour is deemed 'deviant' by public authorities are, essentially, challenging custom and tradition, and cocking a snook at the social structure. Reaction to such challenges can unveil diverse strands of connection within the community, whether the subject is the conduct and habits of a serial killer in the nineteenth century, or of a paedophile of that period, or a lesbian nun in the seventeenth century – this kind of material offers a welcome opportunity to analyse certain crannies of society.[9]

Other sources are subject to yet other rules. As an example, in the Nordic countries and elsewhere, e.g. Lutheran countries, pastors were, for instance, required to catechize their parishioners and assess their reading and writing skills, as well as their knowledge of Christian teachings. The assessment was subjective, and the perspective reflected the fact that the clergyman recording his findings was of a higher social class than most of his parishioners. The corollary of this is that the relationship between the recorder of the source, the individuals who answered the questions he asked, the researcher working with the source and imbuing it with meaning, and the person who reads the findings (contributing his/her own thinking to the understanding of the work), is a dynamic and active one. In microhistorical research the aim is to harness that active relationship, and demonstrate how it is possible to work with conventional sources and with others, less used, in a novel way – on the basis of new approaches. The opportunities which arise through working with the source in this way are endless and first and foremost, perhaps, provide the opportunity to approach new questions from an unexpected perspective. A 'polyphony' of events and paradoxes arising from that perspective is characteristic of such research.

The individual

Microhistorians place great emphasis upon the individual being central to their research. Within the social framework the individual has considerable freedom of action in the view of many microhistorians, and hence it is only reasonable to explore people's diverse responses to a range of circumstances (Corbin 1992; Reay 2002). If one is constantly labelling people according to their conduct, or other norms, there is a risk of overlooking the choices faced by each individual, when he/she considers the possibilities in his/her life.

When the individual as a social being is made the specific subject of research, it is necessary to uncover the informal semiotic systems of human behaviour as manifested in the person's life. Relationships between a person's experience and the historian's interpretation of the events under consideration are very complex. 'In case of memory, it is the informant's own way of remembering that is of paramount importance', as Finnish scholar Jorma Kalela points out in his paper 'The Challenge of Oral History', while warning that meaning should not be read direct from memories. Research on different forms of memory has in many ways chimed well with the ideology of microhistory, opening the way to a better understanding of how the individual lives his/her life (Crane 1997: 1372–85). For it is unavoidable, when the individual is placed at the centre of the study, to seek to look inside his/her head, and explore how memories are formed, and what methods are employed in recalling the past.

Kalela goes on to say: 'In more general terms, the historian must unravel the way the people studied understood their situation and defined their actions. If this is not done, if the actors' concept of reality and their discourse have not been reconstructed, the historian's description cannot be fair' (Kalela 1999: 153). Kalela also maintains that 'the historian's work does not lead to a reconstruction of how things really were. What he/she is able to convey is only a *plausible and fair description*' (Kalela 1999: 153). Kalela points out that, while historians will never succeed in recreating the understanding of those who took part in the events, there is nothing to prevent them expressing a view of that understanding, as many microhistorians do in their research.

It is important to realize that what is proposed here is not that historians should put themselves in the place of historical characters, as favoured by British historian R. G. Collingwood and others, with the concept of *empathy*. I am of the view that it is theoretically impossible to enter into the mental state of a person of long ago. The necessary 'translation' between cultures, periods and individuals from the past is so complex that it is far-fetched to maintain that one can grasp the thoughts of people of long ago. Such an attempt leads only to improvisation or fiction, which by its nature has little to do with the past (Jenkins 1991: 39–47).

The ideology of microhistory consists in bringing out the individual, and applying his/her own testimony, in whatever form it has survived, but without imagining that one can recreate the reality using the existing sources. This can be done both by using the direct testimony of the individuals, and by reconstructing sources which relate indirectly to their lives (Lüdtke 1995: 3–40). In microhistory the focus is on studies relating to individuals – whether famous or unknown – in which they are not studied for their historical significance, but as material for the shaping of our ideas about history. The point is being made here that individuals do not make history; it is scholars who do so. Individual actions can influence that process, but only indirectly.

Microhistory as a pedagogical model

Over the last few years I have made use of the ideology of microhistory both in my research and as a tool to build up a better understanding of the roles and functioning of history as an academic discipline. This has included writing both articles on methodology and book-length historical studies, with the help of the ideology of microhistory as I have understood it. The aim behind all this work has been to develop the ideology further and to make microhistorical methods a firmer basis for historical research in the future. My wish has also been to approach the methods of microhistory from a rather different angle and attempt to investigate whether they can be advanced still further through the combination of teaching and research. It is my view that if microhistory can be developed as a pedagogical method its benefits as an ideology of academic research will become even more clearly apparent. There are certain weighty arguments in favour of this view:

Microhistory has as yet been little used in research on substantive categories, for instance minority groups, race, ethnicity and even gender. Here microhistorians have a significant opportunity to demonstrate what the ideology of microhistory has to offer in such research. It may also be said that there has been little evidence of this approach in the historiography of the United States, by which I mean that historians specializing in the history of the United States have not used it, although a number of US historians doing research into European history and elsewhere have done so in rich measure. But in light of the preoccupation among US historians with the kinds of substantive categories noted above, microhistory might prove an enormously powerful tool in the discussion of US issues at various periods, if they could manage to snap out of the social-historical mode which has directed a lot of the research into those categories mentioned earlier. I am fully convinced that it is only a matter of time before microhistory is applied deliberately and systematically to research relating to American history in a much more direct way than hitherto.[10]

Finally, the methods of microhistory provide an opportunity for the development of teaching via the internet and creating a basis for collaboration between universities in different countries. This is, I believe, an extremely important consideration, and I see it as helping to promote the spread of the approach in the coming years. It should now be possible to offer on-line courses run by specific history departments and serving academic institutions throughout the world. The advantage in such teaching is that it is very easy to adapt the methodology of microhistory to individual regions, places, instances and, indeed, individuals and their aspirations, wherever in the world they may be located.

All the work in this book has had the aim of identifying and defining new channels for microhistory and seeking ways for it to be applied in research on new subjects. By moving the discussion over to the form of the teaching, I feel that new vistas will open up, making it possible to develop the ideology still further in years to come within a fertile international context. This will create opportunities to develop the methodology among those researching new areas where microhistory has not had a major impact, especially from the youngest generation of scholars. That will hopefully be the focus of many microhistorians in the future.

Voices

One of the most renowned historians of our time, a Briton of Austrian descent named Francis Newton, once commented on British feminist Sheila Rowbotham's polemic on women's place in history, *Hidden from History* (Rowbotham 1992 [1973]): 'These were people for whom history was not so much a way of interpreting the world, but a means of collective self-discovery, or at best, of winning collective recognition' (Newton 2005: 296). The problem Newton sees with such an approach is that it 'undermines the universality of the universe of discourse that is the essence of all history as a scholarly and intellectual discipline, a *Wissenschaft* in both the German and the narrower English sense' (Newton 2005: 296). It is not entirely clear what the world-famous historian meant by this reference to the universe, but probably he had in mind the reception of his own work around the world – in all corners of the globe, people apparently understand his views and theories.

'It also undermines what both the ancients and the moderns had in common,' says Newton, 'namely the belief that historians' investigations, by means of generally accepted rules of logic and evidence, distinguish between fact and fiction, between what can be established and what cannot, what is the case and what we would like to be so.' Here Newton provides the reader with an insight into the epistemological ground on which he stands – the manner in which he believes we should approach the world. He imagines a framework of knowledge, agreed upon by all, to work with and to comprehend. But he ignores the fact that it is precisely that framework which feminists, and others who have been marginalized in society, are unable to accept. From painful experience such individuals know that the conventional platform of knowledge in scholarship prevents them from having a space for their views, because it is part and parcel of the power relations in society, which are primarily masculine – based on a masculine perspective – as we are well aware.

Newton, who wrote those words in his old age, warned future generations against the *Zeitgeist* – i.e. postmodernism. He pointed out that, after the end of the Cold War, there was increasing pressure on scholars to become advocates for forgotten groups, those who had been sidelined in the drama of the 'war' which was never literally fought, but is now over (so to speak)! 'More history than ever is today being revised or invented by people who do not want the real past, but only a past that suits their purpose. Today is the great age of histor- ical mythology.' (Newton 2005: 296). This can have been no surprise to Newton, author of such books as *The Age of Revolution 1789–1848* (1962), *The Age of Capital* (1974), *The Age of Empire 1875–1914* (1987), and finally the volume which brought him real global fame, *The Age of Extremes 1914–1991* (1994). 'Francis Newton' was in truth none other than Professor Eric Hobsbawm of the University of London (Birkbeck) and the New School of Social Research in New York. For many years Hobsbawm also wrote about jazz for a British per- iodical under the pen name Francis Newton, as he recounted in his autobiography, *Interesting Times.*[11]

What do Hobsbawm's assertions tell the reader about his ideas about the past, and about history? They are somewhat unexpected, coming from the man who edited *The Invention of Tradition,* which addressed precisely scholars' ideas about the world, and how they were 'invented' in the context of the society from which they sprang (Hobsbawm and Ranger (eds) 1984; Smith 2000). He aligns himself with scholars such as Benedict Anderson and others, who maintained that the nation state was a construct of the Age of Enlightenment, that nationalism was 'invented' rather than emerging from the pulse of history, as has been maintained by another school of historians. The ideas of Hobs- bawm, Anderson and others changed people's thinking about the past, and its place in the sources. Many of those who adopted this ideology went on to become influential in postmodernism, pursuing the idea of the 'social construct' of history, and working in the certain knowledge that the past was to be found inside the scholar's head.

I think it is safe to say that Hobsbawm's ideas about the past, as elucidated in his autobiography, are of quite a different nature – that they are strikingly at odds with the picture presented in the above-mentioned research on nationalism. But paradoxes in the works of scholars need, perhaps, come as no surprise: for within every individual there are 'many people'– every person has many aspects, and within us are many voices. And microhistorians have striven to make this point in their research.

The titles of the *Ages* mentioned above give, however, a clue to how Hobsbawm and his generation saw history – as a tool to bring out the past – 'the real past.' I am quite sure that the 'grand narrative' which imbues his *Ages* may be just as strong an influence on the 'invention' of history which is discussed, as on his conclusions about his own life and history. His own story is at least modelled in a very large framwork – so large, indeed, that he never fully steps forward in his own narrative; reflecting the events of world history appears to be a necessity for him. His whole life is an ongoing dialogue with the events of political history, from his birth until his nineties – Hobsbawm was born in 1917 and died in 2012. I cannot help wondering whether the name Hobsbawm was just another pseudonym. The Hobsbawm the reader meets in *Interesting Times* has no 'self,' or is at least closely tied to the 'universal consciousness' – so closely that it is hard to tell them apart.

Eric Hobsbawm was a most interesting man, who had first-hand experience of much which was created by the twentieth century, for good or for ill. Yet there is something in his weighty tome about Eric Hobsbawm the man which does not work – some kind of paradox that is not explored; not creative, but restrictive. For throughout his career he refused to recognize the process of historical deconstruction, i.e. that history can be broken down, and that one can flourish in the fragments left behind by history. Hence he did not understand the feminist Sheila Rowbotham, when she stood up and demanded that the scholarly world acknowledge that women too had a history. For that history did not fit with the grand narrative which had informed his life and thinking. Thus Hobsbawm becomes a person who does not exist, an illusion within the matrix into which he fits his history and that of the world – a historian without a personal history within the grand narrative!

If the approach of the great Eric Hobsbawm does not work, one may ask how we can deal with a world which is so complex and multifaceted that it is hard to get a grip on history. It is precisely the paradoxes of conventional history that have led to the need for other methodologies, such as the one represented by Sheila Rowbotham, and the one which has been the subject of this book. We, the authors of this book, who are certainly in disagreement over various matters, as has been shown here, realize, however, that the microhistorical method offers an opportunity to approach the past in a different way from how it has been done in the past. We understand that the complex and multifaceted world requires methods that enable us to slow down, so that scholars have the opportunity to explore individual fragments of history with the aim of gaining an understanding of phenomena and events from the past, and of the circumstances of people who were previously not admitted into historians' research. At the same time we are sure that readers of this book will discern paradoxes in both our voices; and when we add to the mix our differences of opinion on how to apply the ideology we call microhistory, we add another layer of complexity. And it must count in our favour that the reader has presumably noticed that we do not seek to conceal our differences – they are out in the open.

István M. Szijártó's approach to his subject is through the works of microhistorians themselves and how they have seen their position within the scholarship of microhistory, especially through the definition of three elements which are found in many microhistorical studies: micro-analysis, agency and the intention of each author to answer a 'great historical question'. Equipped with these analytical tools, he goes around and evaluates books that we tend to think of as microhistorical research: what it is in these works which has shaped the method we call microhistory. His analysis is historiographical in nature, and he takes the development of microhistory through its different manifestations in individual countries such as Italy, Germany and France, and in the English-speaking world. In that way he works towards a working definition of the methods of microhistory based on its fractal-like character and the notion of 'abduction', insisting all the while that microhistorians intend to address a 'great historical question'.

My own approach is a different one. I point out that microhistorians have, in the end, proved to have relatively little influence within the discipline of history. In my view this is precisely because they have been too concerned with the 'great historical questions,' or what I term the 'grand narrative'. Instead of focusing on studying as minutely as possible the fragments they have in their hands, they fall into the temptation of conventional history, of contextualizing their findings. In the end they handle their research as Eric Hobsbawm did in his *Ages*; they are far too busy drawing up the outlines of historical progress, following the pattern of the grand narrative. My approach is an attempt to direct the microhistorian towards focusing primarily on his/her actual subject; I urge microhistorians to ignore the grand narrative as far as possible, and to concentrate on the research model I call 'the singularization of history'. In this way they are likely to gain the opportunity to approach their subject in a new way, without being tied to the received standards of the grand narrative, which will thus cease to determine what research questions are asked, and even sometimes the findings of the research.

In the end, I feel that one of the lessons to be learned from this book is precisely that, even when there is only one author, the reader is likely to 'hear' many voices in the narrative. But if we stick to small units, as microhistorians have generally done, we are likely to gain a better grasp of our subjects, and gain insight into a lost world which would otherwise have remained closed to us.

In my writings I have stated my firm conviction that it is not possible 'to step into the same stream twice', to use the metaphor Socrates is supposed to have attributed to Heraclitus to capture his doctrine that everything is in motion and subject to constant change (Plato, *Cratylus* 402A). According to Aristotle in his *Metaphysics*, Cratylus went even further in this matter, asserting that 'it cannot even be done once' (Aristotle, *Metaphysics* V.5. 1010a13). Historians will, I suppose, just have to accept that the past will never be within their grasp. Recognizing this is, to my mind, history's most powerful defence and it is on this basis that microhistorians of the future will have to operate.

Notes

1 In this context it is worth mentioning special issues of the *American Historical Review* 94 (1989) under the name: 'AHR Forum: The Old History and the New', and of *Central European History* 22 (1989), both of which explored the two phenomena exhaustively. Both marked in a sense the beginning of extensive debate on the influence

of these two concepts on history, although they had been part of the broader scholarly discourse for some time.

2 I reiterate yet again that in this book I consciously use the word *ideology* instead of the concept of *methodology* which is so often used in the context of history. This reflects the fact that in my view the ideology of scholarly research comprises three principal factors: research, narrative, and method. The *ideology* of a work is a function of the relationship between these factors, while the *methodology* refers only to technical aspects of how the subject is handled. When the word methodology is used to refer to the historical approach, the inference is that the historian's perspective and interpretation are merely technical factors, of no greater importance than the system of annotation.

3 See the earlier chapters of this book for a discussion of the trends in different countries. Also papers by the following scholars: (Ginzburg 1993: 10–35; Levi 1992: 93–113). See also: (Gregory 1999: 100–110).

4 See, for example: (Denzin and Lincoln (eds) 1994; Taylor and Bogdan 1984).

5 No-one has addressed the argument better than Carlo Ginzburg in the following study: (Ginzburg 1989a: 96–125).

6 See interesting discussions of the concept in the following books: (Bell, M. 1998; Levine 1997).

7 Archaeology has much to contribute here, as it has many features in common with what has been described. See the following paper on the development of historical archaeology: (Orser 2010: 111–50)

8 It should be stated that historians differ on this matter. For a different view on this subject, see: (Appleby, Hunt and Jacob 1995; Elton 1991).

9 A multitude of studies could be cited here, but a few examples are: (Brown, J.C. 1986; McLaren 1993; Wolff 1988).

10 In recent years outstanding studies have been published in the USA, which apply the approaches of microhistory, without formally aligning themselves with it. These have clearly demonstrated the value of this research method for bringing out previously-hidden aspects of the past. I refer once again to Patricia Cline Cohen and her *The Murder of Helen Jewett*, which was discussed in Chapter 7. In addition I wish to mention two other works which have similar qualities – being based upon detailed study of a defined subject, which shed light on a much larger theme without specifically setting out to do so: (Lewis and Ardizzone 2002; Merwick 1999).

11 Hobsbawm, E. (2005 [2002]) *Interesting Times: A Twentieth-Century Life*, New York: Pantheon. Page numbers in attributions to 'Francis Newton' refer to this book by Hobsbawm.

Bibliography

Manuscripts and archival material

Lbs. Landsbókasafn Íslands [The National Library of Iceland]

Lbs. 1672 4to: Sveitarblaðið Gestur [handwritten local newspaper, 'The Visitor'].

Lbs. 1673 4to: Halldór Jónsson: Í tómstundum ['In idle hours': notebook of Halldór Jónsson].

Lbs. 1674 4to: Halldór Jónsson: Búkolla [Notebook. The name comes from a magical cow in a well-known folktale].

Lbs. 1675–78 4to: Halldór Jónsson Dagbækur [Diaries of Halldór Jónsson].

Lbs. 1857–66 8vo: Halldór Jónsson Dagbækur [Diaries of Halldór Jónsson].

Lbs. 1867–69 8vo, Halldór Jónsson: Samtíningsbækur I, II and IV [Miscellanies I, II and IV].

Lbs. 2503–50 4to: Dagbækur Níelsar Jónssonar [Diaries of Níels Jónsson].

Lbs. óskráð [uncatalogued letter]: Halldór Jónsson to Níels Jónsson.

Lbs. óskráð [uncatalogued letter]: Níels Jónsson to Guðrún Bjarnadóttir.

Þjóðskjalasafn Íslands, Skjalasafn landlæknis: Ársskýrslur lækna [National Archives of Iceland, Archive of the surgeon general of Iceland: Annual doctors' reports] DI & II.

Þjóðskjalasafn Íslands, Skjalasafn sýslu-og sveitastjórna [National Archives of Iceland, Archives of county and local district administrations]: Strandasýsla III, 23: Bréfabækur [Correspondence], 1899–1908.

Þjóðskjalasafn Íslands: Skjalasafn sýslu-og sveitastjórna [National Archives of Iceland, Archives of county and local district administrations]: Strandasýsla V, 7: Dóma-og þingabók [Court records], 1892–1906.

Þjóðskjalasafn Íslands [National Archives of Iceland]: Strandasýsla: Prestsþjónustubækur Tröllatungu [Parish registers of the church at Tröllatungu], 1889–1940.

Þjóðskjalasafn Íslands [National Archives of Iceland]: Strandasýsla X, 7: Manntalsbækur [Census records] 1904–15: Tröllatunga, Húsvitjunarbók [Record of pastoral visits], 1887–1938.

Published works

Ago, R. (2004) 'From the archives to the library and back: Culture and microhistory', in A.-M. Castrén, M. Lonkila and M. Peltonen (eds) *Between Sociology and History. Essays on microhistory, collective action, and nation-building*, Helsinki: SKS – Finnish Literature Society.

Aguirre Rojas, C. A. (2003) *Contribución a la historia de la microhistoria italiana*, Rosario: Prohistoria.

Aljunied, S.M.K. (2011) 'Micro-history and the study of minorities: Working-class Sikhs in Singapore and Malaya', *Social History* 36: 22–35.

Amato, J.A. (2008) *Jacob's Well: A case for rethinking family history*, St. Paul, MN: The Minnesota Historical Society.

Anderson, B. (1991) *Imagined Communities: Reflections on the origin and spread of nationalism*. Revised edn, New York: Verso.

Andrade, T. (2010) 'A Chinese farmer, two African boys, and a warlord: Towards global microhistory', *Journal of World History* 21: 573–91.

Anisimov, Ý. (2003) 'Po tu storonu Yoannovskogo mosta, ili strahi donoschika', *Casus* 5: 111–25.

Ankersmit, F. R. (1995) 'Historicism: An attempt at synthesis', *History and Theory* 34: 143–61.

——(1997) 'Sprache und historische Erfahrung', in K. E. Müller and J. Rüsen (eds) *Historische Sinnbildung. Problemstellungen, Zeitkonzepte, Wahrnehmungshorizonte, Darstellungstrategien*, Reinbeck bei Hamburg: Rohwolt.

——(2003) *A történelmi tapasztalat*, trans. T. Balogh, Budapest: Typotex. (1st edn 1993: *De historische ervaring*)

Appleby, J., Hunt, L. and Jacob, M. (1995) *Telling the Truth about History*, 2nd edn, New York – London: Norton. (1st edn 1994)

Astarita, T. (1999) *Village Justice: Community, family, and popular culture in early modern Italy*, Baltimore – London: The Johns Hopkins University Press.

Auerbach, E. (1959) *Mimesis. Dargestellte Wirklichkeit in der abendländischen Literatur*, 2nd edn, Bern: Francke Verlag. (1st edn 1946)

[author unknown] 'Hættulegir ósiðir' [Dangerous abuses] *Ísland* 1, 11 September 1897: 147.

Baker, K. M. (1987) 'Introduction', in K. M. Baker (ed.) *The Political Culture of the Old Regime*, Oxford – New York: Pergamon Press.

Banner, L.W. (2009) 'Biography as History', *AHR* Roundtable: Historians and Biography, *American Historical Review* 114: 579–86.

Barriera, D. G. (ed.) (2002) *Ensayos sobre microhistoria*, Morelia: Jitanjáfora and Red Utopia and Prohistoria.

Barth, F. (1966) *Models of Social Organization*, London: Royal Anthropological Institute.

——(1981) *Process and Form in Social Life*, London, Boston and Henley: Routledge & Kegan Paul.

Barth, V. (2008) 'The Micro-history of a world event: Intention, perception and imagination at the Exposition universelle de 1867', *Museum and Society* 6:1: 22–37.

Barthes, R. (1968) 'L'effet de réel', *Communications* 11: 84–89.

Behringer, W. (1998) *Shaman of Oberstdorf. Chonrad Stoeckhlin and the phantoms of the night*, trans. H.C.E. Midelfort, Charlottesville, VA: University Press of Virginia. (1st edn 1994: *Chonrad Stoeckhlin und die Nachtschar. Eine Geschichte aus der frühen Neuzeit*)

Bell, M. (1998) *Slow Space*, New York: The Monacelli Press.

Bell, R. M. and Brown, J. C. (1987) 'Renaissance sexuality and the Florentine archives: An exchange', *Renaissance Quarterly* 40: 485–511.

Benad, M. (1990) *Domus und Religion in Montaillou: Katholische Kirche und Katharismus im Überlebenskraft der Familie des Pfarrers Petrus Clerici am Anfang des 14. Jahrhunderts*, Tübingen: J.C.B. Mohr (Paul Siebeck).

Benda, G. (2008) *Zsellérből polgár: Keszthely társadalma, 1740–1849*, Budapest: L'Harmattan.

Berenson, E. (1988) 'The politics of divorce in France of the Belle Epoque: The case of Joseph and Henrietta Caillaux', *American Historical Review* 93: 31–55.

——(1992) *The Trial of Madame Caillaux*, Berkeley, CA and Los Angeles: University of California Press.

Berkhofer, R. F. (1995) *Beyond the Great Story: History as text and discourse*, Cambridge, MA: Harvard University Press.

Bicheno, H. (2008) *Vendetta: High art and low cunning at the birth of the Renaissance*, London: Weidenfeld and Nicholson.

Biernacki, R. (2000) 'Language and the shift from signs to practices in cultural inquiry', *History and Theory* 39: 289–310.

Bisha, R. (1998) 'Reconstructing the voice of a noblewoman of the time of Peter the Great: Daria Mikhailovna Menshikova. An exercise in (pseudo) autobiographical writing', *Rethinking History* 2: 51–63.

Bjarnason, Þ. (1892) 'Fyrir 40 árum', *Tímarit hins íslenska bókmenntafélags* 13: 170–258.

Blok, A. (1974) *The Mafia of a Sicilian Village, 1860–1960: A study of violent peasant entrepreneurs*, New York: Harper and Row.

Bókay, A. (1997) *Irodalomtudomány a modern és a posztmodern korban*, Budapest: Osiris.

Boyer, P. and Nissenbaum, S. (1974) *Salem Possessed: The social origins of witchcraft*, Cambridge, MA and London: Harvard University Press.

Boyle, L. E. (1981) 'Montaillou revisited: Mentalité and methodology', in J. A. Raftis (ed.) *Pathways to Medieval Peasants*, Toronto: Pontifical Institute of Medieval Studies.

Brewer, J. (2004) *Sentimental Murder: Love and madness in the eighteenth century*, London: HarperCollins.

——(2010) 'Microhistory and the histories of everyday life', *Cultural and Social History* 7: 87–109. Also published in CAS LMU e-Series 2010/5: 5–7. Online. Available HTTP: <http://www.cas.uni-muenchen.de/publikationen/e_series/cas-eseries_nr5.pdf> (accessed 12 October 2012).

Brooks, J. F., DeCorse, C.R.N, and Walton, J. (eds) (2008) *Small Worlds: Method, meaning and narrative in microhistory*, Santa Fé, NM: School for Advanced Research Press.

Brown, I. Q. and Brown, R. D. (2003) *The Hanging of Ephraim Wheeler: A story of rape, incest and justice in early America*, Cambridge, MA and London: The Belknap Press of Harvard University Press.

Brown, J. C. (1986) *Immodest Acts: Life of a lesbian nun in Renaissance Italy*, Oxford: Oxford University Press.

Brown, J. M. (2009) '"Life histories" and the history of the South Asia', *AHR* Roundtable: Historians and Biography, *American Historical Review* 114: 587–95.

Brown, K. (2009) 'A place in biography of oneself', *AHR* Roundtable: Historians and Biography, *American Historical Review* 114: 596–605.

Brown, R. D. (2003) 'Microhistory and the post-modern challenge', *Journal of the Early Republic* 23: 1–20.

Brucker, G. (1986) *Giovanni és Lusanna: Love and marriage in Renaissance Florence*, Berkeley, CA and Los Angeles: University of California Press.

Bruegel, M. (2006) 'The social relations of farming in the early American Republic: A microhistorical approach', *Journal of the Early Republic* 26: 523–53.

Bruner, J. S. (1986) *Actual Minds, Possible Worlds*, Cambridge MA and London: Harvard University Press.

Budde, G., Conrad, S. and Janz, O. (eds) (2006) *Transnationale Geschichte: Themen, Tendenzen und Theorien*, Göttingen: Vandenhoeck & Ruprecht.

Burke, P. (1991) 'History of events and the revival of narrative', in P. Burke (ed.) *New Perspectives on Historical Writing*, Cambridge: Polity Press.

——(1996) *The Fortunes of the Courtier: The European reception of Castiglione's Cortegiano*, New York: Penn State Press.

——(2000) 'Carlo Ginzburg, detective', in C. Ginzburg *The Enigma of Piero. Piero della Francesca. New edition with appendices*, London – New York: Verso.

——(2008) *What is Cultural History?* Cambridge: Polity Press. (1st edn 2004)

Burke, V.E. and Gibson, J. (2004) *Early Modern Women's Manuscript Writing: Selected Essays of the Trinity/Trent Colloquium*, Hampshire and Burlington: Ashgate Publishing Ltd.

Cabrera, M. A. (2004) *Postsocial History: An Introduction*, trans. M. McMahon, New York: Lexington Books.

Carr, E. H. (1961) *What is History?* New York: Vintage Books.

Carrard, P. (1992) *Poetics of the New History: French historical discourse from Braudel to Chartier*, Baltimore: The Johns Hopkins University Press.

Cartledge, P. (2002) 'What is social history now?', in D. Cannadine (ed.) *What is History Now?* Houndmills – New York: Palgrave Macmillan.

Castrén, A.-M., Lonkila, M. and Peltonen, M. (eds) (2004) *Between Sociology and History: Essays on microhistory, collective action, and nation-building*, Helsinki: SKS – Finnish Literature Society.

Cerutti, S. (1990) *La ville et les métiers: Naissance d'un langage corporatif (Turin, 17e-18e siècle)*, Paris: Éditions de l'École des hautes études en sciences sociales.

——(2004) 'Microhistory: Social relations versus cultural models?', in A.-M. Castrén, M. Lonkila and M. Peltonen (eds) *Between Sociology and History. Essays on microhistory, collective action, and nation-building*, Helsinki: SKS – Finnish Literature Society.

Chakrabarty, D. (2000) *Provincializing Europe: Postcolonial thought and historical difference*, Princeton – Oxford: Princeton University Press.

——(2009) 'The climate of history: Four theses', *Critical Inquiry* 35: 197–222.

Chambers, P. (2006) *The Cock Lane Ghost: Murder, sex and haunting in Dr Johnson's London*, Stroud: Sutton Publishing.

Chartier, R. (1985) 'Text, symbols and Frenchness', *Journal of Modern History* 57: 682–95.

Chin, C. (2011) 'Margins and monsters: How some micro cases lead to macro claims', *History and Theory* 50: 341–57.

Christiansen, P. O. (1988) 'Construction and consumption of the past: From "Montaillou" to "The Name of the Rose"', *Ethnologia Europea* 18: 5–24.

——(1995) *Kultur og historie: Bidrag til den etnologiske debat*, København: Studiebøger.

Cipolla, C. M. (1973) *Christofano and the Plague: A study in the public health in the age of Galileo*, London: Collins.

——(1979) *Faith, Reason, and the Plague in Seventeenth-Century Tuscany*, trans. M. Kittel, New York: Norton. (1st edn 1977: *Chi ruppe i rastelli a Monte Lupo?*)

Clark, A. (1990) 'Queen Caroline and the sexual politics of popular culture in London, 1820', *Representations* 31: 47–68.

Clifford, J. and Marcus, G. E. (eds) (1986) *Writing Culture: The poetics and politics of ethnography*, Berkeley, CA: The University of California Press.

Cohen, P. C. (1990) 'The Helen Jewett murder: Violence, gender, and sexual licentiousness in antebellum America', *National Women's Studies Association Journal* 2: 374–89.

——(1992) 'Unregulated youth: Masculinity and murder in the 1830s city', *Radical History Review* 52: 33–52.

——(1993) 'The mystery of Helen Jewett: Romantic fiction and the eroticization of violence', *Legal Studies Forum* 17: 133–45.

——(1995) 'Ministerial misdeeds: The Onderdonk trial and sexual harassment in the 1840s', *Journal of Women's History* 7: 34–57.

——(1999) *The Murder of Helen Jewett: The life and death of a prostitute in nineteenth-century New York*, New York: Vintage Books. (1st edn 1998.)

Cohen, T. V. and Cohen, E. S. (1993) *Words and Deeds in Renaissance Rome: Trials before the papal magistrates*, Toronto, Buffalo and London: University of Toronto Press.

Contreras, J. (1997) *Pouvoir et Inquisition en Espagne au XVIe siècle. 'Soto contre Riquelme'*, trans. B. Vincent, Paris: Aubier. (1st edn 1992: *Sotos contra Riquelmes. Regidores, inquisidores y criptojudíos*)

Cook, A. P. and Cook, N. D. (1991) *Good Faith and Truthful Ignorance: A case of transatlantic bigamy*, Durham NC and London: Duke University Press.

Cook, H. J. (1994) *The Trials of an Ordinary Doctor: Joannes Groenevelt in seventeenth-century London*, Baltimore: The Johns Hopkins University Press.

Cook, J. W. (2012) 'The kids are all right: On the "turning" of cultural history', *AHR* Forum: Historiographic 'Turns' in Critical Perspective, *American Historical Review* 117: 746–71.

Corbin, A. (1992) *The Village of Cannibals: Rage and murder in France, 1870*, trans. A. Goldhammer, Cambridge, MA: Harvard University Press. (1st edn 1990: *La Village des cannibales*)

——(1998) *Le monde retrouvé de Louis-François Pinagot: Sur les traces d'un inconnu, 1798–1876*, Paris: Flammarion.

Crane, S. A. (1997) '*AHR* forum: Writing the individual back into collective Memory', *American Historical Review* 102: 1372–85.

Crapanzano, V. (1986) 'Hermes' dilemma: The masking of subversion in ethnographic description', in J. Clifford and G. E. Marcus (eds) (1986) *Writing Culture: The poetics and politics of ethnography*, Berkeley, CA: The University of California Press.

Curthoys, A. and Docker, J. (2006) *Is History Fiction?* Sidney: UNSW Press.

Czoch, G. (1999) 'A társadalmi rétegződés mikro-és makrotörténelmi vizsgálata' *Századvég* 4 (No. 15): 17–38.

Daniel, U. (2004) *Kompendium Kulturgeschichte: Theorien, Praxis, Schlüsselwörter*, 4th edn, Frankfurt am Main: Suhrkamp. (1st edn 2001)

Darnton, R. (1985) *The Great Cat Massacre and Other Episodes in French Cultural History*, New York: Vintage Books. (1st edn 1984)

——(1986) 'The symbolic elements in history', *Journal of Modern History* 58: 218–34.

——(2004) 'It happened one night', *The New York Review of Books*, 51 (No. 11, 24 June 2004): 60–64.

Davis, N. Z. (1983) *The Return of Martin Guerre*, Cambridge, MA: Harvard University Press.

——(1988) 'On the lame', *American Historical Review* 93: 572–603.

——(1990) 'The shapes of social history', *Storia della Storografia* 17: 28–34.

——(1995) *Women on the Margins: Three seventeenth-century lives*, Cambridge MA: Harvard University Press.

——(2006) *Trickster Travels: A sixteenth-century Muslim between worlds*, New York: Hill and Wang.

Dekker, R. (2002) 'Jacques Presser's heritage: Egodocuments in the study of history', *Memoria y Civilización* 5: 13–37.

Deleuze, G. and Guattari, F. (1983) *Anti-Oedipus: Capitalism and schizophrenia*, Minneapolis, MN: University of Minnesota Press.

Demos, J. P. (1982) *Entertaining Satan: Witchcraft and the culture of early New England*, Oxford, New York, Toronto and Melbourne: Oxford University Press.

——(1996) *The Unredeemed Captive: A family story from early America*, London: Macmillan Papermac. (1st edn 1994)

Denzin, N. K. and Lincoln, Y. S. (eds) (1994) *Handbook of Qualitative Research*, Thousand Oaks, CA: Saga Publications.

Domanska, E. (1998) *Encounters: Philosophy of history after postmodernism*, Charlottesville, VA: University Press of Virginia.

——(2010) 'Beyond anthropocentrism in historical studies', *Historein* 10: 118–30.

Droysen, J. G. (1868) *Grundriss der Historik*, Leipzig: Veit & Comp.

Duby, G. (1990) *The Legend of Bouvines*, trans. C. Tihanyi, Cambridge: Polity Press. (1st edn 1973: *Le dimanche de Bouvines*)

Duffy, E. (2001) *The Voices of Morebath: Reformation and rebellion in an English village*, New Haven, CT: Yale University Press.

Duggan, L. (1993) 'The trials of Alice Mitchell: Sensationalism, sexology and the lesbian subject in turn-of-the-century America', *Signs* 18: 791–814.

Editors of the Annales (1988) 'Histoire et sciences sociales: Un tournant critique?', *Annales E.S.C.* 43: 291–93.

——(1989) 'Histoire et sciences sociales: Tentons l'expérience', *Annales E.S.C.* 44: 1317–23.

Egmond, F. and Mason, P. (1997) *The Mammoth and the Mouse: Microhistory and morphology*, Baltimore: The Johns Hopkins University Press.

Eley, G. (2005) *A Crooked Line: From cultural history to the history of society*, Ann Arbor, MI: University of Michigan Press.

Elton, G. R. (1991) *Return to Essentials*, Cambridge: Cambridge University Press.

Englund, P. (1992) *The Battle that Shook Europe: Poltava and the birth of the Russian empire*, trans. P. Hale, London: Victor Gollancz (1st edn 1988: *Poltava: berättelsen om en armés undergång*).

Espada Lima, H. (2006) *A micro-história italiana: Escalas, indícios e singularidades*, Rio de Janeiro: Record.

Evans, R. J. (2002) 'Prologue: What is history – now?', in D. Cannadine (ed.) *What is History Now?* Houndmills and New York: Palgrave Macmillan.

Fairburn, M. (1999) *Social History: Problems, strategies and methods*, New York: Palgrave Macmillan.

Farge, A. and J. Revel (1991) *The Vanishing Children of Paris: Rumor and politics before the French revolution*, trans. C. Miéville, Cambridge, MA: Harvard University Press. (1st edn 1988: *Logiques de la foule*)

Figes, O. (2008) *The Whisperers: Private life in Stalin's Russia*. Penguin: London, 2008. (1st edn 2007)

Finlay, A. (1988) 'The Refashioning of Martin Guerre', *The American Historical Review* 93: 553–71.

Fleming, R. (2009) 'Writing Biography at the Edge of History', *AHR* Roundtable: Historians and Biography, *American Historical Review* 114: 606–14.

Fokasz, N., Kopper, Á., Maródi, M. and Szedenics, G. (1997) 'Az európai nemzeti és regionális vasúthálózatok fraktáljellegéről', in N. Fokasz (ed.) *Rend és káosz. Fraktálok és káoszelmélet a társadalomkutatásban*, Budapest: Replika Kör.

Forth, C. E. (2001) 'Cultural history and new cultural history,' in Peter N. Stearns (editor in chief), *Encyclopedia of European Social History. From 1350 to 2000,* Vol 1, New York: Charles Scribners & Sons.

Fox, J. and Stromquist, S. (eds) (1998) *Contesting the Master Narrative: Essays in social history*, Iowa City, IA: University of Iowa Press.

Fuery, P. and Mansfield, N. (1997) *Cultural Studies and The New Humanities: Concepts and controversies*, Melbourne: Oxford University Press.

Fulbrook, M. and Rublack, U. (2010) 'In relation: The "social self" and ego-documents', *German History* 28: 263–71.

Für, L. (2000) *A berceli zenebona, 1784: Kísérlet a történelmi pillanat megragadására*, Budapest: Osiris.

Gaddis, J. L. (2002) *The Landscape of History: How historians map the past*, Oxford and New York: Oxford University Press.

Garðarsdóttir, Ó (2002) *Saving the Child: Regional, cultural and social aspects of the infant mortality decline in Iceland, 1770–1920*, Umeå: The Demographic Data Base.

Garton Ash, T. (1997) *The File: A personal history*, New York: Vintage.

Geertz, C. (1973) *The Interpretation of Cultures*, New York: Basic Books.

——(1988) 'Being there', in C. Geertz *Works and Lives. The anthropologist as author*, Stanford, CA: Stanford University Press.

Gelbart, N. R. (1998) *The King's Midwife: A history and mystery of Madame du Coudray* Berkeley, CA: University of California Press.

Genette, G. (1997) *Paratexts: Thresholds of Interpretation*, trans. Jane E. Lewin, Cambridge: Cambridge University Press.

Ghosh, D. (2012) 'Another set of imperial turns?', *AHR* Forum: Historiographic 'Turns' in Critical Perspective, *American Historical Review* 117: 772–93.

Ginzburg, C. (1980) *The Cheese and the Worms: The cosmos of a sixteenth-century miller*, trans. J. Tedeschi and A. C. Tedeschi, London and Henley: Routledge and Kegan Paul. (1st edn 1976: *Il formaggio e i vermi. Il cosmo di un mugnaio del '500*)

——(1988) 'Proofs and possibilities: In the margins of Natalie Zemon Davis' *The Return of Martin Guerre*', *Yearbook of Comparative and General Literature*, 37: 113–27.

——(1989a) 'Clues: Roots of an evidential paradigm', in C. Ginzburg *Clues, Myths and the Historical Method*, trans. J. Tedeschi and A. C. Tedeschi, Baltimore: The Johns Hopkins University Press. (1st edn 1979: 'Spie: Radici di un paradigma indiziario')

——(1989b) 'Inquisitor as Anthropologist', in C. Ginzburg *Clues, Myths and the Historical Method*, trans. J. Tedeschi and A. C. Tedeschi, Baltimore: The Johns Hopkins University Press. (1st edn 1986: 'L'inquisitore come antropologo')

——(1992) *Clues, Myths and the Historical Method*, trans J. Tedeschi and A. C. Tedeschi, Baltimore: The John Hopkins University Press.

——(1993) 'Microhistory: Two or three things that I know about it', *Critical Inquiry* 20: 10–35.

——(1999) *History, Rhetoric, and Proof: The Menahem Stern Jerusalem lectures*, Hanover, NH: University Press of New England.

——(2000) *The Enigma of Piero: Piero della Francesca*. New edition with appendices, trans. M. Ryle and K. Soper, London and New York: Verso. (1st edn 1981: *Indagini su Piero: il Battesimo, il ciclo di Arezzo, la Flagellazione di Urbino*)

——(2005) 'Latitude, slaves and the bible: An experiment in microhistory', *Critical Inquiry* 31: 665–83.

——(2010a) 'Postface: Réflexions sur une hypothèse', in C. Ginzburg *Mythes emblemes traces. Morphologie et histoire*, Lagrasse: Verdier.

——(2010b) 'Préface', in C. Ginzburg *Le fil et les traces. Vrai faux fictif*, Lagrasse: Verdier.

——(2011) 'Bevezető a második magyar kiadáshoz', in C. Ginzburg *A sajt és a kukacok. Egy XVI. századi molnár világképe*, 2nd edn, Budapest: Európa, 5–16.

Ginzburg, C. and Poni, C. (1991) 'Il nome et il come: Scambio ineguale e mercato storiografico', trans. E. Branch (first published 1979) 'The Name and the Game: Unequal Exchange and the Historiographic Marketplace', in E. Muir and G. Ruggiero (eds) *Microhistory and the Lost Peoples of Europe*, Baltimore and London: The Johns Hopkins University Press.

Gleick, J. (1999) *Káosz – egy új tudomány születése*, trans. P. Szegedi, Budapest: Göncöl. (1st edn 1988: *Chaos: Making a new science*)

González, L. (1968) *Pueblo en vilo: Microhistoria de San José de Gracia*, México: El Colegio de México.

Gray, M. W. (2001) 'Microhistory as universal history', *Central European History* 34: 419–31.

Gregory, B. S. (1999) '*Is* small beautiful? Microhistory and the history of everyday life', *History and Theory* 38: 100–110.

Greilsammer, M. (2009) *La roue de la fortune: Le destin d'une famille d'usuriers lombards dans les Pays-Bas a l'aube des Temps modernes*, Paris: Éditions de l'École des hautes études en sciences sociales.

Grendi, E. (1977) 'Micro-analisi e storia sociale', *Quaderni Storici* 35: 506–20.

——(1993) *Il Cervo e la repubblica: Il modello ligure di antico regime*, Torino: Einaudi.

——(1996) 'Repenser la micro-histoire?', in J. Revel (ed.) *Jeux d'échelles. La micro-analyse a l'expérience*, Paris: Hautes Études, Seuil and Gallimard.

Gribaudi, M. (1987) *Itinéraires ouvriers: Espaces et groupes sociaux à Turin au début du XXe siècle*, Paris: Éditions de l'École des hautes études en sciences sociales.

——(2004) 'Biography, academic context and models of social analysis', in A.-M. Castrén, M. Lonkila and M. Peltonen (eds) *Between Sociology and History. Essays on microhistory, collective action, and nation-building*, Helsinki: SKS – Finnish Literature Society.

Guðmundsson, B. (ed.) (1952–56) *Skjalasafn landlæknis 1760–1946*, Reykjavík: Þjóðskjalasafn Íslands.

Guðmundsson, J. Kr. (1990) *Skyggir skuld fyrir sjón*, vol. I, *Sagnabrot og ábúendatal úr Geiradal, Reykhólasveit, Gufudalssveit og Múlasveit í Austur-Barðastrandarsýslu, 1703–1989*, Kópavogur: Hildur.

Gumbrecht, H. U. (1997) *In 1926: Living at the edge of time*, Cambridge MA and London: Harvard University Press.

Gundersen, T. R. (2003) 'On the dark side of history: Carlo Ginzburg talks to Trygve Riiser Gundersen.' *Eurozine*. Online. Available HTTP: <http://www.eurozine.com/articles/2003-07-11-ginzburg-en.pdf > (accessed 13 September 2012). First published in *Samtiden* 2/2003 (Norwegian version).

Gyáni, G. (1997) 'A mindennapi élet mint kutatási probléma', *AETAS* 12 (No. 1): 151–62.

Harline, C. (1994) *The Burdens of Sister Margaret: Inside a 17th-century convent*, New York: Doubleday.

Helgason, J. K. (2007) 'Þýðing, endurritun, ritstuldur: Ort í eyður *Fortíðardrauma*', *Íslensk menning*, vol. II: Til heiðurs Sigurði Gylfa Magnússyni fimmtugum, Reykjavík: Einsögustofnunin: 97–113.

Hellbeck, J. (2009) 'Galaxy of black stars: The power of soviet biography', *AHR* Roundtable: Historians and Biography, *American Historical Review* 114: 615–24.

Hill, W. S. (1996) 'Where we are and how we got here: Editing after poststructuralism', *Shakespeare Studies* 14: 38–46.

Hobsbawm, E. (2005) *Interesting Times: A twentieth-century life*, New York: Pantheon. (1st edn 2002).

Hobsbawm, E. and Ranger, T. (eds) (1984) *The Invention of Tradition*, Cambridge: Cambridge University Press.

Hoffer, P. C. (2004) *Past Imperfect: Facts, fictions, fraud – American history from Bancroft and Parkman to Ambrose, Bellesiles, Ellis, and Goodwin*, New York: Public Affairs.

Hollow, M. (2009) 'Introducing the historian to history: Autobiographical performances in historical texts', *Rethinking History* 13: 43–52.

Holt, J. C. (1982) *Robin Hood*. London: Thames and Hudson.

Hsia, R. P. (1992) *1475. Stories of a Ritual Murder Trial*, New Haven, CT and London: Yale University Press.

Hsü, K. J. and Hsü, A. J. (1989) 'Fractal geometry of music', *Proceedings of the National Academy of Sciences of the USA* 87: 938–41.

Hughes-Hallett, P. (2002) *The Immortal Dinner: A famous evening of genius and laughter in literary London, 1817*, Chicago: New Amsterdam Books.

Hunt, L. (1998) 'Postscript', in E. Domańska *Encounters. Philosophy of history after postmodernism*, Charlottesville, VA: University Press of Virginia.

Iggers, G. G. (1997) *Historiography in the Twentieth Century: From scientific objectivity to the postmodern challenge*, Hanover, NH: University Press of New England.

Imhof, A. E. (1984) *Die verlorene Welten: Alltagsbewältigung durch unsere Vorfahren – und weshalb wir uns heute so schwer damit tun*, München: Beck.

Ísberg, J. Ó. (2005) *Líf og lækningar: íslensk heilbrigðissaga*, Reykjavík: Hið íslenska bókenntafélag.

Jacobson Schutte, A. (1986) 'Book review on Giovanni Levi: *Inheriting Power: The story of an exorcist*', *Journal of Modern History* 58: 961–62.

Jager, E. (2004) *The Last Duel: A true story of crime, scandal, and trial by combat in medieval France*, New York: Broadway Books.

Jarrick, A. (1999) *Back to Modern Reason: Johan Hjerpe and other petit bourgeois in Stockholm in the Age of Enlightenment*, Liverpool: Liverpool University Press.

Jenkins, K. (1991) *Re-Thinking History*, London: Routledge.

Jónsson, G. and Magnússon, M. S. (eds) (1997) *Hagskinna: Icelandic historical statistics*, Reykjavík: Hagstofa Íslands.

Jónsson, Þ. (ed.) (1994) *Ormsætt: ættir Íslendinga*, Niðjatal IX 3, Reykjavík: þjóðsaga.

Justice, G. L. and Tinker, N. (2002) *Women's Writing and the Circulation of Ideas: Manuscript publication in England 1550–1800*, Cambridge: Cambridge University Press.

Kagan, R. L. (1990) *Lucrecia's Dreams: Politics and prophecy in sixteenth-century Spain*, Berkeley, CA and Los Angeles: University of California Press.

Kalela, J. (1999) 'The challenge of oral history: The need to rethink source criticism', in A. Ollila (ed.) *Historical Perspectives on Memory*, Helsinki: SHS: 139–54.

Kastan, D. S. (1996) 'The mechanics of culture: Editing Shakespeare today', *Shakespeare Studies* 14: 30–37.

Kates, G. (1995) *Monsieur d'Eon is a Woman: A tale of political intrigue and sexual masquerade*, Baltimore: The Johns Hopkins University Press.

Kessler-Harris, A. (2009) 'Why Biography?', *AHR* Roundtable: Historians and Biography, *American Historical Review* 114: 625–30.

King, M. L. (1994) *The Death of the Child Valerio Marcello*, Chicago: The University of Chicago Press.

Kingdon, R. M. (1995) *Adultery and Divorce in Calvin's Geneva*, Cambridge, MA: Harvard University Press.

Klaniczay, G. (1998) 'Montaillou harminc éve', *BUKSZ* 10: 168–78.

Klapisch-Zuber, C. (1985) 'Kin, friends and neighbors', in: Klapisch-Zuber, C. *Women, Family and Ritual in Renaissance Italy*, trans. L. G. Cochrane, Chicago – London: The University of Chicago Press. (1st edn 1976: 'Parenti, amici, vicini')

Klein, K. L. (1995) 'In search of narrative mastery: Postmodernism and the people without history', *History and Theory* 34: 275–98.

Koselleck, R. (2004) *Futures Past: On the semantics of historical time*, trans. K. Tribe, New York: Columbia University Press. (1st edn 1979: *Vergangene Zukunft. Zur Semantik geschichtlicher Zeiten*)

Kosheleva, O. E. (2002) 'Odin iz Ivanov v epohu Petra (opit personalnoy istorii)', *Casus* 4: 305–25.

Kracauer, S. (1969) *History: The last things before the last*. Completed by Paul Oskar Kristeller, New York: Oxford University Press.

Kuehn, T. (1989) 'Reading microhistory: The example of Giovanni and Lusanna', *Journal of Modern History*, 61: 512–34.

——(1991) *Law, Family, & Women: Toward a legal anthropology of Renaissance Italy*, Chicago and London: The University of Chicago Press.

LaCapra, D. (1985) 'The Cheese and the Worms: The cosmos of a twentieth-century historian', in D. LaCapra *History and Criticism*, Ithaca, NY and London: Cornell University Press.

——(1988) 'Chartier, Darnton, and the great symbol massacre', *Journal of Modern History* 60: 95–112.

Lake, P. (2001) *The Boxmaker's Revenge: 'Orthodoxy', 'heterodoxy' and the politics of the parish in early Stuart London*, Stanford, CA: Stanford University Press.

Lamoreaux, N. R. (2006) 'Rethinking microhistory: A comment', *Journal of the Early Republic* 26: 555–61.

Lepetit, B. (1993) 'Architecture, géographie, histoire: Usages de l'échelle', *Genèses* 13: 118–38.

Lepetit, B. (ed.) (1995) *Les formes de l'expérience: Une autre histoire sociale*, Paris: Albin Michel.

Lepore, J. (2001) 'Historians who love too much: Reflections on microhistory and biography', *Journal of American History* 88: 129–44.

Le Roy Ladurie, E. (1978) *Montaillou: The promised land of error*, trans. B. Bray, New York: Braziller. (1st edn 1975: *Montaillou, village occitan de 1294 à 1324*)

——(1980) *Carnival: A people's uprising at Romans, 1579-1580*, trans. M. Feeney, New York: Braziller. (1st edn 1979: *Le Carneval de Romans*)

——(1987) *Jasmin's Witch*, trans. B. Pearce, Aldershot: Scolar Press. (1st edn 1983: *La sorcière de Jasmin*)

Levi, G. (1985) 'I pericoli del Geertzismo', *Quaderni Storici* 20: 257–78.

——(1988) *Inheriting Power: The story of an exorcist*, trans. L. G. Cochrane, Chicago and London: The University of Chicago Press. (1st edn 1985: *L'eredità immateriale: Carriera di un esorcista nel Piemonte del seicento*)

——(1991) 'On microhistory', in P. Burke (ed.) *New Perspectives on Historical Writing*, Cambridge: Polity Press.

——(1992) 'On microhistory', in P. Burke (ed.) *New Perspectives on Historical Writing*, 2nd edn, University Park, PA: Pennsylvania State University Press.

——(2004) 'Historians, psychoanalysis and truth', in A.-M. Castrén, M. Lonkila and M. Peltonen (eds) *Between Sociology and History. Essays on microhistory, collective action, and nation-building*, Helsinki: SKS – Finnish Literature Society.

Levine, R. V. (1997) *A Geography of Time: The temporal misadventures of a social psychologist, or how every culture keeps time just a little bit differently*, New York: Basic Books.

Lewis, E. and Ardizzone, H. (2002) *Love on Trial: An American scandal in black and white*, New York: W. W. Norton & Company.

Li, H. (2009) *Village China Under Socialism and Reform: A micro history, 1948–2008*, Stanford, CA: Stanford University Press.

Lima, H. E. (2006) *A micro-história italiana: Escalas, indícios e singularidades*, Rio de Janeiro: Civilização Brasileira.

Linden, M. van der (2003) 'Gaining ground', *Journal of Social History*, Special Issue: *The Futures of Social History* 37: 69–75.

Linehan, P. (1997) *The Ladies of Zamora*, University Park, PA: Pennsylvania State University Press.

Loriga, S. (2010) *Le petit X: De la biographie a l'histoire*, Paris: Seuil.

Lüdtke, A. (1994) 'Stofflichkeit, Macht-Lust und Reiz der Oberflächen: Zu den Perspektiven von Alltagsgeschichte', in W. Schulze (ed.) *Sozialgeschichte, Alltagsgeschichte, Mikro-Historie. Eine Diskussion*, Göttingen: Vandenhoeck & Ruprecht.

——(1995) 'Introduction: What is the history of everyday life and who are its practitioners?' in A. Lüdtke (ed.) *The History of Everyday Life: Reconstructing historical experiences and ways of life*. Princeton, NJ: Princeton University Press.

——(ed.) (1995) *The History of Everyday Life: Reconstructing historical experiences and ways of life*, trans. W. Templer, Princeton, NJ: Princeton University Press. (1st edn 1989: *Alltagsgeschichte. Zur Rekonstruktion historischer Erfahrungen und Lebensweisen*)

Lugosi, A. (2001) 'A tünetektől az interpretációig: Esszé egy homeopata jellegű történetírói gyakorlatról: a mikrotörténelemről', *Szociológiai Figyelő* 2nd series 5: 24–42.

McCloskey, D. N. (1991) 'History, differential equations, and the problem of narration', *History and Theory* 30: 21–36.

McCormmach, R. (1982) *Night Thoughts of a Classical Physicist*, Cambridge, MA and London: Harvard University Press.

McDonald, T. J. (ed.) (1996) *The Historical Turn in the Human Sciences*, Ann Arbor, MI: University of Michigan Press.

Macfarlane, A. (1970) *Witchcraft in Tudor and Stuart England: A regional and comparative study*. London: Routledge & Kegan Paul.

——(1977) *The Family Life of Ralph Josselin: A seventeenth-century clergyman. An essay in historical anthropology*, New York and London: W. W. Norton.

Macfarlane, A. in collaboration with S. Harrison (1981) *The Justice and the Mare's Ale: Law and disorder in seventeenth-century England*, Oxford: Blackwell.

McKenzie, D. F. (1986) *Bibliography and the Sociology of Texts*, London: British Library.

McLaren, A. (1993) *A Prescription for Murder: The Victorian serial killings of Dr. Thomas Neill Cream*, Chicago: The University of Chicago Press.

Magnússon, S. G. (1993) *The Continuity of Everyday Life: Popular culture in Iceland, 1850–1940*, PhD thesis, Carnegie Mellon University, USA.

——(1995) 'From children's point of view: Childhood in 19th-century Iceland', *Journal of Social History* 29: 295–323.

——(1997) *Menntun, ást og sorg: einsögurannsókn á íslensku sveitasamfélagi 19. og 20. aldar*, Reykjavík: Háskólaútgáfan.

——(1998) *Brœður af Ströndum: dagbækur, ástarbréf, almenn bréf, sjálfsævisaga, minnisbækur og samtíningur frá 19. öld*, Reykjavík: Háskólaútgáfan.

——(2001) 'The contours of social history: Microhistory, postmodernism and historical sources', in C. T. Nielsen, D. G. Simonsen and L. Wul (eds), *Mod nye historier*. Rapporter til Det 24. Nordiske Historikermfide, Vol. 3, Århus: Historisk Institut.

——(2003) 'The singularization of history: Social history and microhistory within the postmodern state of knowledge', *Journal of Social History* 36: 701–35.

——(2006) 'Social history as "sites of memory"? The institutionalization of history: microhistory and the grand narrative', *Journal of Social History* 39: 891–913.

——(2007) *Sögustríð: Greinar og frásagnir um hugmyndafræði*, Reykjavík: ReykjavíkurAkademían.

——(2010) *Wasteland with Words: A social history of Iceland*. London: Reaktion Books.

Magnússon, S.G. and Ólafsson, D. (2002) 'Barefoot historians: Education in Iceland in the Modern Period', in K-J. Lorenzen-Schmidt and B. Poulsen (eds) *Writing Peasants. Studies on Peasant Literacy in Early Modern Northern Europe*, Århus: Landbohistorisk Selskab: 175–209

——(2012) 'Minor knowledge: Microhistory, scribal communities, and the importance of institutional structures', *Quaderni Storici* 140/a.XLVII, n.2, agosto: 495–524.

Majtényi Gy. (2001) '"Uraltak" vagy "önfejűek": Diktatúrák mindennapjai a német társadalomtörténet-írásban', *Korall* 2:5–6: 242–52.

Mann, S. (2009) 'Scene-setting: Writing biography in Chinese history', *AHR* Roundtable: Historians and Biography, *American Historical Review* 114: 631–39.

Marshall, A. (1999) *The Strange Death of Edmund Godfrey: Plots and politics in Restoration London*, Stroud: Sutton Publishing.

Martin, J. (1992) 'Review essay: Journeys to the world of the dead: The work of Carlo Ginzburg', *Journal of Social History* 25: 613–26.

Martin, R., Scott, J. W. and Strout, C. (1995) 'Forum: Raymond Martin, Joan W. Scott, and Cushing Strout on *Telling the Truth About History*,' *History and Theory* 34: 320–39.

Martines, L. (2003) *April Blood: Florence and the plot against the Medici*, Oxford: Oxford University Press.

Mattíasson, S. (1906) 'Um þrifnað og óþrifnað', *Eimreiðin* 12: 161–75.

Medick, H. (1994) 'Mikro-Historie', in W. Schulze (ed.) *Sozialgeschichte, Alltagsgeschichte, Mikro-Historie. Eine Diskussion*, Göttingen: Vandenhoeck & Ruprecht.

——(1995) '"Missionaries in the rowboat"? Ethnological ways of knowing as a challenge to social history', in A. Lüdtke (ed.) *The History of Everyday Life: Reconstructing historical experiences and ways of life*, trans. W. Templer, Princeton, NJ: Princeton University Press. (1st edn 1984: '"Missionare im Ruderbot"? Ethnologische Erkenntnisweisen als Herausforderung an die Sozialgeschichte')

——(1996) *Weben und Überleben in Laichingen 1650–1900: Lokalgeschichte als Allgemeine Geschichte*. Göttingen: Vandenhoeck & Ruprecht.

Megill, A. (1995) 'Grand narrative and the discipline of history,' in F. Ankersmit and H. Kellner (eds) *A New Philosophy of History*, Chicago: The University of Chicago Press.

——(2007) *Historical Knowledge, Historical Error: A contemporary guide to practice*, Chicago: The University of Chicago Press.

Merwick, D. (1999) *Death of a Notary: Conquest and change in colonial New York*, Ithaca, NY: Cornell University Press, 1999.

Millman, J. S. and Wright, G. (2005) *Early Modern Women's Manuscript Poetry*, Manchester: Manchester University Press.

Mímisson, K. (2012) 'Twisted lives: On the temporality of materiality of biographical presences', *International Journal of Historical Archaeology* 16: 455–71.

Molho, A. (1987) 'Review: *Giovanni and Lusanna*', *Renaissance Quarterly* 40: 96–100.

——(2004) 'Carlo Ginzburg: Reflections on the intellectual cosmos of a 20th-century historian', *History of European Ideas* 30: 121–48.

Monod, P. K. (2003) *The Murder of Mr. Grebell. Madness and civility in an English town*, New Haven, CT and London: Yale University Press.

Moorhead, J. K. (ed.) (1930) *Conversations of Goethe with Eckermann*, London and New York: J. M. Dent and Sons.

Mosley, S. (2006) 'Common ground: Integrating social and environmental history', *Journal of Social History* 39: 915–33.

Muir, E. (1991a) 'Introduction: Observing trifles', in E. Muir and G. Ruggiero (eds) *Microhistory and the Lost Peoples of Europe*, Baltimore and London: The Johns Hopkins University Press 1991.

——(1991b) 'Review: Clues, myths, and the historical method: by Carlo Ginzburg', *Journal of Social History* 25: 123–25.

——(1998) *Mad Blood Stirring: Vendetta in Renaissance Italy*. Reader's edition, Baltimore and London: The Johns Hopkins University Press. (1st edn 1993)

Muir, E. and Ruggiero, G. (eds) (1990) *Sex and Gender in Historical Perspective: Selections from the Quaderni Storici*, Baltimore and London: The Johns Hopkins University Press.

——(1991) *Microhistory and the Lost Peoples of Europe: Selections from the Quaderni Storici*, Baltimore and London: The Johns Hopkins University Press.

——(1994) *History from Crime: Selections from the Quaderni Storici*, Baltimore and London: The Johns Hopkins University Press.

Munslow, A. (1997) *Deconstructing History*, London: Routledge.

Munslow, A. and Rosenstone, R. A. (eds) (2004) *Experiments in Rethinking History*, New York and London: Routledge.

Muraközy, Gy. (1997) 'A káosz elmélete és tanulságai', in N. Fokasz (ed.) *Rend és káosz. Fraktálok és káoszelmélet a társadalomkutatásban*, Budapest: Replika Kör.

Nagy, Á. (2010) 'Társadalmi mobilitás a kapcsolatok hálózatában – visszatérés a társadalom konfigurációs szemléletéhez', in Papp, G. and I. M. Szijártó (eds) *Mikrotörténelem másodfokon*. Budapest: L'Harmattan.

Nasaw, D. (2009) 'Introduction', *AHR* Roundtable: Historians and Biography, *American Historical Review* 114: 573–78.

Novick, P. (1988) *That Noble Dream: The 'objectivity question' and the American historical profession*, Cambridge: Cambridge University Press.

Nyikos, L. and Balázs, L. and Schiller, R. (1997) 'A kubizmustól a fraktálizmusig', in N. Fokasz (ed.) *Rend és káosz. Fraktálok és káoszelmélet a társadalomkutatásban*, Budapest: Replika Kör.

Obeyesekere, G. (1997) *The Apotheosis of Captain Cook: European Mythmaking in the Pacific*, Princeton: Princeton University Press. (1st edn 1992)

Ollila, A. (ed.) (1999) *Historical Perspectives on Memory*, Helsinki: SHS.

Orgel, S. (1996) 'What is an editor?', *Shakespeare Studies* 14: 23–29.

Orser, C. E. Jr (2010) 'Twenty-first century historical archaeology', *Journal of Archaeological Research* 18: 111–50.

Ouwenell, A. (2005) *The Flight of the Shepherd: Microhistory and the psychology of cultural resilience in Bourbon central Mexico*, Amsterdam: Aksant.

Ozment, S. (1986) *Magdalena and Balthasar: An intimate portrait of life in sixteenth-century Europe revealed in the letters of a Nuremberg husband and wife*, New York: Simon and Schuster.

——(1990) *Three Behaim Boys: Growing up in early modern germany. A chronicle of their lives*, New Haven, CT: Yale University Press.

——(1996) *The Bürgermeister's Daughter: Scandal in a sixteenth-century German town*, New York: St. Martin's Press.

Pallares-Burke, M. L. G (2002) *The New History: Confessions and conversations*, Cambridge: Polity Press.

Passeron, J.-C. and Revel, J. (2005) 'Penser par cas: Raisonner a partir de singularités', in J.-C. Passeron and J. Revel (eds) *Penser par cas*. Paris: Éditions de l'École des Hautes Etudes en Sciences Sociales.

Peltonen, M. (2001) 'Clues, margins, and monads: The micro-macro link in historical research', *History and Theory* 40: 347–59.

——(2004) 'After the linguistic turn?', in A.-M. Castrén, M. Lonkila, and M. Peltonen (eds) *Between Sociology and History. Essays on microhistory, collective action, and nation-building*, Helsinki: SKS – Finnish Literature Society.

Perényi, R. (1999) 'Egy Montaillou-kép a '80-as évek végéről', *Sic itur ad astra* 11: 307–12.

Perl-Rosenthal, N. (2012) 'Comment: Generational turns', *AHR* Forum: Historiographic 'Turns' in Critical Perspective, *American Historical Review* 117: 804–13.

Phillips, M. S. (2003) 'Histories, micro- and literary: Problems of genre and distance', *New Literary History* 34: 211–29.

Plamper, J. (2010) 'The history of emotions: An interview with William Reddy, Barbara Rosenwein, and Peter Stearns', *History and Theory* 49: 237–65.

Polanyi, K. (1944) *The Great Transformation*, New York: Rinehart.

Pomata, G. (1998) 'Close-ups and long shots: Combining particular and general in writing the histories of women and men', in H. Medick and A.-C. Trepp (eds) *Geschlechtergeschichte und Allgemeine Geschichte: Herausforderungen und Perspektiven*, Göttingen: Wallstein Verlag.

——(2000) 'Telling the truth about micro-history: A memoir (and a few reflections)', *Netværk for historieteori og historiografi*, Arbejdspapirer No. 3: 28–40.

Pucci, I. (1997) *The Trials of Maria Barbella: The true story of a 19th-century crime of passion*, New York: Vintage Books.

Putnam, L. (2006) 'To study the fragments/whole: Microhistory and the Atlantic world', *Journal of Social History* 39: 615–30.

Raggio, O. (1990) *Faide e parentele: Lo stato genovese visto dalla Fontanabuona*, Torino: Einaudi.

Ramella, F. (1983) *Terra e telai: Sistemi di parentela i manufattura nel Biellese dell'Ottocento*, Torino: Einaudi.

Rappaport, J. (1994) *Cumbe Reborn: An Andean ethnography of history*, Chicago: The University of Chicago Press.

Reay, B. (1996) *Microhistories: Demography, society and culture in rural England, 1800–1930*, Cambridge, New York and Melbourne: Cambridge University Press.

——(2002) *Watching Hannah: Sexuality, horror and bodily de-formation in Victorian England*, London: Reaktion Books.

Reddy, W. M (2008) 'Emotional styles and modern forms of life', in N. Karafyllis and G. Ulshöfer (eds) *Sexualized brains: scientific modeling of emotional intelligence from a cultural perspective*, Cambridge, MA: MIT Press.

Redfield, R. (1955) *Little community: Viewpoints for the study of the human whole*. Chicago: The University of Chicago Press.

Redondi, R. (1987) *Galileo: Heretic*, trans. R. Rosenthal, Princeton, NJ: Princeton University Press. (1st edn 1983: *Galileo eretico*)

Reinhard, W. (2009) *Paul V. Borghese (1605–1621): Mikropolitische Papstgeschichte*, Stuttgart: Anton Hiersemann.

Renders, H. and De Haan, B. (2011) 'The limits of representativeness: Biography, life writing and microhistory', *Storia della Storiografia* 59–60: 32–42.

Revel, J. (1995a) 'L'institution et le social', in B. Lepetit (ed.) *Les formes de l'expérience. Une autre histoire sociale*, Paris: Albin Michel.

——(1996a) 'Micro-analyse et construction du social', in J. Revel (ed.) *Jeux d'échelles. La micro-analyse a l'expérience*, Paris: Hautes Études, Seuil and Gallimard, trans. A. Goldhammer (1995b) 'Microanalysis and the construction of the social', in J. Revel and L. Hunt (eds), *Histories: French constructions of the past*, New York: New Press.

——(1996b) 'Présentation', in J. Revel (ed.) *Jeux d'échelles. La micro-analyse a l'expérience*, Paris: Hautes Études, Seuil and Gallimard.

——(2001) 'Retour sur l'évènement', in J-L. Fabiani (ed.) *Le goût de l'enquête. Pour Jean-Claude Passeron*, Paris: L'Harmattan.

Revel, J. (ed.) (1996) *Jeux d'échelles: La micro-analyse a l'expérience*, Paris: Hautes Études, Seuil, and Gallimard.

Richardson, B. (1994) *Print Culture in Renaissance Italy: The editor and the vernacular text, 1470–1600*, Cambridge: Cambridge University Press.

Ricoeur, P. (1981) 'The hermeneutical function of distanciation', in Ricoeur, P. *Hermeneutics and the Human Sciences*, ed. and trans. J. B. Thompson, Cambridge: Cambridge University Press and Paris: Editions de le Maison des Sciences de l'Homme.

——(1984) *Time and Narrative*, Vol. 1, trans. K. McLaughlin and D. Pellauere, Chicago: The University of Chicago Press.

——(2000) *La mémoire, l'histoire, l'oubli*, Paris: Seuil.

Rosenblatt, P. C. (1983) *Bitter, Bitter Tears: Nineteenth-century diarists and twentieth-century grief theories*, Minneapolis, MI: University of Minnesota Press.

Rosenstone, R. A. (1988) *Mirror in the Shrine: American Encounters with Meiji Japan*, Cambridge MA and London: Harvard University Press.

Rosental, P.-A. (1996) 'Construire le "macro" par le "micro": Fredrik Barth et la microstoria', in J. Revel (ed.) *Jeux d'échelles: La micro-analyse a l'expérience*, Paris: Hautes Études, Seuil and Gallimard.

Rosenwein, B. H. (2002) '*Review Essay:* Worrying about emotions in history', *American Historical Review* 107: 821-45.

——(2006) *Emotional Communities in the Early Middle Ages*, Ithaca, NY: Cornell University Press.

Ross, D. (1995) 'Grand narrative in American historical writing: From romance to uncertainty', *American Historical Review* 100: 651–77.

Rowbotham, S. (1992) *Hidden from History: 300 years of women's oppression and the fight against it*, London: Pluto Press. (1st edn 1973).

Rowland, I. D. (2004) *The Scarith of Scornello: A tale of Renaissance forgery*, Chicago and London: The University of Chicago Press.

Ruggiero, G. (1993) *Binding Passions: Tales of Magic, Marriage, and Power at the End of the Renaissance*, Oxford and New York: Oxford University Press.

——(2001) 'The strange death of Margarita Marcellini: *Male*, signs, and the everyday world of pre-modern medicine', *American Historical Review* 106: 1140–58.

——(2007) *Machiavelli in Love: Sex, self, and society in the Italian Renaissance*, Baltimore: The Johns Hopkins University Press.

Sabean, D. W. (1984) *Power in the Blood: Popular culture and village discourse in early modern Germany*, Cambridge: Cambridge University Press.

——(1990) *Property, production and family in Neckarhausen, 1700–1870*, Cambridge: Cambridge University Press.

——(1998) *Kinship in Neckarhausen, 1700–1870*, Cambridge: Cambridge University Press.

Sahlins, M. (1985) 'Captain James Cook; or, the dying god', in M. Sahlins, *Islands of History*, Chicago – London: The University of Chicago Press.

——(1995) *How 'Natives' Think: About Captain Cook, for example*, Chicago: The University of Chicago Press.

Sandwell, R. W. (2008) 'History as experiment: Microhistory and environmental history,' in A. McEachern and W. Turkel (eds) *Method and Meaning in Canadian Environmental History*, Toronto: Nelson Education.

Schama, S. (1992) *Dead Certainties (Unwarranted speculations)*, New York: Vintage Books. (1st edn 1991)

Schlumbohm, J. (1994) *Lebensläufe, Familien, Höfe: Die Bauern und Heuerleute des osnabrückischen Kirchspiels Belm in proto-industrieller Zeit, 1650–1860*, Göttingen: Vandenhoeck & Ruprecht.

Schulze, W. (1994) 'Einleitung', in W. Schulze (ed.) *Sozialgeschichte, Alltagsgeschichte, Mikro-Historie. Eine Diskussion*, Göttingen: Vandenhoeck & Ruprecht.

Scribner, R. W. (1997) 'Historical anthropology of Early Modern Europe', in R. P. Hsia and R. W. Scribner (eds) *Problems in the Historical Anthropology of Early Modern Europe*, Wiesbaden: Harrassowitz.

Sebeok, T. A. and Umiker-Sebeok, J. (1980) *'You Know my Method': A juxtaposition of Charles S. Peirce and Sherlock Holmes*, Bloomington, IN: Gaslight Publications.

Serna, J. and Pons, A. (2000) *Cómo se escribe la microhistoria: Ensayo sobre Carlo Ginzburg*, Madrid: Cátedra.

Sewell, W. H. Jr. (2005) *The Logics of History: Social theory and social transformation*, Chicago: The University of Chicago Press.

Shapiro, J. (2005) *1599: A year in the life of William Shakespeare*, London: Faber and Faber.

Sharpe, J. (1999) *The Bewitching of Anne Gunter: A horrible and true story of football, witchcraft, murder and the King of England*, London: Profile Books.

Sherr, R. (1991) 'A canon, a choirboy, and homosexuality in late sixteenth-century Italy: A case study', *Journal of Homosexuality* 21: 1–22.

Shifflett, C. (1995) 'Book review on Gary W. Gallagher' (1995) *The Fredricksburg Campaign: Decision on the Rappahannock*, Chapel Hill, NC and London: The North Carolina Press, H-Net book review. Online. Available HTTP: <http://h-net.msu.edu/cgi-bin/logbrowse.pl?trx=vx&list=h-review&month=9509&week=b&msg=7MUsJv2SB/HV00fvFGlfOQ&user=&pw=> (accessed 11 October 2012).

Simon, Z. B. (2013) 'Tapasztalat, jelenlét, történelem', forthcoming in *AETAS* 29.

Skidmore, C. (2010) *Death and the Virgin: Elizabeth, Dudley and the mysterious fate of Amy Robsart*, London: Weidenfeld & Nicolson.

Smith, A. D. (2000) *The Nation in History: Historiographical debates about ethnicity and nationalism*, Hanover, NH: University Press of New England.

Sogner, S. (1995) 'History of mentalities – History of cultures', in William Hubbard et al. (eds) *Making a Historical Culture. Historiography in Norway*, Oslo: Scandinavian University Press: 347–59.

Sparks, R. J. (2004) *The Two Princes of Calabar: An eighteenth-century Atlantic odyssey*, Cambridge, MA and London: Harvard University Press.

Spence, J. D. (1978) *The Death of Woman Wang*, New York: Viking Penguin.

Spiegel, G. M. (1990) 'History, historicism and the social logic of the text in the Middle Ages', *Speculum* 65: 59–86.

——(2005) 'Introduction', in G. M. Spiegel (ed.) *Practicing History. New directions in historical writing after the linguistic turn*, New York: Routledge.

——(2007) 'Revising the past/revisiting the present: How change happens in historiography', *History and Theory*. Theme Issue 46: Revision in History 46:4: 1–19.

Spufford, M. (1974) *Contrasting Communities: English villagers in the sixteenth and seventeenth centuries*, Cambridge, London, New York and Melbourne: Cambridge University Press.

Srebnick, A.G. (1995) *The Mysterious Death of Mary Rogers: Sex and culture in nineteenth-century New York*, Oxford and New York: Oxford University Press.

Stanley, L. (1992) *The Auto/Biographical I: Theory and practice of feminist auto/biography*, Manchester: Manchester University Press.

Stearns, P. N. (2003) 'Social history, present and future', *Journal of Social History*, Special Issue: *The Futures of Social History* 37: 9–20.

——(2007) 'Debates about social history and its scope', in S. G. Magnússon, *Sögustríð. Greinar og frásagnir um hugmyndafræði*, Reykjavík: The Reykjavík Academy.

Stearns, P. N. (ed.) (1994) *Encyclopedia of Social History*, New York – London: Garland Publishing.

Stearns, P. N. and Stearns, C (1985) 'Emotionology: Clarifying the history of emotions and emotional standards', *American Historical Review* 90: 813–36.

Stewart, G. R. (1987) *Pickett's Charge: A microhistory of the final attack at Gettysburg, July 3, 1863*, Boston: Houghton Mifflin. (1st edn 1959)

Stone, H. S. (2002) *St. Augustine's Bones: A microhistory*, Amherst, MA and London: University of Massachusetts Press.

Surkis, J. (2012) 'When was the linguistic turn? A genealogy', *AHR* Forum: Historiographic 'Turns' in Critical Perspective, *American Historical Review* 117:3: 700–722.

Szekeres, A. (1999) 'Mikrotörténelem és általános történeti tudás', *Századvég* 4 (No. 15): 3–17.

——(2003) 'Carlo Ginzburg, a morfológia és a történelem. A bizonyítás új meghatározása felé', in Zs. K. Horváth, A. Lugosi and F. Sohajda (eds) *Léptékváltó társadalomtörténet. Tanulmányok a 60 éves Benda Gyula tiszteletére*, Budapest: Hermész Kör and Osiris.

Szijártó, I. M. (2002) 'Four arguments for microhistory', *Rethinking history* 6: 209–15.

——(2008) 'Puzzle, fractal, mosaic: Thoughts on Microhistory', *Journal of Microhistory*, Online. Available HTTP: <http://www.microhistory.org/pivot/entry.php?id=47> (accessed 1 May 2011).

Taylor, A. (1995) *William Cooper's Town: Power and persuasion on the frontier of the early American Republic*, New York: Alfred A. Knopf.

Taylor, B. (2009) 'Separations of soul: Solitude, biography, history', *AHR* Roundtable: Historians and Biography, *American Historical Review* 114: 640–51.

Taylor, S. J. and Bogdan, R. (1984) *Introduction to Qualitative Research Methods: The search for meaning*, New York: Wiley.

Thomas, J. A. (2012) 'Comment: Not yet far enough', *AHR* Forum: Historiographic 'Turns' in Critical Perspective, *American Historical Review* 117: 794–803.

Tilly, C. (1984) *Big Structures, Large Processes, Huge Comparisons*, New York: Russell Sage Foundation.

Tillyard, S. (1994) *Aristocrats: Caroline, Emily, Louisa, and Sarah Lennox 1740–1832*, London: Chatto & Windus.

Tomich, D. (2008) 'The order of historical time: The *longue durée* and micro-history', paper presented at 'The *Longue Durée* and World-Systems Analysis' Colloquium to Commemorate the 50th Anniversary of Fernand Braudel, *Histoire et sciences sociales: La longue durée. Annales E.S.C.*, XIII, 4, 1958. 2008 October 24–25. Fernand Braudel Center, Binghamton University, Binghamton, NY 13902. Online. Available HTTP: <http://www2.binghamton.edu/fbc/archive/tomich102508.pdf> (accessed 13 October 2012).

Torre, A. (1987) 'Antropologia sociale e ricerca storica', in P. Rossi (ed.) *La storiografia contemporanea. Indirizzi e problemi*, Milano: Il Saggiatore.

Ulbricht, O. (2009) *Mikrogeschichte: Menschen und Konflikte in der Frühen Neuzeit*, Frankfurt and New York: Campus Verlag.

Ulrich, L. T. (1990) *A Midwife's Tale: The life of Martha Ballard, based on her diary, 1785–1812*, New York: Alfred A. Knopf.

Vardi, L. (2009) 'Rewriting the lives of eighteenth-century economists', *AHR* Roundtable: Historians and Biography, *American Historical Review* 114: 652–61.

Vivo, F. de (2010) 'Prospect or Refuge? Microhistory, History on the Large Scale: A Response', *Cultural and Social History* 7: 387–97.

Wachtel, N. (2001) *La foi du souvenir: Labyrinthes marranes*, Paris: Seuil.

Weis, R. (2000) *The Yellow Cross: The story of the last Cathars, 1290–1329*, London: Viking.

White, H. (1973) *Metahistory: The historical imagination in nineteenth-century Europe*, Baltimore: The John Hopkins University Press.

White, L. (2000) *Speaking with Vampires: Rumor and history in colonial Africa*, Berkeley, CA and Los Angeles: University of California Press.

Wilder, G. (2012) 'From optic to topic: The foreclosure effect of historiographic turns', *AHR* Forum: Historiographic 'Turns' in Critical Perspective, *American Historical Review* 117: 723–45.

Wilson, N. J. (1999) *History in Crisis? Recent directions in historiography*, Upper Saddle River, NJ: Prentice Hall.

Wolff, L. (1988) *Child Abuse in Freud's Vienna: Postcards from the end of the world*, New York – London: NYU Press.

Wrightson, K. and Levine, D. (1995) *Poverty and Piety in an English village: Terling, 1525–1700*, 2nd edn, Oxford: Clarendon Press. (1st edn 1979)

Wroe, A. (1995) *A Fool & His Money: Life in a partitioned medieval town*, London: Jonathan Cape.

Wul, L. (2000) 'Microhistory in practice – a reply to Hans Henrik Appel', in L. Egholm and L. Wul (eds) *Microhistory – Towards a new Theory of History?* Papers fra seminaret d. 13. November 1999 på Syddansk Universitet Odense, Netværk for historieteori & historiografi. Arbejdspapirer Nr. 3: 23–27.

Zammito, J. H. (1998) 'Ankersmit's postmodernist historiography: The hyperbole of "opacity"', *History and Theory* 37: 330–46.

Zamoyski, A. (2004) *1812: Napoleon's fatal march on Moscow*, London: HarperCollins.

Þórðarson, Þ (1936–40) 'Lifnaðarhættir í Reykjavík á síðari helmingi 19. aldar' [Modes of living in Reykjavik in the latter part of the 19th century], Landnám Ingólfs: *Safn til sögu þess: Ýmsar ritgerir* II., Reykjavík.

Index